Captain George Day in the cockpit of an F-84F in 1956.

Perhaps no pilot was more skilled or accomplished than Colonel Bud Day, particularly in Vietnam, where the unit he led was renowned for its daring missions into enemy airspace to destroy SAM sites and rescue downed comrades. But on his sixty-seventh raid, Day's F-100F jet was shot down over North Vietnam. He managed to escape from the enemy forces that discovered him, and after a grueling three-week ordeal, he made it to South Vietnam. But just a few miles from safety, he was recaptured and taken to the infamous Hanoi Hilton...

Also by Robert Coram

Boyd: The Fighter Pilot Who Changed the Art of War

AMERICAN PATRIOT

The Life and Wars of Colonel Bud Day

Robert Coram

BACK BAY BOOKS
Little, Brown and Company
New York   Boston   London

To my daughter, Kimberly Drew.
And to my grandchildren, Anna Katherine and Ryan.
Every story has at least two sides.

Back Bay Books / Little, Brown and Company
Hachette Book Group
1290 Avenue of the Americas, New York, NY 10104
littlebrown.com

Originally published in hardcover by Little, Brown and Company, May 2007
First Back Bay paperback edition, June 2008

Back Bay Books is an imprint of Little, Brown and Company, a division of Hachette Book Group, Inc. The Back Bay Books name and logo are trademarks of Hachette Book Group, Inc.

The publisher is not responsible for websites (or their content) that are not owned by the publisher.

All insert photographs are from the family collection of Doris and Bud Day, unless otherwise indicated.

Library of Congress Cataloging-in-Publication Data
Coram, Robert.
   American patriot : the life and wars of Colonel Bud Day / By Robert Coram.
      p. cm.
   Includes index.
   ISBN 978-0-316-75847-5 (hc) / 978-0-316-06739-3 (pb)
   1. Day, George E.   2. Medal of Honor—Biography.   3. United States. Air Force—Officers—Biography.   4. Fighter pilots—United States—Biography.   5. Vietnam War, 1961–1975—Prisoners and prisons, North Vietnamese.   6. Prisoners of war—United States—Biography.   7. Prisoners of war—Vietnam—Biography.   8. Lawyers—United States—Biography.   9. Retired military personnel—United States—Biography.   I. Title.
   UG626.2.D39C67 2007
   959.704'37—dc22   2006022736

10 9 8 7 6

LSC-H
Book design by Bernard Klein
Printed in the United States of America

Contents

ACKNOWLEDGMENTS

Thanks to the "Red Bulls," the 87th Flying Training Squadron at Laughlin Air Force Base, hosts of my first Dining Out. Also to Mark Mattison, then commanding officer of the 87th, for his splendid exegesis of these events.

Honor Bound, by Stuart Rochester and Frederick Kiley, is far and away the best book about the POW experience. I borrowed liberally from it, and I thank the authors.

Thanks be to: Dr. Grant Hammond of the Air War College for his explanation of true heroism; Grace Linden, Curator of History at the Sioux City Public Museum; and Olivia Anastasiadis and Kirstin Julian at the Nixon Presidential Library.

Thanks to Richard Belcher and Steven Sears, both of whom have sharp eyes and extraordinary knowledge.

Also Dr. Richard Bernstein, Eric Caubarreaux, Bill Kaczor, Mike McGrath, Larry Myhre, David Nordan, Jack Shanahan, David Strickland, Bill Walters, and Greg Young.

While I had the best of sources, any mistakes herein are mine alone.

A special thanks to Lin and Jimmy Rogers of Pleasure Bluff; you lightened the load.

Finally, as always, to Jeannine. My heart song.

Preface

It is no compliment when a writer's colleagues read his work and say he has "gone native." To "go native" not only means a writer has been suborned by his subject but means he is unprofessional, that his work lacks objectivity.

Nevertheless, I hereby serve notice that in writing this book I went native. Every time I was with Bud Day and the Mistys or the POWs, I recalled that line from James Michener when the admiral is standing on the bridge of an aircraft carrier watching his pilots take off against the terrible defenses at Toko-Ri and says to himself, "Where do we get such men?"

I think this business about going native comes from writers who believe that the only true biography is one in which the subject's head is served on a platter. Both the idea and the people who hold it are narrow. Readers don't care a whit if a writer has gone native. Readers don't care if a writer admires the person he writes about.

In the interest of full disclosure I must confess there is a personal element to my admiration for Bud Day. As background, my daddy was an Army top sergeant who spent thirty-three years in uniform. I never had a childhood; I had an extended boot camp and I fought it every day. I rejected everything my daddy represented. He often threatened me with the specter of a military school where I would be "straightened out." He died when I was sixteen and that was the greatest day of my young life. For reasons I am not quite sure of, I briefly attended a military college. I say "briefly" because I flunked out. Then, again for reasons I don't understand, I enlisted in the Air Force, where I became what the military calls a "shit bird," a misfit who was always in trouble. I was in so much trouble that I was court-martialed three times and given an Undesirable Discharge.

Thereafter, my life was spent as far as possible from all things military.

But now, as I approach The River, it has become my job to write biographies of military men. This has enriched my life beyond all measure.

Military men are better than most of us. They live their lives based on clear values—a code of honor and loyalty, a patriotism, a commitment, and a discipline that place them on a moral high ground. It is their job to fight for and, if necessary, to die for their country. They willingly accept that contract. Bud Day and John McCain and Robbie Risner and James Stockdale and Orson Swindle and Larry Guarino and Jack Van Loan and Paul Galanti and Jack Fellowes and several hundred others spent years in the prisons of North Vietnam. Among those POWs were men crippled for life, men driven insane, men killed by their captors, and men who simply disappeared. But those who came home showed the world what Americans are made of.

Now, even though I went native, it would be a mistake to assume that I abandoned the professionalism gained from more than forty years as a writer. If there is a bias here, it is in the selection of Bud Day as a subject, not in the execution of the book. Only two or three more books are in me, and I want them to be the best I can do. Even though I have unbounded admiration for Bud Day, I did my job.

More than three years were spent researching and writing this book. In that time, I came to sense an ironic circularity to my life. All that I have run from for so many years—that is, anything to do with the military—I now embrace. All that I have criticized about the military, I now revere. Bud Day's life revealed to me the truths my daddy tried to teach me more than a half century ago. And the companionship of Bud Day became a surrogate for the affection that never existed between my daddy and me. Today I weep at the knowledge that I rejected the greatest gift a father could pass on to his son. And each military biography I write is a message to my daddy that now I understand.

Robert Coram
Moonpie Studio
Harris Neck, Georgia
2006

AMERICAN
PATRIOT

Prologue

THE colonel wore a soft cotton shirt with a ruffled front, a clip-on bow tie, and dark blue formal trousers. A waist-length jacket—what Air Force officers call the mess dress blouse—was draped over a chair. On his feet were highly polished black boots with a zipper on the inside, the sort of boots that only a fighter pilot could wear—and carry off—with formal dress.

It had been almost three decades since the colonel retired, and here he was at Laughlin Air Force Base (AFB) near Del Rio, Texas, in the Distinguished Visitors Quarters. He sat solitary amid a sprawling suite usually reserved for generals. The colonel was almost eighty, and as he pulled himself out of a chair, his left hand shot involuntarily to his upper left thigh. The pain was always there. When he sat for a while and then stood up, the sting and throb radiated down his leg. Over the years the pain had pulled his body into a perpetual stoop. He limped to the refrigerator, where his hosts had provided a bottle of his favorite "white Z"—the zinfandel that was the only thing he drank these days. He poured a glass and walked slowly back across the room, sank into the chair, and shifted uncomfortably. For thirty years he had searched unsuccessfully for a chair in which he could sit and not feel pain.

He glanced at the heavy gold watch on his left wrist. The Republican Party of Arizona had given him the big Omega in 1973, the year he always referred to as "the year I got out of jail." On the back of the watch, in block letters, was written OUR HUMBLE THANKS.

His escort would soon arrive. He reached up and checked his bow tie. The clip-ons had a tendency to break loose on one side and dangle from his collar. Then his left hand massaged his right forearm; it was bowed, and even a casual observer could see it once had been broken and improperly set. His right hand did not have a baby's strength. Tonight he would be shaking hands with dozens of officers, and afterward his hand would hurt for days. The colonel stood up again and walked into the bedroom. When he returned, a heavy medal in the shape of a star was draped around his neck. It was surrounded by a wreath and hung from a sky-blue ribbon.

The colonel's hand caressed the medal for a moment as he remembered the price he paid to earn it and the price he paid every day to wear it. A military doctor who specialized in traumatic orthopedic injuries had told him that the price would become higher with every passing year. But it was not just the pain. It was the memories, the memories and the nightmares. Nights were hell revisited. The man who had permanently crippled him — "the Bug" — was never far away. The ropes used to truss him into a pretzel and to wreck his body were never far away. Sleeping pills only dulled the pain and pushed the Bug into the middle distance for a few hours. With morning, and many cups of strong coffee, came a few good hours. Then in the afternoons he saw not only the lengthening shadows of the day but the growing shadow of the everlasting night. And he knew that when darkness fell, the back door of hell would open and the Bug would beckon.

The colonel reached for the glass of wine and shook his head. He was here because of his past; that was what his hosts wanted — history's glory. For his hosts, his past was valor and bravery and courage. He was immensely proud of his life, but he was also *haunted* by what had happened. Burned into his psyche forever were the words that kept him alive during those terrible years:

Return with Honor.

Return with Honor.

Return with Honor.

The old man did not want to think of the past. For him the present was far more important; he was in the midst of what he suspected would be his last great battle, and the outcome would affect more than a million military retirees. But his hosts knew nothing of that fight, so tonight he would talk of the past.

"It was all so long ago," he murmured. "So long ago." He shook his head almost in despair and said, "It was forever ago."

A loud knock sounded. As the colonel stood up and limped across the room, a big smile transformed his face. He opened the door.

"Good evening, sir," said a young Air Force captain.

"Come in. Come in." The two men shook hands.

The captain stepped into the room, his eyes locked on the medal around the colonel's neck: the Medal of Honor. Except for those pictured in the medal recognition books the young officer had studied, it was the first he had ever seen. It is the only medal awarded by the president of the United States. It is the only medal worn around the neck. It identifies its wearer as one who risked his life in combat; whose service to his country was above and beyond the call of duty. It is the only medal that defines a military man for all his days.

"Sir, I'm here to escort you, if you are ready." His eyes never left the medal.

"Of course. Let me put on my jacket." The colonel's voice was soft and the boyish smile never left his face.

He picked up the jacket on the chair and struggled with it. His right arm just wouldn't straighten enough to slide into the sleeve.

The captain moved behind the colonel to help. The colonel shrugged and felt the jacket settle into place. "Let's go," he said.

The captain stepped around in front of the colonel and froze, his eyes locked on the colonel's left breast and row after row of ribbons and medals. Several carried palms or clusters indicating the medal had been awarded multiple times.

When one Air Force officer meets another, he can tell with a split-second look at the other man's uniform all he needs to know. Does the man wear wings? If so, are they the wings of a pilot, a navigator, or an astronaut? The colonel wore wings with a wreath topped by a star—the wings of a command pilot, the highest pilot ranking in the Air Force.

The medals of an officer reveal if he is a warrior or a staff person. A warrior wears medals awarded for combat. A bureaucrat wears meritorious service medals and commendation medals. The medals are stacked in descending order of importance. Thus, one officer can look at the left breast of another, identify the medals, and know the story of that man's career.

The captain had never seen so many combat medals on one person.

There on the top was the Air Force Cross, the highest medal awarded by the Air Force. The captain had never seen an Air Force Cross before. His gaze swept down the colonel's chest. The Silver Star. The Distinguished Flying Cross with cluster after cluster. What outfit had the colonel been with to fly so many combat missions?

The Air Medal with nine oak-leaf clusters. Twelve campaign battle stars.

The arc of a thirty-year military career was there on his chest, beginning with medals from the Pacific Theater of World War II, then Korea, and then Vietnam.

Three wars. Three wars. My God, the man had served his country during three wars.

And under the U.S. medals was the National Order of Vietnam, the Vietnamese equivalent of the Medal of Honor.

The colonel wore the highest award for valor granted by TWO countries.

The captain regained his composure and escorted the colonel across the street to the officers' club. Tonight was a Dining Out hosted by the 87th Flying Training Squadron, the famed "Red Bulls" of Laughlin AFB, part of the Air Education and Training Command. The Red Bulls and their begowned ladies were gathered next door in the bar at the officers' club.

The Red Bulls train the last true knights of warfare.

Astronauts, or "rocketeers," as fighter pilots call them, ride the most powerful beasts; but they usually do it only once. Fighter pilots mount up several times each week. Their first training is "basic fighter maneuvering": one pilot against another at twenty thousand feet and the closest thing there is to jousting. Played out for real in combat, it is the ultimate sport: the loser goes down in flames and makes a big hole in the ground.

Every fighter pilot has an ego large enough for a separate zip code. And with good reason. In all the wars since Vietnam, Air Force pilots have flown into enemy territory, stomping down Main Street, beating their chests and daring enemy fliers to rise against them. Overwhelmed in every way, most enemy air forces never left the ground. As a result, in the last three decades, few Air Force pilots have been bloodied in combat.

The Dining Out is a formal affair rooted in ancient history. From pre-Christian Roman legions, to marauding Vikings, to King Arthur's knights, a banquet to celebrate military victories has long been customary among warriors. British soldiers brought the practice to colonial America, where it was adopted by George Washington's army. Close bonds between U.S. Army Air Forces pilots and Royal Air Force (RAF) officers during World War II cemented the custom in the U.S. military.

The goal for any Dining Out, no matter the branch of service, is to have a speaker who embodies the highest ideals of the military; preferably a combat leader, a man who has demonstrated in battle that he carries on the tradition of ancient warriors, a man whose deeds will forever inspire young men. Such an ideal has become more and more difficult to reach. But tonight a great warrior was speaking to the Red Bulls. And the opportunity to be in his presence was something they would talk about for the remainder of their days.

A retinue of colonels greeted the old man as he entered the officers' club. Some military courtesies are dropped when officers are indoors. For instance, protocol does not call for saluting or standing at attention in the presence of a senior officer, much less an officer of equal rank. And officers of equal rank do not say "sir" to each other. But every colonel came to attention and said "sir" as they greeted the visitor.

A few lieutenant colonels and majors approached the colonel, but the junior officers hung back, drinking and whispering to each other as they stared, hesitant to even approach.

Some of the colonels wore a row of medals, a few had a couple of rows. But most of their medals were not combat decorations; they were basic "attaboy" awards for showing up for duty. Every colonel there looked at the old man's medals, and their envy was almost palpable.

After numerous visits to the "grog bowl," a commode filled with a napalmlike mixture of various liquors, everyone was in a jovial mood. The younger lieutenants and captains became bold enough to approach the colonel. Those on the outer edges of the circle jostled and elbowed one another as is the nature of young fighter pilots. But as they drew closer to the colonel, they became quiet and respectful, almost like small boys.

Snatches of their conversation were audible over the rowdiness of the party.

He's got more combat medals than all the other medals in this room put together.

The squadron pilots plus officials from the wing of which the squadron was a part totaled fifty-four officers. That one man wore more combat medals than all the other officers in the room combined was mind-boggling.

Yeah, plus he's got THE medal.

Which president awarded it?

I don't know. But I do know he is the most decorated living American officer.

You mean . . . ?

He's got more medals than any other person in any branch of the U.S. military.

The young officers looked upon this man and tried to figure out what was different about him, what there was about him that might rub off on them. In the history of the Air Force, only seventeen men have received the Medal of Honor. Five of those men remain alive. Those five received the medal in Vietnam, and the Vietnam War ended before these young officers were born.

The colonel ignored the stares. He had never expected to receive the Medal of Honor. Hell, he never expected to *live*. Others, many others, who performed as well as he were dead. So many of his friends died in jail, so many good men lost in terrible and heartrending conditions. They died protecting the right of young men back home to flee to Canada in order to avoid being drafted. They died protecting the rights of college students to take to the streets and demonstrate against the Vietnam War. They died that Americans might sleep in peace.

Once, all this had angered the colonel immensely. But it was such a long time ago and no longer seemed to matter so much. What did matter, what would always matter, were the acts of bravery he had witnessed when he was in jail, acts of bravery that would live forever in his heart; acts of bravery that still caused him to weep when he remembered them.

I heard he was shot down in Vietnam and . . .

He was the first commanding officer of a highly classified outfit that flew F-100s. He was shot down and captured, and was the only American to escape from North Vietnam into South Vietnam. Then he was shot and recaptured and taken to Hanoi. He was a POW almost six years. They tortured him pretty badly.

Is that how he got the medal?

He got that for his escape. He got the Air Force Cross for his leadership while he was a POW. They tortured him for months on end. Almost killed him. He was in solitary for years, but they never broke him. He is one tough son of a bitch.

The young officers stared at the colonel, who was smiling and kneading his forearm. His face was almost beatific, and were it not for his uniform and the medals, he would have looked like everyone's favorite uncle. One said what the others were thinking.

Hard to believe.

Gentlemen, the colonel kept the faith. Remember this night because you are looking at a great man, a warrior, and you will not gaze upon his like again.

The squadron commander of the Red Bulls called the Dining Out to order. The colonel walked to his place at the head table, looked at the hard chair, and exhaled softly. The next hour or so was going to be agony. He took his seat near the middle of the table, and the rituals of the evening unfolded. The flag was brought into the mess, a procedure known as the Posting of the Colors, and then there was a series of formal toasts to the flag, to allied comrades, to the president of the United States, to the senior officers of each branch of the service, and, finally, a toast with water "to all that could not return," the absent comrades dead or imprisoned in foreign countries.

Protocol dictates that no matter what high-ranking officers are in a room, a Medal of Honor recipient always is introduced first. But the squadron commander ignored protocol and introduced those sitting on his right and then those on his left, saving the colonel for last.

A rigid rule of a Dining Out is that applause is not permitted. Instead, guests rap their spoons on the table. As the head-table guests were introduced, each was greeted by a courteous tapping of perhaps five seconds. Then the colonel was introduced, and the gentle tapping turned into a rumble and then rose to a thunderous bass roar that went on and on and on. Around the room officers began standing. The thunder of the spoons became louder. Now everyone in the room was standing. Officers leaned over and crashed their spoons on the table. The building trembled. Wide-eyed cooks and waiters came from the kitchen to see what was happening as the thunder of the spoons rolled on and on and on until it seemed it would never stop.

The colonel beamed. To receive the approbation of fellow officers did not begin to make worthwhile all that he had gone through, all those years when he was absent from his wife, from his beloved Dorie, whom he had loved since he was a teenager, and from his four children, but it helped; it was a temporary balm for the pain and the nightmares and a cushion against the specter of the Bug.

The open adulation on the faces of the officers, the trembling of their lips and the moistness of their eyes as they looked upon him, sent his thoughts back to the beginning, back to the wrong side of the tracks in Sioux City, Iowa, back to Riverside, where, even in his most ambitious and outrageous dreams, he never thought his life would take this course, never dreamed that such cruelty would befall him, never imagined the honors that would come his way.

As the deep thunder of the spoons continued, the colonel's thoughts tumbled down the decades.

It was all so long ago, so very long ago.

1

Siouxland

OUT in the clean and sweetly rolling plains of the Midwest, out where Iowa and Nebraska and South Dakota come together, is a region called Siouxland — a place far removed from the swirling trends that wash over the dynamic cities of the East and West Coasts. This is the heartland, the stable and rock-solid core of America, and here the virtues long thought of as uniquely American are as real and ever-present as the wind across the prairie. Sophisticated people say the Midwest is "flyover country," a dull and boring place where exciting things rarely happen. But the people of Siouxland know that the very things America finds amusing about them are, in fact, their greatest strengths.

Sioux City, Iowa, is the best-known town in Siouxland.

Only a few generations earlier, Sioux City had been the edge of civilization, the place where people stocked up on provisions before jumping into the wild Dakota Territories. Sioux City was as far up the Missouri as steamboats could travel. The railroad ended here. The first burial of a soldier west of the Mississippi River was that of Sergeant Charles Floyd, a member of Lewis and Clark's Corps of Discovery who sickened and died here on August 20, 1804. The largest monument honoring a member of the Corps of Discovery is the one-hundred-foot-tall sandstone obelisk known as the Floyd Monument in Sioux City. Afterward, Sioux City became a trail-end sort of town where cowboys brought cows and hogs to local meatpacking houses. Brothels and gambling and useless violence were big in Sioux City.

Two prominent geographic features help define Sioux City: the Missouri River and the Loess Hills. The mighty Missouri is one of America's most fabled and historic rivers while the Loess Hills are sharp-crested sand dunes formed centuries ago from windblown silt. Comparable hills are found in China, but the Loess Hills that run along the western border of Iowa and up through Sioux City are the longest in the world. On the edge of Sioux City, the Missouri is joined by the Big Sioux River. On the alluvial plain along the Big Sioux is a jam-packed suburb of small frame houses. This is Riverside, separated from Sioux City by the Loess Hills.

Riverside is a big part of the reason that Iowa and the rest of the Midwest looked down on Sioux City for much of the twentieth century. Riverside was the bad side of town — the home of roughnecks, the uneducated, and those on the windy side of the law. Here, grifters, hustlers, and bootleggers lived alongside railroad workers and those who worked in meatpacking houses. During the 1920s, tunnels under many Riverside homes served as hideouts for bank robbers who terrorized the Midwest; there were even stories that Al Capone visited when things got hot in Chicago. Dozens of illegal rat-hole bars were here, open seven days a week and known far and wide for their bloody fights. People in Riverside were so poor that in the winter they went over to the South Bottoms and waded into the Floyd River, where they scooped up buckets of fat, formed by congealed runoff from the stockyards, to use for cooking or for making soap.

Most people in Riverside accepted their lot in life. They were too busy eking out an existence to do otherwise. Only a few had the desire to get out and get up — to seek a better life. And of those few with the desire, even fewer made it.

George Day was one of those who did.

George Everette Day was born February 24, 1925, the second child and only son of John Edward and Christine Day. He was named George for his father's brother and Everette for one of his mother's brothers. From the beginning he was known only as "Bud."

John Edward Day, called "Ed," was fifty-four when Bud was born, an old man at a time when many men died in their sixties. He was five foot seven and slender, a taciturn fellow with a hard face. When he spoke, more often than not he was crabby. Some thought him mean.

Both Ed and Christine had been married previously. Ed divorced his first wife when he discovered there were other men in her life. He never spoke of his previous family except in dismissive and critical terms, and Bud grew up knowing little about them. Ed's sour disposition could have been caused in part by his first marriage or it could have been caused by what he called his "nervous stomach," for which he frequently took medicine. But more than likely his disposition was born in his poverty and in the knowledge that because he had only a sixth-grade education, his life would never be any better.

For a big part of Bud's childhood, Ed was unemployed, doing little but tending to a vegetable garden planted in the rich soil on the banks of the Big Sioux. The Day family had no car and no telephone. Ed sometimes could not afford to pay his rent, and several times the family was evicted. Bud's childhood was spent in a series of frame houses, none larger than about nine hundred square feet. In one of those houses, Bud's mother and sister slept in the single bedroom while he and his father slept on the porch. The houses were not insulated and the woodstoves strove mightily during the fierce prairie winters. Summers were blazing and there was no air-conditioning. A well provided water. An outhouse was about ten feet from the well.

It was a daily fight for existence, but Bud's father never complained. Like most Midwesterners, Ed was a man of fortitude who assumed he could and would handle whatever life threw at him.

He was a stubborn man who simply did not know how to give up. The example he set in dealing with adversity was his greatest gift to his son.

Few parts of America were hit as hard by the Great Depression as was the Midwest. Siouxland became a dust bowl. Prairie grass died, the wells dried up, and the relentless wind blew away the dreams of a generation. For days, sometimes weeks, Bud never saw the sun.

Until the Depression, Siouxland was Republican country. But economics reversed the polarity of local politics. Like many of his neighbors, Ed Day went from being a ho-hum Republican to an evangelical Democrat who conferred almost godlike status upon President Franklin Delano Roosevelt. Most afternoons Ed turned on the radio to listen to Fulton Lewis Jr., a Republican commentator, so that every few minutes he could shout, "Lying son of a bitch!" Ed blamed the Republicans for every bad thing in his life. Years later Bud would remember, "If we had a year when there were not many pheasants and hunting was bad, he blamed it on the Republicans."

Ed's passion for politics was another gift he passed to his son.

To Ed Day, a man who did not vote was beneath contempt, right down there with men who borrowed money, drank liquor, or ran around on their wives. "If you don't vote, you can't complain," he said. "A no-vote is a vote for the status quo. Change will not come until a man exercises his right to vote."

But the Day household was not a democracy. When Ed told Bud to do something, it was always with a loud voice, and he never issued orders but once. If Bud moved slowly, his father slapped him into compliance. And no detail of Christine's appearance or demeanor escaped Ed's carping. She and her family were Danish immigrants, and Ed was particularly fond of ridiculing her accent and her family. He grumbled that her family did not speak English and said they were "stupid" to teach their children Danish. "If they are going to be real Americans, they've got to speak English," he said. Sioux City had a large Scandinavian population, and Ed referred to them derisively as "Eric" or "Eric the Red." He also had favorite slurs for other ethnic groups.

It is human nature that a man of pride, a man with no education and no job, must have someone to belittle. Perhaps Christine realized this; in any case, she never responded to the criticism. Her first husband had died and left her with four children. Ed put those children to work on Iowa farms in a form of indentured servitude, and they all moved to Chicago as soon as they could get away. Fatalistic about life, Christine did whatever Ed told her to do. She was a drudge, ruling nothing except her kitchen. She baked bread, cooked, and cleaned, and would not dream of taking a job outside the house; only a woman of doubtful virtue worked outside the home.

She was in her late forties when Bud was born. No one knew her age, as she told no one the date of her birth.

Every morning Christine cooked the same meal for her husband: one egg, fried very hard, along with a piece of fat pork and a couple of buckwheat pancakes.

Bud remembers also eating pancakes, as well as oatmeal and Cream of Wheat with raisins and milk and sugar, though during his childhood he never had a salad or a steak. As for his mother's diet, he can't remember; he recalls only that she was always running between the table and the stove and rarely sat down.

Bud's sister, Joyce, was six years older than he. She was so intelligent that twice she was moved ahead a year in school and would have been moved a third time if her mother hadn't forbidden it, saying she should not be in a class with girls who were three years older. Independent and headstrong, Joyce, had she been born a few decades later, could have been a militant feminist.

Ed was as verbally abusive to his daughter as he was to his wife. But Joyce was not intimidated. She and her father had tremendous fights. Bud particularly remembers one disagreement concerning Gypsy Rose Lee, the famous "hoochie koochie" dancer of the time whom Ed thought was a "strumpet." Joyce liked Gypsy Rose Lee and told her father, "Times are changing. A woman can do anything she wants as long as she does not break the law. If she was breaking the law, she would be arrested." And Joyce was so angry about Ed's constant criticism of Christine that many times she said to her mother, "Divorce him. You don't have to take his abuse. You don't have to live like this."

Bud was nine years old when Joyce — at fifteen — graduated from high school and moved to Chicago to live with a half sister. When she announced she was entering college in Oklahoma City, Ed sputtered and spouted and issued edicts, but all to no avail. This was not an issue in which he had a vote.

Joyce blazed through college as quickly as she did high school and, by nineteen, had graduated and was working in southeast Iowa. Then one day, while carrying a load of laundry downstairs, she tripped, tumbled down the stairs, and broke her neck. She died instantly.

Older people in Riverside still shake their heads when they talk of Joyce's death. She was a pretty girl, and they believe there was something mysterious about her death. Agile nineteen-year-olds don't fall down stairs. But there was no investigation, only bitter acceptance.

After the funeral, Ed found he was the beneficiary of Joyce's $500 life-insurance policy. He used the money to invest in a house at 2222 Riverside Boulevard. It was the only house Ed ever owned. The property had no bathroom, only a toilet. Ed wired the house, dug a basement with pick and shovel, braced it up, bricked it, and installed a furnace and a coal chute, then added an enclosed back porch and a toolshed. Ed was not the introspective sort who would have found irony in the fact that the only house he ever owned came through the death of an estranged daughter.

One of the few things Bud did with his father on a regular basis was to get on the streetcar in the early fall and ride down to lower 4th Street to the pawnshop owned by "Little Joe." There his father bought him a pair of shoes and a coat for the coming winter. By then Bud's shoes from the previous year were falling apart. (Time after time his mother took a cereal box and cut out a piece of cardboard in the shape of Bud's feet to fit inside his shoes. The mothers of Bud's friends did the same. It was a matter of pride among Riverside mothers that there were no holes in the socks of their children.)

Ed was convinced that Little Joe gave him great deals. So one day when the pawnbroker offered him an old single-barrel .410-gauge shotgun, Ed bought it and gave it to Bud, figuring that a Riverside boy ought to be able to shoot, to put meat on the table, even if he was only ten years old.

The .410-gauge shotgun was a small, low-powered shotgun with a very tight spread of shot. Hunters consider it something of a toy. But Bud became an excellent wing shot. Every year thousands of ducks covered the surface of sloughs along the Big Sioux, and Bud shot many of them for his mother's table. He also shot pheasants and pigeons. During the winter when he brought home game birds, his mother hung them on a wire in the yard, where they froze, not thawing out until maybe late March. When the family wanted one for the table, Bud's mother pulled it from the line and dressed and cooked it, supplementing domestic chickens and turkeys with pheasant, rabbit, pigeons, ducks, and geese.

Providing for the family meant more than finding food. Bud was expected to work. Though a boy had to be twelve to become a caddy at what then was called the Elmwood Golf Course, Bud somehow got one of the jobs when he was ten. As is sometimes the case with poor children, Bud was particularly observant. One of the first things he noticed at Elmwood, beyond the obvious fact that golfers had the money to indulge in an expensive sport and the leisure time to enjoy it, was that golfers wore expensive clothes and had manners far smoother than those of Riverside men. Their conversation was more worldly. And every man who played golf had been to college.

For a Riverside boy growing up in the Depression, there were no professions higher than being a doctor or lawyer. Bud Day decided he would be a doctor. But he told no one. The idea of a boy from Riverside going to college was outrageous. Only one boy in the neighborhood had ever gone to college: the preacher's son. For a Riverside boy to go to college and then to medical school . . . well, to talk of such dreams would evoke only scorn and ridicule.

Bud discovered reading about the same time he discovered golf. Down the street was a police officer who was the father of a classmate. The officer had taken an early retirement because of an injury and spent his days on a recliner or in bed. His friends brought him books and magazines, so many that they stacked up in his small house. One day he invited Bud to look through the piles and take whatever he wanted. It was a revelation for the youngster.

As sometimes happens with children who are not happy with their lives, Bud found a better world between the covers of a book. Subsequently, he began checking books out of the city library. The limit was two volumes, but Bud went through books so fast and returned them so promptly that the librarian — as is the way of good librarians everywhere — increased his limit to four. During the summer he read from seven to nine books each week, many of them while lying on the roof of his house in the shade of an oak tree.

Ed, for all his rigidity in other matters, was lenient in the extreme about Bud's reading, probably because he thought reading would help Bud graduate from high school. A high school diploma was considered as far as a Riverside boy could go. College was not even a dream. Again and again Ed used his most emphatic tone to tell Bud, "You *will* be a high school graduate."

Bud read with the undisciplined enthusiasm of a boy who has discovered a secret. He quickly burned through books in the children's section, books about Daniel Boone, and books by Nathaniel Hawthorne and James Fenimore Cooper, and moved on to books about Nathan Hale and Thomas Paine and Daniel Webster and Thomas Jefferson. His boyhood hero became Charles Lindbergh. Bud considered Lindbergh almost a local; after all, he flew out of St. Louis, which was not that far away. Bud bought a leather pilot helmet and goggles and daydreamed of duplicating Lindbergh's exploits, of mounting up with wings as eagles. But of course it was only daydreaming. Boys from Riverside did not become officers and pilots; they became enlisted men and infantry soldiers.

By the time Bud was ten, he had several friends with whom he would remain close all his life.

The one thing they had in common was that they were afraid of Ed. Sometimes when they knocked on Bud's front door, Ed appeared with his angry scowl. The boys were already backing away when Ed announced, "He's not coming out." There was no rhyme or reason as to why Ed sometimes kept Bud at home.

Bud inspired a fierce loyalty among his childhood companions. One of Bud's friends was Paul Jackson, a Serb (the family name was Jaksik until it was changed to Jackson) whose parents spoke heavily accented English. When Jackson was in his late seventies, battling cancer and a host of other illnesses, he met a person inquiring about Bud and said, "I'll fight any man who says anything bad about Bud Day." He meant it.

And there was Frank Work, a tough kid from a big family, all of whom lived in a tiny apartment for which the rent was $5 per month. Even in Riverside some people looked down on Frankie Work. But not Bud. "He treated me with dignity and respect," Work recalled, and it was clear from his tone that few other people had. Work often was in trouble with the cops and was widely known for his fighting abilities, and from an early age he made it his mission in life to protect Bud. Once, when he was tossed out of his own home, he came to Bud's house and slept with Bud. Work remembers that Bud's bed "was hard as burled oak," and he still wonders how his friend slept on it night after night.

Another buddy was Dick Skavhdahl, whose older brother, "Skinks," was an enlisted Marine — one of the old-timers known as China Marines — who sometimes wore his dress blues when he came home. He was a bigger-than-life figure, a recruiting-poster kind of military man who, in a few years, was to have an enormous influence on the boys of Riverside.

And finally there was Jim Brodie. Brodie's father, John, was a lawyer with considerable political influence. In a few years he would have a significant impact on Bud's life.

The boys spent much of their time in the Loess Hills, "running the hills," they called it, and shouting, "Radook," a nonsense word that became their rallying call. An old buffalo wallow was up in the hills, as were several Indian burial grounds where Bud and his friends found arrowheads and partial skeletons. In the summers they swam nude in "Greenie Pond" or they swam the Sioux River to steal watermelons on the South Dakota side. During the winter they rode sleds down Catholic Hill (which they called "Cat-licker Hill"), and when the Big Sioux froze, Bud and his friends played ice hockey using a tin can as a puck and willow limbs as hockey sticks. In the spring, when the ice broke up, it was a big deal among the boys to see which one first dove in.

There were two illegal whiskey stills in Riverside. Bud and Frankie found them and studied their construction.

Bud turned eleven in 1936. Even today, people in Sioux City who are of a certain age shake their heads when they remember 1936, a brutal year that included one of the coldest winters and hottest summers in history. That summer the temperature was around 100 degrees for weeks, so hot that many people in Riverside slept on the grass in local parks.

That same year, Ed was hired by the Works Progress Administration (WPA) — one of President Roosevelt's programs to get Americans relief during the Great Depression — to be a night custodian of equipment kept on the banks of the Floyd River as part of a flood-control project. Ed went to work every day at 5 p.m. and returned at about 8 a.m. He slept a few hours, then supervised Bud's chores and puttered in his garden until it was time to return.

By the time he was twelve, Bud not only was a caddy but had a job at the Lakeshore Inn on McCook Lake. The Lakeshore Inn was a place where the food was cheap and the booze was bad — a dimly lit place where older men brought younger girls. Bud cleaned the floor of vomit when he arrived and then cooked ribs for the dinner crowd. He spent what little extra money he had on Bing Bars, a candy bar made by the local Palmer Candy Company. With their cherry-cream center and a chocolaty-peanut coating, Bing Bars would be a lifelong passion for Bud Day.

WHEN the time came, Bud attended Central High School, a monstrous building made of Sioux Falls granite that everyone referred to as the "castle on the hill." There he made Bs and Cs. He used study periods at school to do all his homework and never once took a book home. He played hooky often and used those absences to walk up to the north side of town and admire the two-story brick homes of wealthy people. He marveled at the cars in the driveways and vowed that one day he too would live in a large house, preferably a two-story brick house, and that he would drive what then was the ultimate sign of success — a Cadillac.

Bud was in numerous fights at school, not because he picked them — he was too small to pick fights (about five feet tall and a hundred pounds) — but because he was from Riverside and everyone picked on River Rats. Though frequently beaten up, Bud also held his own many times. In fact, he became known as something of a scrapper who never backed down, no matter the size of his challenger. He did not tell his father about the fights; to go home and whine that a big kid had picked on him was unthinkable. He knew what Ed would say: *Take care of yourself. Pick up a stick and do whatever it takes, but don't let anybody run over you.*

When Bud was fifteen, someone, he doesn't remember who, gave him a dog — an Irish water spaniel. Bud named it "Curly" and set about teaching him to hunt. In so doing, he found he was a gifted dog trainer. Before long the eighty-pound chocolate-colored spaniel had a reputation throughout Siouxland. Bud and Curly spent countless hours roaming the sloughs near the Missouri.

By the time he was sixteen, Bud had still another job delivering the Sunday *Des Moines Register.* Through this job he met Sonwald

Sorensen. The Sorensen family was immensely proud of its Norwegian heritage; at home they spoke only Norwegian.

Bud often took Curly with him when he met Duffy and Stanley Sorensen and played basketball in the Sorensens' driveway. A nearby streetlight enabled the boys to play well into the evening. Duffy had a younger sister, Doris, who, when the boys got hot and sweaty, brought them water. Bud, focused on his friends, the game, and his dog, did not know she existed.

In high school, Bud dated a cheerleader for a while and flirted with a few other girls before meeting — and finally noticing — Doris again. She was twelve but appeared to be years older. They encountered each other at the empty lot on Riverside Boulevard that, during October, was flooded by the fire department. The "skating pond" remained frozen all winter. Bud wanted to skate with Doris, but ice-skating meant holding hands, and she did not want her parents to drive by and see her holding hands with a boy. So the two skated independently, smiling at each other.

Bud, sixteen at the time, thought Doris was his age, maybe a year younger, a mistake easy to make. She worked part-time for her father, ordering paint and lumber and paying bills and answering the phone — chores usually reserved for an older person. In addition, pictures of her taken during that time show she had the physical attributes not only of an older girl but of a much-blessed older girl.

ON Sunday, December 7, 1941, the Japanese bombed Pearl Harbor. The next day as Bud rode the streetcar to school, passing the post office at the corner of Pearl and 6th Street, he stared at the double line of young men stretching around the block and halfway around in a second loop. These were young men from age eighteen up to their early thirties. They were locals who had taken the streetcar down to the post office to enlist in the military. It was a cold December in Sioux City, but few of the men wore coats. They were too poor.

Bud kept his eyes on the men until the streetcar rounded a corner. Something about the long line resonated with him. Although he was too young to articulate his feelings, he sensed the young men were standing on the street for two reasons: America had been dealt a serious blow and needed soldiers for the long war that was ahead. The young men of Siouxland were simply answering the call. But another reason, the unspoken reason, was that the military was a jobs program. The Depression still lay heavily on America. Boys graduating from high school knew they faced the same bleak future that thousands of men in their middle and late twenties were facing. The military would teach them a trade. They could serve their country, do their bit for America, then come home and get on with their lives.

That afternoon after school Bud walked downtown and saw that the line around the post office was longer than it had been that morning.

Bud wanted to be part of it. But he was only sixteen and it was not yet his time.

In the months after Pearl Harbor, the war did not go well for America. The Japanese controlled almost half the Pacific, and the Germans were defeating the British in North Africa. A glimmer of good news came in April 1942, when the Doolittle Raiders bombed Japan. In August, the U.S. Marines landed on Guadalcanal and took horrendous casualties. Felt all across America was a desperate urgency for a battlefield victory. Young men volunteered to do their part.

Abroad and at home, America was still struggling. Twenty-eight percent of the population had no income. Tenants could not pay rent. Cities could not provide services. People could not cover their mortgages and were forced out of their homes. One-fourth of America's schoolchildren were malnourished, and no place in America suffered more than the Midwest.

In the summer of 1942, Bud hitchhiked to Chicago to spend the summer with a half brother. He says he left home because he "grew tired of the old man's constant griping and carping." He says too, "There was some pushing and shoving," and that he wrestled his old man to the floor and pinned him. He denies that it was a real fight. Whatever it was, it led to his first venture away from Sioux City. He worked in a Chicago bowling alley all summer and then hitchhiked home for his final year of high school.

That fall he won a golf tournament with other caddies at the country club, shooting a 75. Life went on.

SONWALD Sorensen became successful enough to leave Riverside and move into Sioux City. But on Fridays the family came back to Riverside so Mrs. Sorensen could have her hair done. On one of these trips, Doris ran into Bud again, this time at the ice-cream parlor. They shared a chocolate malt and caught up. She was now thirteen and Bud was a senior in high school. He walked her home, and Doris thought he was the most polite boy she had ever met. She went inside to tell her parents she was outside talking to a friend. She and Bud then stood in the bitter cold of an Iowa winter and talked more than an hour, oblivious of the cold. Bud said he wanted to meet her again next week at the skating rink. She agreed and he leaned over and kissed her good night.

That kiss was the beginning of one of the great love stories of our time — a love story in which, years later, during a time of great adversity, both Bud and Doris manifested the finest qualities of the Midwest and of America for all the world to see. Thus, their stories, like their lives, cannot be separated. From that moment there was never really anyone else for either of them.

IN the fall of 1942 came an announcement that eighteen-year-olds would be drafted in January. Bud thought that meant he would be drafted when he turned eighteen, and the idea of being drafted was anathema. When your country was in trouble, you voluntarily came to her aid. It was that simple.

One day he heard Dick Skavhdahl say, "I'm joining the Marines next week," and without thinking he said, "Me too."

When Bud told his parents he was dropping out of school to join the Marines, Ed exploded. "You haven't graduated from high school," he pleaded. "You get your diploma in a few weeks. Wait that long."

"I'm joining up," Bud said.

"You are disobeying me," his father said.

This is the painful moment when the boy becomes a man, when the father must step aside or be pushed aside.

Because he was underage, Bud had to have his parents' permission to join the Marines. Even though Ed did not want Bud to drop out of school, the men of Siouxland did not stand in the way of sons who wanted to fight for their country. Reluctantly, he signed the waiver.

About the time Bud announced he was joining the Marines, Curly disappeared. Bud assumed someone had stolen the spaniel because of its reputation. But he was too wrapped up in details about joining the Marines to search for Curly. All things had to be put on hold while he readied himself for war.

Bud was five foot two — not exactly what the Marine Corps had in mind when they went looking for a few good men — and weighed 114 pounds. For several days he stuffed himself with bananas, but when he walked into the post office, the Marine Corps recruiter took one look at him, gave him a dime, and sent him across the street to buy more. Bud returned with his stomach protruding. Yet when he climbed atop the scales, he topped out at 116 pounds. The minimum weight for a man joining the Marine Corps was 120 pounds. Nevertheless, the Marines granted him a waiver.

Ironies abound here. The man who, more than three decades later, would become America's most highly decorated military man had to have two waivers to begin his military career: a waiver from his parents because of his age and a waiver from the Marine Corps because of his size.

Bud was sworn into the Marine Corps on December 10, a day that, for the rest of his life, would remain special.

The day he left Sioux City to begin his training, Bud and his mother rode the streetcar down to the train station. (Ed was still angry that his only son was a high school dropout, so he stayed home.) At the station, Bud kissed his mother good-bye and walked toward the train. He looked over his shoulder to see his mother leaning against the tan brick wall, and as mothers always do when their sons go away to war, she was weeping.

What is going on with this woman? Bud thought. *This is not a thing to be crying about.*

And with that, the teenage River Rat boarded the train and headed off to become a Marine.

2

War and Peace

BUD Day rode the train across Iowa to Des Moines, the collection point for recruits from Iowa, Illinois, and Missouri. After a physical examination, he boarded a troop train bound for California.

Today troops travel by air, but in 1942 trains were America's primary mode of mass transportation, and troop trains funneling recruits to training bases on the East and West Coasts were a common sight across Middle America.

Pulling out of Des Moines, the slow-moving train dropped down through the corner of Nebraska and across Kansas and Oklahoma and trudged through the deserts of New Mexico and Arizona and then into California. Most of the young men aboard had never been away from home, and many were riding a train for the first time.

Through the carriage windows, the boys saw, some for the last time, the country they were about to defend. Bud Day was agog. New Mexico was barren and dusty, not at all like the green prairies of Siouxland, and the heat was stifling. When they opened the windows for fresh air, the young men often were covered with soot and stung by cinders. A dining car was available, but few aboard had the money to buy meals.

Bud was excited the entire trip. Except for last summer's visit to Chicago, he had never been out of Sioux City. Now he was crossing the America he had read so much about, and he spent hours staring out the window. His companions were all as young and green as he. They were homesick for much of the trip.

After three days, they arrived in San Diego amid the organized chaos of the Marine Corps Recruit Depot, the MCRD.

To understand the mood and atmosphere of the Marines at the time, a bit of background is necessary. When Pearl Harbor was bombed, the Marine Corps consisted of about 54,000 officers and men. A year later, when Bud Day joined the Corps, that number had risen to about 142,500. By the end of the war, the number would reach 475,604. Almost 87,000 of those Marines would be wounded or killed, most of them in the bloody island-hopping campaigns of the Pacific.

Marine recruits, as was the case with recruits in other branches of the military, did not sign up for a two- or three-year hitch; they signed up until the end of the war plus six months or "for the duration." The recruits found nothing unusual in this. America was in desperate trouble against fearful odds, and winning this thing might take a while.

Training Marine recruits was an around-the-clock, seven-day-a-week business done at two bases. Recruits from the eastern half of America went to Marine Corps Recruit Depot Parris Island on the coast of South Carolina. Recruits from the western half of America went to Marine Corps Recruit Depot San Diego. Parris Island, or PI, was the older of the two and had the reputation of being far tougher. Marines who went through Parris Island looked down their noses at their West Coast counterparts, whom they called "Hollywood Marines."

Nevertheless, a Hollywood Marine received the same training as one at Parris Island. For many of the recruits, basic training, or boot camp, was their first taste of harsh discipline. Bud and his fellow members of Platoon 12-08, a designation that meant they were the eighth platoon to go through basic training in December, were met by a drill instructor (DI) whose greeting began with

"I am your father. I am your mother. I am Jesus Christ. You people are shitheads."

Marine Corps training of recruits always has been the most rugged of any branch of the military. And Day went through in the "Old Corps," long before there were any considerations of recruits except hammering them into Marines. For many of the boys, boot camp was entirely outside any experience they had ever known. But for Bud Day, the training was an upgraded version of his childhood. Drill instructors were tough but not that much tougher than Ed Day. Life in the Marine Corps was about discipline, and discipline was about following orders and not breaking the rules. Back in Siouxland, there was only one way to do things and that was the Ed Day way. Now there was only the Marine Corps way.

Recruits found it impossible to please a DI. For eight miserable weeks they were told every hour of every day that they were shitheads who were not good enough to be Marines. They suffered through endless inspections. When they were in the field, they drank water from a creek. (Pills dropped into the water were supposed to kill the fecal coliform that came from runoff in the nearby pastures where herds of cattle grazed, but these lads were training to become U.S. Marines, so what was a little cow shit in the water?) The DIs filled the pockets of the recruits' uniforms with sand and marched the burdened youngsters around the base. They put buckets on the recruits' heads and banged away. Recruits learned the Manual of Arms, how to fire an M1 while prone, standing, or zigzagging across a field. They learned map reading and navigation and how to exist off the land.

From the day the recruits walked onto the hallowed ground of the MCRD, they were taught that Marines were superior to all other forms of life, that they were the greatest warriors ever to tread the earth, and that soldiers were mere "dogfaces" while sailors were "swabbies" or "squid." You never yield, Day was told. You never give up. You are a leader. You will take charge. You represent America. It is mandatory that you succeed. Failure is not an option. And the Marines are the greatest fighting force the world has ever known, always ready, willing, and able to accept whatever job they are assigned. Their war plan is simple: kill everyone they meet. If they are not shooting, they are reloading.

More than a decade later, General William Thornson of the U.S. Army said, "There are two kinds of people that understand Marines: Marines and the enemy. Everyone else has a secondhand opinion." He wrote that Marines treat their military service as if it were a kind of cult, that they are cocky and foulmouthed but that their sense of brotherhood sets them apart, and, further, that they are "the most professional soldiers and the finest men and women I have ever had the pleasure to meet."

MCRD meant growing up in all sorts of ways. The Marine Corps insisted that recruits shave every morning. So Bud Day began shaving for the first time. Early in boot camp, Bud ate the first salad of his life. He also had his first steak. Being a Marine Corps steak served in a Marine Corps chow hall, it was not a good steak, not even a mediocre steak. In fact, it was little more than a hunk of gristle, far tougher than any pheasant or duck or pigeon that he had ever eaten. He was not impressed.

About halfway through his basic training, Bud came down with "cat fever," a pneumonia-like malady that sent him to the hospital for three weeks. Any disorder severe enough to send a seventeen-year-old to a military hospital for three weeks is serious. But Day's stay was particularly painful because, during war, any recruit in sick bay was considered a malingerer.

As soon as Bud was ambulatory, he was put to work operating an elevator in the hospital. There he saw an endless parade of military dependents: pregnant women, old men, crippled veterans. Many older veterans — men in their sixties or seventies, many wounded or disabled in World War I — lived in the hospital. As part of training, the recruits all had studied the "Red Book," which included, among other things, the benefits of a military career.

One of the strongest points made was that if a man gave the U.S. military twenty years, the military would, for the remainder of his life, give him free medical benefits. Bud knew that the old veterans believed this to be one of the most important benefits of a military career. But he was a seventeen-year-old shithead, and his level of interest in free medical benefits was too low to be measured.

When Bud was released from the hospital, he was put on light duty for several weeks. The hospital stay, followed by light duty, meant he had to drop back several recruit classes. Considering what happened later, cat fever may have saved his life.

DORIS had not seen Bud for several weeks at the skating pond. She asked about him and was told, "He's gone. He joined the Marines." She wondered why he had not said good-bye.

But he had not forgotten her. While Bud was in the hospital, he called a friend in Sioux City and said, "Tell that Sorensen girl with the big smile to write me."

When the friend called Doris, she said, "I never write first to a boy. You tell Bud to write me." As she and Bud's friend were negotiating the protocols of who should first write, her mother walked into the room and told Doris to hang up the phone, that her father was expected to call. Doris quickly said to Bud's friend, "Okay, give me his address."

So Doris wrote first, and soon the letters were flying back and forth. Doris read the first letters to her mother. Then, over the next several years, as the tenor of the letters changed and Bud became more expressive about his feelings, she began to omit parts of the letters when reading.

BUD graduated from boot camp in early March, a few days after he turned eighteen. No longer a recruit, no longer a shithead, he now belonged to Mother Green. He had been taught — and since the teaching came from a DI, it had ecclesiastical weight — that when dogfaces go to war, the soldiers sew a combat patch on the shoulder of their uniform and call for the Marines. When swabbies go to war, they sip their coffee and call for the Marines. When Army Air Forces weenies go to war, they have a drink and call for the Marines. All men are born equal. But then some become Marines.

In years to come, great honors would be showered upon Bud Day. But up there at the top of the list of the things of which he was most proud was that he was a Marine. Not that he once had been a Marine but that he *was* a Marine.

UPON graduation from boot camp, Bud attended the combat rifleman school, the final course before being assigned to a unit. He expected to be ordered to Hawaii, where the 2nd Marine Division had been formed and was finishing training. Scuttlebutt was that they were about to ship out to a combat zone. Bud Day expected to be with them — and that is what would have happened had it not been for the long arm of John Brodie.

Brodie, the Sioux City lawyer and father of his good friend, had been a Democrat back when almost everyone else in the Sioux City power structure was a Republican. With the Depression conversion of many of them to Democrats, Brodie was elevated to a position of some influence. He now used his political connections to request that the Marine Corps grant Bud a week's leave. The purpose: to take a battery of tests, receive his high school diploma, and graduate as a member of the Central High School class of 1943. The Marine Corps granted the request.

Ed Day could not have been more pleased. When Bud received his diploma, his father nodded in approval and said, "That was one of the few smart things you ever did."

Bud left Sioux City with twenty-five cents in his pocket. On the long bus trip back to California, he had nothing to eat, only a few small cartons of milk. This was not a hardship for a Riverside boy. It was simply how things were. And, of course, worse was to come.

FEW armies anywhere have ever done what the Marine Corps did in the Pacific in the early 1940s. Marines were island-hopping:

taking real estate away from the Japanese and paying for it with blood. Their casualties were horrendous. But the glory was everlasting. By the spring of 1943, Marines were manning dozens of islands in the Pacific. Christmas Island, Wake Island, Midway, Johnston, and Palmyra — all were garrisons in the island chain.

In early April, Bud shouldered his seabag, boarded the *Henderson*, and shipped out for Pearl Harbor. The Marines were preparing to land on Bougainville. Bud Day soon would be in the thick of the fighting. But Bud Day's great exploits as a warrior were not to take place in the Pacific in World War II; it is almost as if the gods of war were saving him for another conflict, for another form of battle.

The *Henderson* was three days out of Pearl Harbor when the captain thought an enemy submarine was nearby and ordered general quarters. Bud moved swiftly toward his appointed position. As he climbed through a hatch on an upper deck, the gunner of a heavy caliber machine gun opened fire to clear the barrel. Bud was so close that the noise ruptured his right eardrum. Within a day the ear was infected. A corpsman administered a sulfa drug, but Bud was allergic to the drug and became sicker. The corpsman gave him more of the drug. When the ship arrived at Pearl Harbor, Bud was hospitalized and underwent a mastoid operation. After the operation, doctors administered a new drug called penicillin. Bud was so allergic to penicillin that he almost died.

He was in the hospital five months, during which doctors considered giving him a medical discharge. The long illness took a heavy toll, and Bud, never a big man, became downright puny. Doctors put him on light duty and assigned him to the nearby Navy Yard, where he could gain a few pounds and they could keep an eye on him. He was given a job in the mess hall, peeling potatoes. All around him Marines were being ordered to islands in the Pacific where heavy fighting was going on. But Bud's personnel records were at the hospital rather than at the Replacement Depot, and the doctors thought Bud Day was too weak for combat.

After a few weeks, he received orders sending him to Johnston Island, a thousand-yard-long atoll 717 miles west-southwest of

Hawaii that served as a refueling stop for Navy ships. It was an island caught in the backwaters of the war. The 3rd Marine Defense Battalion, about forty civilian construction workers, and a squadron of small bombers called Scout Bombers–Dive (SBD) were based there. The island was to be a staging area for B-29s when America attacked the Mariana Islands.

When Bud arrived late in the fall of 1943, the civilian contractor had almost finished extending the runway. Some fifteen hundred troops lived on Johnston Island and nearby Sand Island. Bud's first job was as the powder man for a five-inch gun. Every day, from an hour before sunrise to an hour after sunset, he stood by the gun. Had the island come under attack, it would have been his job to toss bags of gunpowder down the barrel.

About a year later, Bud was promoted to corporal and became the noncommissioned officer in charge (NCOIC) of a searchlight battery that was integrated with a 90 mm antiaircraft artillery (AAA) gun. As a corporal, Bud supervised the duties of men under his command and wrote reports on their activities.

That he had so much responsibility at such a low rank illustrates a crucial point about the Marine Corps. Men of comparable enlisted rank in the Army Air Forces were taught about machines, about equipment, about technology. Enlisted soldiers were taught about weapons and small-unit tactics. But from the first time a Marine wears the green uniform, he is taught leadership. Being a Marine is about taking charge.

But in any capacity, duty on Johnston Island was boring. After the Battle of Midway, Johnston Island found itself in a deserted part of the vast Pacific. Bud spent his days looking for Japanese ships that never came.

Because Johnston Island was so remote, the Navy provided plenty of recreational outlets for young Marines. Fishing equipment and an extensive library were both offered. Bud's reading, or at least the nature of what he read, was relatively unusual among eighteen-year-old Marines. He became a fan of John Steinbeck and Hemingway. He read Erskine Caldwell and thought it was the most salacious material ever printed. He read every work of history he could find. Perhaps because of the reading, perhaps because of what he had observed thus far in the Marine Corps, he was coming to realize that one aspect of the military was the same as civilian life: educated people had privileges.

Bud certainly did not spend all his free time with a book in hand. Young Marines are as famous for alcohol consumption and hell-raising as they are for their combat skills. The line between boyish exuberance and illegality can be thin. The drinking aspect of Bud's time on Johnston Island marks the beginning of his wild-rabbit days, the time when his rambunctious side came out and he flirted with activities beyond the pale.

Johnston Island brought out a side of Bud that, even today, few people know about. Before the story of his drinking can be told, a fish story must be told.

It was Marine Corps policy to serve fish to all hands on Friday. The salted fish came from a warehouse. Officers began griping that they were in the middle of the ocean, surrounded by fish-filled waters, and were eating salted fish. They wanted fresh fish.

The Navy cook suddenly was under pressure. He put out the word that he wanted fresh fish for the officers' mess.

Bud had provided food for the family table since he was ten years old, and gathering fish for a chow hall did not seem that big of a challenge. He approached the cook and offered a deal. "I can get you fresh fish, not only for the officers' mess but for all the enlisted troops on Johnston Island."

A cook on a remote island has little chance of moving up the ranks. It would have been a real coup to provide fish for the officers. But to do so for the officers *and* more than a thousand enlisted men — well, the Marine Corps appreciates initiative and results. The cook was looking at a sure promotion.

He also knew that Corporal Day was not doing this out of the goodness of his heart. There had to be a catch. He stared at Bud and said, "What do you want in return?"

"All the syrup off every can of peaches. And yeast."

The cook raised his eyebrows. Marines ate canned peaches two or three days a week. Bud was talking about gallons of syrup. That much syrup could be used for only one thing. But the cook decided that was none of his business. The two men shook hands.

Bud then "liberated" — that is the military term for "stole" — a 25-horsepower outboard engine from the civilian contractor. He hid the engine for a few days until the civilians finished the runway extension and were transferred off the island. They left behind a beamy fifteen-foot wooden boat. Bud also "liberated" the boat.

Next, between the protective sandbagged walls of the searchlight battery, Bud built a whiskey still modeled on the ones he had found in Riverside. Once the still was completed, he gave the cook a heads-up: expect fresh fish for Friday.

A reef surrounded much of Johnston Island. Three days each week a Navy scow went outside the reef and dumped the garbage of fifteen hundred men. Thousands of fish gathered for the feast: white tuna, sea bass, dozens of species. Several hours before the first garbage run of the week was to take place, Bud took his purloined vessel into the shallows near the island. At his feet was a box of "liberated" hand grenades. Schools of mullet numbering in the thousands took refuge in the three-feet-deep waters. When Bud saw a school of mullet, he pulled the pin on a grenade and threw it into the water. Scores of stunned fish covered the surface. Day scooped up a few dozen and then motored to where the garbage scow was moving offshore. As the Navy enlisted guys began throwing garbage overboard, the big pelagic fish were swarming.

Bud hooked a mullet on a fishing rig and tossed it overboard, and a few seconds later he was fighting a forty-pound tuna. One after another, fish after fish was pulled in. When his boat was in danger of swamping from the load, he motored back and presented his catch to the cook. He did the same thing the next time the garbage scow went out. On Friday the officers and men feasted on fresh fish, and Bud received his gallons of peach syrup and boxes of yeast.

Bud took the fixings back to his still and began brewing moonshine. But either he had the wrong kind of yeast or he had not paid enough attention to construction details of the still back home, since he produced only a weak, milky liquor that he called "Horrible Hooch." The stuff was too bad to sell even to Marines, so he gave it away to a few friends.

Every Friday until April 1945, when Bud rotated back to Hawaii, the officers of Johnston Island, unlike Marines elsewhere in the Pacific, feasted on tuna only hours out of the ocean. And Bud Day and a few friends regularly became sick on Horrible Hooch. Had Bud's moonshining activities been discovered, he would have been court-martialed and sent to the brig.

ONE day Doris and her mother were talking about Bud's letters, and her mother said, "He has nice handwriting." Doris agreed. What she did not know was that her sister was reading all of Bud's letters and showing them — unedited — to their mother. But it seemed to make no difference.

Doris and her mother had developed a daily ritual. Each afternoon when Doris came home from school, her mother would have ready a plate of pastries. The two snacked, read passages from the Bible, and prayed for the safety of Bud Day.

Even though the tone of the letters between Bud and Doris had changed, Doris remained careful in her letters to Bud. She rarely used the word "I" but instead used the word "we," meaning herself and her mother. "We pray for you every day and are waiting for you to come home," she wrote.

Bud was moved. No one ever said they were waiting for him or that they were praying for his safety. He wrote his parents often, but their responses were slow and almost impersonal.

BUD returned to Hawaii in April 1945, on the same day President Franklin Roosevelt died. He was assigned to a guard company, a unit of Marines who pulled sentry duty at military installations.

The unit was sandwiched between the Navy submarine base and Hickam Field. Hickam was the Army's principal air base in Hawaii and was adjacent to Pearl Harbor. The Marines in the Pacific were building up their forces to invade Japan, and Hawaii remained very much on a wartime footing. It was almost impossible for enlisted Marines to obtain a liberty pass and go into Honolulu. This restriction was greatly appreciated by most locals. The mere sight of a Marine caused local parents to go on full alert. They thought GIs in general and Marines in particular were primitive beings who sought carnal knowledge of anything with a heartbeat.

There is a considerable body of anecdotal evidence to support this belief.

Bud was not big enough to hold much liquor. His ID card showed he was now five foot seven and weighed 123 pounds. Nevertheless, he was a Marine, and Marines are known to drink. On a rare trip into Honolulu, he drank more bourbon than he could handle. He did not want to vomit in the bar — he had seen too much of that back at the Lakeshore Inn — so he lurched outside, sat on the curb, and threw up into the gutter. A local bus driver was outraged at the sight and veered toward the curb. Had Bud not had quick reflexes and rolled over backward, the bus would have run over his legs.

On August 6, an atomic bomb fell on Hiroshima. Three days later, another fell on Nagasaki. Everyone knew the war was over and America's young men soon would be going home. But liberty still was scarce — too scarce for Bud Day. The countless hours he spent running the hills and hunting along the Big Sioux had heightened skills that remain undeveloped in most of us. He soon figured out a way to weave between fences, climb over buildings, and thwart Marine Corps security. On one of his illegal forays into town, he walked by the officers' club at Hickam Field, where he saw a Navy officer jump out of a jeep and leave it at the curb while he went inside on what must have been a quick errand.

It was not quick enough, because Bud stole the jeep and drove into Honolulu.

Shortly thereafter, the shore patrol saw him and figured — as Day says — *Something is wrong with this picture* (only officers had jeeps) and pulled him over. The shore patrolman did not ask a single question. Instead he walked up to Bud and said, "You're under arrest."

Bud was tossed into the brig and charged with two offenses: "Spec 1: Knowingly and willfully applying to his own use a one-quarter-ton truck, license #87230, the property of the U.S. Navy on 10 Sept. 45. Spec 2: AWOL from 10:00 p.m. to 10:30 p.m. 10 Sept. 45 when he was apprehended by the Shore Patrol."

On September 26 he faced a summary court-martial. He was convicted, sentenced to twenty-eight days in the brig, and reduced in rank to PFC.

The Marine Corps imposed harsh discipline on its members. But the war was all but over, and liberating an officer's jeep was understood to be more of a prank than a serious crime. Day served his time in the brig, but his reduction in rank was remitted on the condition that he be a good boy until he shipped home.

ONE day in November 1945, Bud's mother looked out the kitchen window of the house on Riverside Boulevard and saw Curly, Bud's Irish water spaniel that had been missing for almost three years. Curly was sitting by the road, waiting. Christine turned to Ed and said, "Bud's coming home."

Ed walked out to the street and stood beside Curly. The two looked up and down the road. "Bud's coming home," Ed said to everyone who passed.

Bud did not know it, but his father was fiercely proud of him and often boasted about his son's serving in the Pacific. He kept all of Bud's letters and read them to anyone who would listen.

On the boat ride from Hawaii to California, Bud did a lot of thinking. His Marine Corps record was not spectacular. His first year in the Corps was spent in training and in hospitals. Then some eighteen months on an island far from combat where he passed the time reading and fishing and moonshining. This was topped off with a court-martial and time in the brig.

Nevertheless, he had learned much. Years later he looked back and said, "When I came out of the Marine Corps, I was going to become a professional. I was going to do something. The Marines got me motivated."

Bud went to Chicago to the Great Lakes Naval Training Center, the closest release point to Sioux City for Marines, and on November 24, 1945, he was discharged as a corporal. Because he had been court-martialed, he was not eligible for the Good Conduct Medal that most enlisted men receive upon discharge.

Not sticking around, he jumped aboard a train for the twelve-hour ride back home to Sioux City, took a streetcar out to Riverside, stepped down, and began walking the last few blocks to 2222 Riverside Boulevard. He was in his Marine Corps uniform, and his seabag was over his shoulder.

Ed and Curly were waiting in front of the house.

3

Preparation

AMERICA was thrumming with energy when, in 1945, the sixteen million young men who had gone away to war as boys came home as hardened young warriors. The country's great economic engine was running on all cylinders, and the young veterans were running at full throttle. Their best young years had been spent fighting across Europe or slogging through Pacific hellholes. But now the job was done and it was time to move on.

On behalf of a grateful nation, the government opened wide the public coffers. To ease the transition into civilian life, every veteran received $20 per week for fifty-two weeks. Recipients called themselves the "52-20 Club." But far more important was the GI Bill, one of the most beneficial and far-reaching domestic programs in American history. The legislation gave every GI a month of college for every month spent in the military, plus a bonus for being overseas or in a combat zone. The GI Bill also paid each veteran $50 per month and covered the cost of books and supplies, enabling a generation of men to get a college education, to move beyond their circumstances.

Bud Day would take full advantage of the GI Bill. But when he returned to Riverside, there were more immediate priorities. One of the first things Day did after moving back into the house was to stand face-to-face with his father and lay down the law.

"There will be no more abuse of Mom," he said. "No more carping, no more criticizing, no more sarcasm. You will treat her with respect."

Thereafter Ed's treatment toward his wife softened. He was still critical and demeaning — that was his nature — but not to the degree he once had been.

Bud did not call Doris immediately. Even though they had been writing to each other for almost three years, and even though their letters had moved into a realm more serious than correspondence between friends, it was not yet time to renew their relationship. Bud was still in his wild-rabbit days, and he wanted to raise hell and howl at the moon. He wanted to run with his old friends and catch up on the lost years; he wanted to eat Bing Bars and drink something other than Horrible Hooch.

Some veterans would spend years riding the hoot-owl trail. But for Day this period would not last long. Bud contacted a few other Riverside boys, all members of the 52-20 Club. One was Frank Work. Even in the Marines, the fighting skills of Frank Work were such that he had been picked to serve as the enlisted Marine aide and bodyguard to Admiral William "Bull" Halsey. Work was with Halsey on the deck of the battleship *Missouri* during the Japanese surrender ceremony in Tokyo Bay, and for the rest of his life, whenever that historic moment was replayed on the History Channel or on documentaries, and the camera panned across the American delegation, Work would point and say, "That's me standing behind Halsey."

Day and Work and Paul Jackson and several other young Riverside veterans set off on a period of drinking and hell-raising. Their favorite bar was the Beer Cave, a basement bar down on Pierce Street where young women hung out. Day had a debonair and courteous manner that women found attractive. "Three or four of us would walk into a bar, and within minutes Bud had a girl on his arm," Work remembers.

Sometimes Day and his Riverside friends went out to the Lakeshore Inn, drank Cuba libres, and fought with anyone who looked at them crossways. Work remembers that one night he and Day were drinking and listening to the band play the "Clarinet Polka" when he noticed Day staring at a man across the bar. Suddenly Day stood and hitched up his belt.

"Where you going?" Work asked.

"I'm going over there and whip that guy's ass."

Work looked at the man and then looked back at his friend. Day was five foot seven and weighed 135 pounds. The guy he wanted to fight was about six foot two and weighed well over 200 pounds.

"Don't do that," Work said.

But Day picked a fight and was holding his own until the manager tossed him out.

Then Work went over, picked a fight with the same guy, and wiped the floor with him before he too was tossed out, and he and Day went laughing into the night.

Another time, he and Jim Brodie were drinking at a downtown bar when a pretty girl came in. Day was quite taken with her. But when the bar closed, she left with several band members. Day stormed out of the bar, got in his car, and a few minutes later stopped for gas. He and Brodie were standing by the pump when, coincidentally, the band members arrived with the girl. Day said something. He doesn't remember what, only that "words were exchanged." When other band members piled out of the car, Day reached into his trunk, pulled out a shotgun, and fired it into the air "just to scare them." The police arrived and Day was charged with discharging a firearm in the city limits.

Day paid a $10 fine and thought it was all over. But several years later the incident would come back to haunt him. Firing the shotgun kept him from realizing his boyhood dream. Firing the shotgun changed his life.

THERE was an ineffable something in Day that singled him out from everyone else Work knew. When Day walked into a room, every eye was drawn to him. He was small and slight, but there was something in his eyes, something in his bearing, something about the way he took command of every gathering, that set him apart. Years later, when his military comrades in arms were asked about him, they always spoke of his leadership abilities.

One measure of that difference was seen in his attitude toward the military. Other Riverside boys, once discharged, were through with the military. But Day's extensive reading and his passion for politics convinced him that a war was imminent with the Soviet Union. "They were looking for trouble all over the world," Day remembers. "I knew we were going to war. We had to be prepared."

Day wanted to join the Marine Corps Reserves. Unfortunately, the closest Marine station was in Minneapolis, some three hundred miles away. Prairie winters were such that the roads between Sioux City and Minneapolis were often closed. But the Marines were unforgiving about absences.

So Day did the unthinkable. On December 11, 1945, several weeks after he was discharged from the Marine Corps, he joined the Army Reserves. He became a dogface.

He also took a weeklong series of placement tests in order to enroll in college. (Several of Day's friends took the same tests and entered college but lasted only a quarter or two.) Day's placement-test results were high enough that he could enter college as a second-quarter sophomore but not high enough for him to enter a premedical program. So many thousands of veterans wanted to study medicine that medical schools had raised entry requirements to new heights. As a result, Day was stuck with his second choice: law. He was disappointed. But decades later, as a lawyer, he would change the lives of more than a million people.

Day enrolled in Morningside College on the east side of Sioux City and was scheduled to begin classes in January. He was eligible for four years of the GI Bill. But college and law school usually required seven years. Even though he was starting as a sophomore, he was going to have to double up on courses almost every quarter.

* * * *

ONE bitterly cold afternoon in December, Day found himself at loose ends. Snow covered the ground, Christmas was just around the corner, his first Christmas home in three years, carols playing on every radio station. All at once he felt compelled to call "that Sorensen girl."

Day's parents still had no phone and he had not yet bought a car, so he walked several blocks to the drugstore, where there was a pay phone. Doris was surprised to hear from him. She did not know he was back in town.

"I'm so glad you are home," she said.

"I'd like to come up and see you," Bud ventured.

To visit Doris, he rode a streetcar downtown, then caught another streetcar to her house — a trip of about forty-five minutes. He was astonished at how much she had changed. She could be described only as voluptuous. And her smile could light up a room. Bud Day was overwhelmed.

He looked around and noticed that on the wall was a crocheted Viking ship — a constant reminder to the Sorensen family of their proud heritage. A still dazed and dazzled Bud nodded, turned to Doris, and said, "You are a Viking."

For the rest of his life, he would refer to her as "The Viking."

One Friday, Bud and Doris were in the recreation room at her house. A fire burned in the fireplace. They were playing Ping-Pong when Bud said he was about to begin classes at Morningside. "Are you going to Briar Cliff?" he asked.

"No. That's a Catholic college," she said with a smile. "And I'm Lutheran. Besides, I'm not in college."

Bud stopped and ignored the Ping-Pong ball that went sailing by. "Are you a senior in high school?"

"No."

"Are you a junior?"

"No."

He was flabbergasted. "My God. You're not a freshman?"

She laughed. "No, I'm a sophomore."

Day put down his paddle and lit a cigarette. He smoked and paced, not saying a word. He had become smitten with Doris three years earlier. How old must she have been at the time? Twelve? Impossible. He didn't want to think about that. Now she was only a sophomore in high school. What would his friends say? He was a former Marine, about to turn twenty-one, and he was dating a sixteen-year-old girl.

He looked at her again.

She looked twenty.

He smoked and paced and looked. She was a smart and level-headed girl with a good sense of business. She had held down a responsible job in her father's business since she was twelve. Plus, she was the prettiest girl he knew. And, as Day remembered many decades later, "God, what a body."

As Bud anxiously deliberated, Doris stood at the end of the table, watching, smiling, and waiting. Bud took a final puff from his cigarette, threw the butt into the fireplace, and said, "Oh, hell. What difference does it make?"

Doris's father had grown fond of Bud back when Bud delivered the Sunday paper. And Doris's mother, having read Bud's letters to her daughter for the past three years, knew the relationship could become serious. But Doris was so young. There must be rules. Doris was a devout Lutheran and was very unworldly. Bud's friends were too old for her, and her friends were too young for him. They could not leave the house on dates. And Bud could visit only on Friday or Saturday evening.

The rules said nothing about phone calls, so every afternoon at 4:30, Bud hiked down to the drugstore, called Doris, and talked for an hour or so. And he began showing up at St. John Lutheran Church on Sunday mornings, as Doris sang in the choir. Bud sat with Mr. and Mrs. Sorensen.

In January 1946, Day entered Morningside College. The primary purpose of the small Methodist college was to train young men for the ministry. Religion courses were obligatory for all students.

The school was prudish and strict — that is, until it was inundated by the tsunami of iconoclastic, beer-drinking, swearing, skirt-chasing, cigarette-smoking veterans, men who had been killing people for the past few years, men who knew every whorehouse in the Pacific and Europe, men usually more interested in a degree than in an education.

Few events in American history have had such an effect on the American university system as when millions of government-funded veterans entered college after World War II. Officials at Morningside realized, as did college officials all across America, that the veterans were a financial boon. When Day signed up for Morningside, the tuition was $35 per quarter. By the end of his first year, tuition had jumped to $100. Then it was raised again. (GI Bill payments were raised commensurately.)

But colleges and universities found that with financial blessings came a trade-off: veterans were often disruptive. Dozens of new professors were hired to teach the flood of GIs. Professors quickly found that while they were looked up to and deferred to by traditional college students, such was not the case with the GIs. These scarred men had built-in bullshit detectors that made them laugh openly at the professors or challenge them on every point. Veterans found that much about college life was shallow and nonsensical — and it was nearly impossible to change their opinion. At the beginning of 1946, Morningside College was trying to close a beer joint about a block south of the campus. Then the ex-GIs landed and the bar owners were suddenly making such profits that a competing beer joint was opened a block north of the campus. Both bars thrived, and Morningside had to swallow some of its Methodist ideals.

For young veterans, the automobile was the metaphor for their upward mobility. Like many others, Bud borrowed money and soon was driving a 1940 Mercury convertible, metallic red with a white top. He was very much the man about town, a handsome young vet going to school at Morningside and shouting, "Radook!" every time he saw one of his Riverside buddies.

Even though he was living at home, the car payments left him terribly pressed for money.

He gave his mother the $50 discretionary income he received from the government every month, and his spending money came from a series of jobs that he worked after class and on weekends. For a while he drove an armored car. Then he was a security guard at the gate of the Zenith assembly plant. He was employed at an abstracting company, checking property titles. And he worked at a bar. But the jobs that paid best — about eighty-five cents per hour — were in the stockyards and meatpacking companies. There, he chased cows into pens owned by meat packers. It was dangerous work. When the cows were off-loaded from trucks into the yards, they were crazed, bellowing wide-eyed behemoths, unpredictable and dangerous. Dozens of times Day was chased up a fence by a charging steer. A mistake in timing or a misstep on the fence would have had serious consequences.

After the cows were slaughtered, they were suspended from hooks and moved down a line of meat cutters. Day's job was to cut out the heart, lungs, and liver. The production pace was such that he had to work quickly. Workers wore metal mesh gloves. Even so, many sliced their hands and fingers.

In the yards, the stench of urine and fecal matter from half-crazed animals was overpowering. And in the packinghouse the entire malodorous process — the blood and viscera, the hooves and offal that boiled day and night — was so powerful and so penetrating that it floated like a miasma over Sioux City. The smell of the packinghouses was the smell of Sioux City. Every evening Bud walked out the gate with the stench imbedded in his clothes, and he thought there was no more repulsive odor in the world.

One day he would find something almost as bad.

The danger of Day's work, the odor and the fatigue, the extra courses and long hours of study, stretched him to the limit. Not surprisingly, he did not enjoy college. Several of his Riverside friends dropped out. But Bud Day knew that an education could lift him out of Riverside.

In later years, Day would remember only two of his teachers. The first was a history professor who encouraged and structured his interest in the past. The second taught English literature and required her students to memorize poems and a dozen or so of Shakespeare's sonnets. At the time, Day thought the assignments silly and time wasting, not knowing that decades later, recalling those poems and sonnets would do much toward maintaining his sanity.

Doris went to choir practice every Wednesday night and rode the streetcar home. It was a big step when her parents decided Day could drive her home — no dawdling permitted. Then the Sorensens allowed Bud to take Doris to movies downtown at the Orpheum Theater. They knew what time the movies ended and calculated within five minutes when Doris should be home.

But increasingly exhausted from work, bored with the inanities of college, and now enduring what he considered oppressive dating rules, Bud grew discouraged about his romance with Doris. Then one day her father said to him, "You come to church every Sunday. Why don't you join our church?" Bud was confirmed as a Lutheran. Slowly and inexorably his life and the life of Doris Sorensen were becoming intertwined.

One day Doris's mother asked her, "Do you love Bud?"

"I don't know," stammered Doris. She was in high school. Why was her mother talking to her about love?

"Well, if you don't, break off this relationship right now because Bud is in love with you."

Doris was stunned. "How do you know when you are in love?" she asked.

"You know. You just know. Bud loves you. I don't want him hurt or you hurt."

Less than a year later, in December 1946, Doris's mother died. Doris thought often about what her mother had said and thus was not surprised when, one night at dinner, Bud looked at her across the table and said, "Doris, when are we going to get married?"

That was his way of proposing.

"Well, I want to wait until I am twenty," she said.

That was her way of saying yes.

WHEN Doris graduated from high school, her father took her to Norway for five months to become more proficient in Norwegian and to learn more of her family history. Before she left, she and Bud made a pact. While she was gone they both would date other people. If they still felt strongly about each other when she returned, they would make plans to get married.

Doris and her father traveled the length and breadth of Norway, meeting the oldest and most distant members of the family. Doris heard of relatives who played crucial roles in the Resistance; of men who had been POWs and tortured by the Germans almost to the point of death. But, it was stressed, they had never betrayed the Resistance. Because the Norwegian resistance to the Germans had been so weak, there were few notable Norwegian patriots. Thus, the bravery of her own relatives assumed even more importance.

Doris sent Bud a letter giving him the time she and her father would return to Sioux City. When the two Sorensens stepped down from the train, Bud was waiting. Doris knew they would be married.

Doris's father accepted this but issued more rules. If Doris went to college, she had to promise she would not get married until she graduated and worked for a while. Sonwald Sorensen did not want to send his daughter to college unless she intended to put her education to use in a practical fashion. Otherwise, it was a secretarial school.

Doris picked secretarial school.

By late 1947, Day lacked only the obligatory religion courses before he could graduate from Morningside. But he had enough hours to enter law school at the University of South Dakota in Vermillion, which, in the pre–interstate highway days of the late 1940s, was forty-two miles north of Sioux City, so he dropped out of college and entered law school. Still feeling the pressure of the four-year time frame for the GI Bill, Bud took extra courses every quarter.

His early-morning ride to Vermillion was relieved by the fact that it was pheasant-hunting season. Every morning before daylight, Bud picked up his shotgun, an act that sent Curly into a frenzy of running and leaping, loaded the dog into his car, and drove up Highway 77. In Vermillion he parked near the white granite building that housed the law school. Curly followed him to class, claws clicking on the oak flooring. During class, Curly slept under Day's chair. (Few students wanted to sit near Day because Curly often passed noxious gas con brio.) At the end of class, Day and Curly jumped back into his car and "road hunted" on the way home. Day drove slowly down 77, shotgun by his leg. When he saw a pheasant, he stopped and released Curly. The dog followed the bird into the tall grass, then flushed it, giving Bud a clear shot. Some days he came home with three or four pheasants for the table.

Every student, if he is fortunate, finds a professor who, in an intellectual sense, sets him on fire. For Bud Day that man was Marshall McKusick, dean of the law school. McKusick was the first true scholar the River Rat had ever met, and he would have a tremendous impact on Day's life.

The dean had a shock of white hair and looked like the movie version of a Supreme Court justice. He spent summers in Maine and was the most worldly man Day had ever met. McKusick spoke Latin fluently and sometimes in class jumped back and forth between English and Latin, an ability that awed Bud and made the classes sparkle. He also was a man of vision and principle. He horrified many when, in 1948, he allowed women into the law school.

As dean, he decreed that his law school would not follow the lead of colleges and universities throughout America and expand just to take advantage of revenues through the GI Bill. The freshman class of the law school had always consisted of forty students; in order to give those students the best possible education, the freshman class would continue to have only forty students.

McKusick took a special interest in Day. During long chats in his office, the dean made Day believe that anything in life was possible. And he reinforced values that Day had learned from his father, ideas about principles and integrity and holding on to one's integrity no matter the outside pressure.

In the spring of 1948, Iowa gave its World War II veterans a one-time bonus of $300 to supplement their GI Bill. Day used the money to buy Doris an engagement ring. They would have to wait more than a year to get married, until Day's mother began receiving a welfare check that would replace the money Bud was giving her every month.

During his first year of law school, Day worked Friday and Saturday nights at a bar called Pheasant Acres. School and work made for eighteen-hour days. But by going to summer school and taking a heavy course load, he would finish in two years. He also joined the Reserve Officers' Training Corps (ROTC).

During the last quarter of law school, Day's schedule finally got the best of him. After class and after work or after visiting Doris, he went to the law library in the courthouse and studied until 2 a.m. Then he staggered home. Because he had a 7:30 a.m. class, he had to get up at 5 a.m. "We have to get married," he said to Doris. "I can't see you in the evenings, then get up and drive to Vermillion and go to class and then go to my job. This is not working out."

By now Doris's father had remarried and was happy to have Doris move out.

On Memorial Day weekend, May 28, 1949, about six weeks before Doris turned twenty and a little over two months before

Bud was to graduate from law school, George Everette Day and Doris Merlene Sorensen were married in St. John Lutheran Church in Sioux City.

Theirs was to be an extraordinary marriage, a match in which both would be called upon to give more and to pay a higher price than most couples could ever imagine.

THE new couple spent their honeymoon at Nest Lake in southwest Minnesota. They had barely settled into their one-room cabin when there was a fearful racket out front and a host of voices shouting, "Radook!" It was the four ushers from the wedding. They had stolen a case of bourbon from the reception and were ready to party.

Frank Work, in his understated fashion, remembers that "Bud and Doris were real surprised to see us."

Nevertheless, Day smiled and said, "Hey, guys. Good to see you. How long you staying?"

"All week," said Frank Work. The four ushers had rented the adjacent cabin.

Day's friends could not cook, so over the course of the next several days, they visited Bud and Doris for every meal. Doris could not cook either, so most meals were boiled eggs, sandwiches, and fish. Not only did the ushers eat every meal with Bud and Doris but they went bass fishing with them during the day and played cards with them every night. There was no bathroom in the cabin. An outhouse was fifty feet from the back door. And there was no privacy, as the bed was separated from the room by a curtain. So when Frank Work and the others visited, Doris had to sit with them.

Today when Doris tells the story, she laughs. But there is an edge to her laughter.

Upon the honeymooners' return, Bud's parents found a place for the newly married couple to live: Bell's Motel at the corner of Riverside Boulevard and St. Paul Avenue. The motel was near the railroad tracks and only two blocks from Day's old home on

Riverside Boulevard. For two rooms and a bath, the rent was $50 per month. The front room was a combination living room–dining room–kitchen and the back room was the bedroom. They had no checking account. Everything was paid in cash. Bud was earning about $110 per month. He set aside $50 for rent and $50 for car payments, and used the remaining $10 for meals and cigarettes. Doris was a secretary with the Western Adjustment Agency, where she made fifty cents an hour and worked five and a half days each week. Her check went for groceries, the $25-a-month payments on the refrigerator and stove, and streetcar tokens. The young couple set aside $5 each month so that on the twenty-eighth — their anniversary date — they could have a celebratory dinner, usually at the Gantz Steakhouse, where Day favored frog legs, a great delicacy in Sioux City. The budget was so tight that, once, Doris did not have $1.50 to pick up her dry cleaning. The clothes stayed at the cleaners more than a year.

To their new apartment, Bud brought a chair, a lamp, and a phonograph. Doris brought a typewriter, a bed, a cedar chest, a sewing machine, several rugs, and a lace tablecloth. They received a kitchen table and four chairs as a wedding gift. Two of the chairs were put together with an afghan draped over them to serve as a "love seat."

The motel was about thirty feet from a railroad track, and several times daily the train from Sioux Falls to Omaha rumbled through, blowing its whistle and causing the building to tremble. Day had heard the train for years and was not bothered. But it took Doris months to get used to the noise.

Day's friends continued with the running shivaree, coming to the motel several nights each week, standing outside shouting, "Radook!" and blowing horns. One evening about six months later, Day opened the door and walked outside. He was smiling. But his eyes were as cold as arctic ice when he said in a calm voice, "I think it is about time this ended." And it did. Right then.

When Christmas came, Bud and Doris could afford only one string of lights for their first Christmas tree. They had no washing machine, so Bud's mother washed their clothes. Television had not come to Sioux City and they did not have a radio and could not afford a telephone, so they spent hours every evening talking. They spent time with her father and his new wife and with Bud's parents. The long conversations strengthened the bond between Bud and Doris, and for the remainder of their lives, they savored long evening discussions.

They lived in the motel for eight months before moving to the top floor of a Victorian house on South Palmetto, a street marked with enormous oaks and elms. The apartment was a few blocks from Morningside College, and except for his stint in the Marine Corps, this was the first time Bud Day lived outside Riverside. Their apartment windows included stained glass, and sometimes they felt as if they were living in a church.

THE day before he graduated from law school, Bud took Curly in the front door of the school and out the back door. Afterward he told people Curly was the smartest dog in Siouxland. "That dog has been through law school," he said.

Day then returned to Morningside to pick up the fifteen hours of religion courses he needed to graduate. He received his degree in January 1950.

He and Frank Work borrowed $3,000 — a lot of money at the time — and bought the Fidelity Detective and Collection Agency in Sioux City, a somewhat shady operation that they intended to make legitimate. Day used his membership in the South Dakota Bar to file a few proceedings in collection matters, but he did not have a law practice. Soon the detective agency was making a profit and growing. Day, like his father, was a staunch Democrat and became president of the Sioux City chapter of Young Democrats. He was beginning to make his presence felt in the community.

Then came an incident that is important because of what it reveals both about Day's sense of duty and about his ability to subjugate friendship to what he considers higher concepts. Years later, after he was released from prison in North Vietnam, he would rise above the brotherhood of the POWs to prosecute fellow officers whom he believed to have shirked their duties. And still later, when he was an old man and engaged in the great legal battle of his life, a colleague would observe his lonely fight and say, "Bud Day, by his very nature, is incapable of allowing injustice to go unchallenged."

Late one night, Day and Work were conducting what detectives call "a domestic surveillance." The target was a bartender whose wife suspected he was too friendly with female customers. As Day and Work watched the bartender through a window, Day looked around and noticed that across the street, the door of a clothing store was ajar. He told Work to call the police.

Day should have simply kept his eye on the door of the clothing store and waited for the cops. That would have been the prudent thing to do. But instead Day did what police officers say is one of the most dangerous tasks in law enforcement: he entered a darkened building where a criminal was inside, plying his trade.

"He walked in and never batted an eye," Work says. "He had more guts than brains."

One of the highest compliments that one police officer can bestow on another is to say, "He is always the first one through the door." This means not only that the officer is brave but that he does not shirk his duty.

Day stepped inside and pulled the .32-caliber pistol he carried. As his eyes adjusted to the semidarkness, he noticed an area closed off with a sheet of canvas — a good place for a burglar to hide. Day approached and in the faint light from the street saw a bulge in the canvas. The burglar had seen Day and was lying in wait. Day ordered the man out. When the burglar stepped from behind the canvas, he had a .45-caliber pistol in his hand. "Drop the gun," Day ordered.

His tone and his confidence made the burglar do just that.

Bud marched the man out of the store and waited for the police to arrive. But Work was having a hard time convincing the police to come to Day's assistance. The police knew Work and thought this was a hoax. It was more than an hour before an officer arrived. During that time, the burglar, who not only was from Riverside but was the brother of one of Day's schoolmates, kept saying, "How about turning me loose?" Riverside people, he stressed, stick together.

But to Bud Day, duty was a higher concept than friendship.

"No. You're going to jail."

The police arrived and took the burglar into custody. Then they found the burglar's heavily armed partner waiting in a nearby car. The car was loaded with goods taken from the clothing store. Both burglars had prior convictions and were considered dangerous men.

Work still remembers the respect in the eyes of the police when they realized what Day had done.

IN April 1950, backed by a college degree, a law degree, and two years of ROTC courses, Day wrote the Marine Corps asking that his records be cleared of his "nonrecurrent violation" — the court-martial for stealing a jeep — so he could apply for a reserve commission. The Marine Corps refused and he appealed. Before a decision was rendered, the Iowa Army National Guard offered Day a commission. He accepted.

In May 1950, Day filed an application to take the Iowa bar exam. His application was returned with a note saying that because of his misdemeanor conviction — firing a shotgun in the city limits — he would not be allowed to take the exam. And he could not practice in Iowa until he passed the bar.

Today he makes light of not being allowed to take the Iowa bar exam by saying, "I couldn't have cared less." He says he could have appealed and prevailed. He says that America was about to go to war in Korea, that he had a commission and knew he would spend his career in the military. Being a Sioux City lawyer just wasn't that important.

Perhaps he is right. But consider the context. Here was a Riverside boy, a bright boy and voracious reader who had learned through books both how mean was his world and how limitless was that outside it. He had done what no Riverside boy had ever done: graduated from both college and law school. But the rewards, the commission in his beloved Marine Corps and becoming a lawyer in Sioux City, had just been snatched from his grasp.

Frank Work still shakes his head in sadness when asked about this time in Day's life. He says Day was devastated. Work recalls how, after Day received the terrible news, the two of them went to have a beer and to talk. Day began bemoaning the consequences of getting drunk in Hawaii and the incident with the shotgun. He took a bar napkin and wrote on it that his wild-rabbit days were over; that henceforth he would be more serious about life; that he would buckle down and seek out every opportunity to make something of himself. He slid the napkin across the table to Work, tapped the napkin, and nodded his head in a silent promise.

Most young men would have left the napkin on the bar and forgotten about it as another beer-fueled bugle of ambition. But Frank Work looked at the napkin and knew his friend was bound for glory. He kept the napkin more than forty years. And later, when people in Sioux City read of Day's acclaim, Work said, "I could have told you that." And he brought out the napkin to show them when it all began.

DAY went to summer camp with the Army National Guard in 1950. Concurrently, North Korea invaded South Korea. Day was terribly disappointed when his Guard unit was not called to active duty, and when he applied for active duty, he was rebuked for his temerity.

When a friend suggested he switch his commission to the Air Force, he was noncommittal. Then the friend talked to a general who not only offered a commission but said Day could go on active duty. It is easy to understand why the Air Force wanted Day. At the time, the military was still something of a jobs program. Most officers did not have college degrees. Efforts to build a professional officer corps were only just beginning. As a result, someone like Day was hot property.

On November 28, 1950, Bud Day moved his commission to the Air Force Reserves. He was assigned to a unit in Sioux City and told to expect a call to active duty. The call came on March 15, 1951.

In April, Bud Day left Sioux City for the beginning of a career that would last almost twenty-seven years and would take him to the distant corners of the earth. He would never again live in Sioux City.

Because of his law degree and his experience as a detective, the Air Force called up Day as a special investigator. But the Air Force needed pilots, and Day took the physical and passed. However, there was a problem. Flight training took a year. Day had just turned twenty-seven, and Air Force regulations said a man had to finish flight training within six months after reaching that age.

For the third time, Bud Day needed a waiver to go to war.

4

The Wild Blue Yonder

In the spring of 1951, the Air Force was gearing up for war so rapidly that prospective pilots were accepted faster than flight schools could accommodate them. Thus, young men were sent to Air Force bases around the country and assigned menial jobs until a new flight-training class opened. Bud Day was ordered to Goodfellow AFB in San Angelo, Texas. When the provost marshal, the top cop at Goodfellow, read Day's personnel records, he thought Bud was a godsend. Usually, prospective pilots are placed in charge of officers' clubs, supply facilities, and motor pools. In "pipeline status," they do not receive an officers efficiency report (ER), the periodic report card that forms the basis for promotion. But Day was given a real job training air policemen and advising the provost marshal on legal matters. As a result, Day received his first ER a year before his contemporaries received theirs.

An ER is awarded by the officer's immediate superior and may be endorsed by a higher-ranking commander. There is no better way to evaluate the arc of an officer's career than by thumbing through his ERs and seeing what his superiors thought of him at given intervals.

Bud Day's first ER covers a short period — June 4 through August 19. But the provost marshal wrote that Day did "an outstanding job," that he had a "keen and alert appearance," that he "eagerly accepts the responsibility of control, supervision, direction, and instruction of subordinates," and that he "exacts rigid conformance with the standards of discipline and conduct expected of Air Force officers." Finally, the ER said Day "makes a continuous effort toward self-improvement" by taking extension courses and completing them with record speed.

Much about this is significant. The military considers second lieutenants among the most useless creatures on earth, and here was a second lieutenant receiving what the military calls a "water-walker" ER. In fact, the ER was so laudatory that a colonel subsequently downgraded it, saying no second lieutenant could be so good.

To a civilian, the comments regarding Day's appearance may seem of little importance, even trivial. But military officers are expected to have a "keen and alert appearance." So by singling this out in Day's ER, his superiors were stating that he was exceptionally well turned out. This, in turn, spoke volumes about his pride in being an Air Force officer. That pride was balanced by a perfect combination of ambition and humility. Day was better educated than his boss — something that would be true for most of his career. Yet he was driven at Goodfellow, as he would be at future assignments, to further his education.

Doris was also getting quite an education. Life at Goodfellow was unlike anything in her experience. Her father was a successful businessman, and her last years at home had been quite comfortable. But at that time the Air Force did not pay to move an officer, and Bud could not afford to move their furniture from Sioux City. Now all he and Doris had were a roll-away bed, an ironing board, a hot plate, a coffeepot, a few plates, and a couple of wicker chairs. The ironing board also served as the dining room table. In the bedroom window was a radiator-like device that Day called the "swamp cooler." A garden hose pushed water through the device and a fan sucked in outside air over the water-cooled container and lowered bedroom temperatures to almost tolerable levels. Doris, generations of Norwegian blood coursing through her veins, found the Texas heat so oppressive that she slept about twelve hours a day. Insects of a type never seen in Sioux City were everywhere. When storms came and the wind blew for days, dust filled the house. No matter how often Doris cleaned, the house was always dusty. One day she walked into the bathroom and saw what she thought was a bug emerging from the sink. She had earlier seen the same sort of bug crawling up the bedroom wall. "Bud, look at that funny bug," she said as she lifted her bare foot to step on it.

"Doris, don't touch it. That's a scorpion."

Doris remembers two things in particular about Goodfellow: From the beginning, Bud rarely talked about his work. "You can't repeat what you don't know," he told Doris. He explained about wartime security, and because of her family's experiences in Norway, she understood. She also remembers how messy Bud was. Never mind that his tailored uniform shirt had razor creases that lined up with the creases in his trousers. Never mind that his haircut was short and that his shoes gleamed; at home he was a slob. When he walked in the door, he took off his shoes and socks and left them in the middle of the floor. Doris grew weary of picking up his sweaty socks but accepted this as one of Bud's quirks and as part of learning to be a good wife.

In August, Day entered flight training at Hondo AFB. Hondo is about forty miles west of San Antonio, out in the middle of nowhere. The base had been closed since the end of World War II and was now reopened because of the demand for pilots in Korea. Most facilities were decrepit, broken, or nonexistent, but the runway was in good shape and that was all that mattered.

Flying a jet aircraft in the early 1950s was a dangerous business.

The flying class ahead of Day was filled with two groups: new Naval Academy and West Point graduates (there was not yet an Air Force Academy) who wanted to fly, and the sons of Air Force generals. Many members of the class were given flying time before their training class began, anything to give them a leg up on their contemporaries. Academy graduates and generals' sons were programmed for success.

About 80 percent of Day's class consisted of cadets, young men without college degrees accepted for pilot training who had not yet received their commission. (They would be commissioned when they were awarded their wings.) This means, of course, that the overwhelming bulk of new pilots, many of whom would make a career of the military, had no college degree. It would be another generation before the Air Force had an officer corps of educated professionals.

The other 20 percent of the class were retreads from World War II, Day among a handful of newly commissioned officers. While the cadets were eighteen or nineteen years old, the retreads were generally in their thirties. Day was in the middle: seven years or so older than the cadets and about ten years younger than the retreads.

Flight training begins with weeks in the classroom, studying the theory of flight, meteorology, navigation, radio procedures, and a host of other technical subjects. Then the student flies with an instructor.

A student's first solo flight is always a career milestone. On the afternoon that he soloed, Day came home to find a candlelight dinner. He smiled, thinking that somehow Doris had heard and this was a celebratory feast.

"I have news for you," he said.

She smiled. "I have news too."

"You go first."

Her smile grew wider. "I got my driver's license today."

An overjoyed Day laughed and congratulated Doris. Soloing an aircraft, he truly believed, took second place to the fact that Doris, at twenty-one, had her first driver's license. It was the beginning of what would be a lifelong pattern for Day: no matter his deeds of valor, his awards and honors, he would always place his wife's accomplishments ahead of his own.

Because Bud and Doris had so few material things, they continued their practice of long afternoon and evening conversations. And while Day was learning to be a pilot, both he and Doris were learning about life in west Texas. It was like an exotic foreign country. Everyone talked slowly, and it seemed they all had two first names. Bud and Doris lived in the upstairs portion of a house where the landlady was named Ella Mae. She had two daughters, Meda Jane and Barbara Joann.

Back home in Iowa, one name was enough for anybody.

Everything was different. Doris had never heard of Mexican food, had never eaten fried shrimp, hot peppers, black-eyed peas, or pinto beans. And as isolated as Texas could feel, it was also strangely cosmopolitan to someone as sheltered as Doris. Back home, she had never heard of spaghetti.

In other ways, it was as small as a shoe box. So many people went barefoot here. They even drove cars while barefoot. Everyone made it his or her business to know everyone else's business. There was only one phone in the house where Bud and Doris boarded, and the landlady listened to every conversation. Once, Doris returned from a grocery trip to San Antonio and was talking to her father on the phone. She told him about a frightening thunderstorm she had experienced. A few minutes after Doris went back upstairs, the landlady called a friend and said, "Did you hear they had a really big storm in San Antonio today?"

Sometimes on Fridays, Bud and Doris went into Hondo to a dance. The sides of the building were raised to let in a vagrant breeze. Men wore cowboy boots, jeans, hats, and T-shirts. They apparently did not bathe before coming, and Doris could smell cowboy from across the room. The locals danced in a fashion Bud and Doris had never seen: arms flapping, legs pumping, and boots stomping, and whooping and laughing and holding their women tightly.

In Sioux City, Lutherans did not dance.

ONCE finished with basic flight school, Day, in February 1952, was ordered up to Big Spring, Texas, for additional training as a fighter pilot, specifically as a fighter-bomber pilot. He would fly the T-33, part of the first generation of notoriously underpowered Air Force jets, and would learn strafing and bombing techniques — how to put "iron in the mud."

At Big Spring, Day picked up one of those habits so revelatory of fighter pilots: he began using JP-4 — jet fuel — in his cigarette lighter. JP-4 was a high-grade kerosene with an odor that many found unpleasant but that was beloved by early fighter pilots. If the pilot was in civilian clothes, every time he lit a cigarette, he sent out an unspoken message: *Hey, I'm a fighter pilot.*

Day's instructor at Big Spring had flown propeller aircraft in World War II and resented being called out of civilian life to teach. He was an overly cautious man who never pushed aircraft to the outer edge of the performance envelope and, as a result, did not teach budding combat pilots the full limits of what they and the machines could and could not do. The instructor also was a screamer who shouted obscenities at students who — as students inevitably do — made mistakes. On one flight he called Day a "dumb son of a bitch."

Many students think such abuse is part of training. Not Day. He was a Riverside boy and a former Marine. When the aircraft landed, Day skidded down the ladder, shucked his parachute, and shouted up to the instructor, "Get down here! I'm going to kick your ass!"

The instructor refused to dismount. Day eventually stalked off and told his flight commander that he did not want to fly again with "that chickenshit instructor." Thereafter, he was assigned another instructor, a man who knew how to bank and yank, a man who knew how to fly a jet aircraft at maximum performance, a man who showed Day what six Gs felt like. This instructor could put the T-33 on the edge of a stall and hold it there longer than anyone Day had ever seen. The natural tendency of a jet aircraft is either to fly or to fall out of the air. To put an aircraft on the edge of a stall and hold it there, nibbling at the stall while still maintaining flying speed, was a virtuoso performance. It was also a skill that every air-to-mud pilot needed, because if he pulled too many Gs coming off a bomb run, the aircraft could stall and depart flight — which meant it assumed the flying characteristics of a brick.

Thus, Day fared well the first time he challenged a nominal superior. As a young man, Day was a curious mixture of excellent manners and thin-skinned and prickly aggressiveness — a typical Riverside boy. With age he would become more temperate, and his manners would be ascendant. But throughout his military career, he never had any reluctance about criticizing his superiors. In the hierarchical Air Force, this would have serious consequences.

Day graduated in September 1952 and received his wings. He was one of the few lawyer–fighter pilots in the U.S. Air Force. And as one of the top graduates in class 52-F, the sixth flying class to graduate in 1952, Day had his choice of assignments.

His overarching desire was to fly combat in Korea. But he faced a dilemma. If he chose to go to Luke AFB in Arizona or Nellis AFB in Nevada and take the "hard polish" course to become a combat pilot, he probably would go to Korea. But not all Luke and Nellis graduates went to Korea. Day wanted a sure thing.

A lot of talk was going around about Operation Fair Play, a plan to use the F-94 Starfire, America's first all-weather jet aircraft, as a night fighter and attack aircraft in Korea. At the time, the Air Force was limiting its fighting in Korea almost entirely to daylight hours. The reason was simple: fighter pilots in the new Air Force did not have the instrument-flying skills for night flying or for severe weather — too many were killing themselves in rather spectacular fashion by crashing into mountains. The very premise of Operation Fair Play acknowledged this deficiency. An Air Force that flies only in daylight hours and good weather is not truly an Air Force. Pilots accepted for Operation Fair Play would receive an advanced six-week course in instrument flying before going to Korea — and they would definitely go to Korea.

Day volunteered and received orders for Moody AFB in Valdosta, Georgia.

Valdosta was in central-south Georgia, a few miles from the Florida line. In 1952, it was, and remains today, a pissant little town that, if not at the end of the world, is in the same zip code. Here people married their cousins, spoke as if they had a mouthful of mush, and carried all manner of guns in their trucks and on their persons. For two people from Sioux City, this was another strange land.

Every time Day took off with an instructor, he flew "under the hood"; that is, he wore a device over his head that restricted his vision to the instrument panel. Unusual attitudes, intercepts, landings, all were done under the hood.

Often, pilots had a chance for real instrument flying. Powerful thunderstorms sweep off the Gulf of Mexico and cut across the area where Florida and Georgia meet. Pilots out of Moody went hunting for this fierce weather and, when they found it, tightened their seat belts, turned up the cockpit lights, and flew into the darkest and most violent parts they could find. Naturally, the trainees had some apprehension about this. But the standard response of the instructor as he pointed the aircraft into the heart of the storm was "Faint heart never fucked a pig," and that became the watchword of young pilots who went through instrument training at Moody in the early 1950s. For years afterward, when facing an onerous task, they declared, "Faint heart never fucked a pig," and then they did the job.

When pilots graduated from Moody, they received a "green card" as proof of their proficiency in all-weather flying. Green cards were relatively rare. Having the card meant that in bad weather, the holder — and not an operations officer on the ground — made the decision as to whether or not he would fly. He could take off in zero-zero weather — that is, when the weather reduced both vertical and horizontal visibility to zero. Some considered the green card a license to go out and get killed. But as much as anything that happened to the operational Air Force in the 1950s, the school at Moody and the green card made a professional Air Force.

Not only did Day demonstrate his flying proficiency by receiving his green card at Moody, but he also first demonstrated his intuitive genius as a pilot there.

In late 1952, Day survived the first of a series of incidents that had killed more experienced pilots.

To understand the nature of Day's initial brush with death, one must first know a bit about a design peculiarity of the T-33.

To oversimplify a complex problem, a jet engine always needs more air. The greater the amount of air, the greater the venturi effect at the rear of the engine, and therefore the greater the thrust. In the T-33, not enough air came through the intake during the takeoff run to generate the thrust necessary for the jet to become airborne. As a result, the T-33 had what were known as "sucker doors" atop the fuselage. The spring-loaded doors inhaled air when the engine was idling and during taxi and takeoff. When the aircraft reached a speed of about 130 knots, the doors automatically closed. The sucker doors were directly behind the main ninety-gallon fuel tank, and the fuel tank was directly behind the pilot.

The fuel tank had a screw-on lid — not unlike that of a Mason jar — that had a rubber gasket that did not always seat properly. Part of the pre-takeoff checklist was to pressurize the fuel tanks on the tip of each wing to ensure a positive flow to the main tank. If the air pressure broke the seal on the gasket, fuel siphoned out of the tank, through the sucker doors, and into an engine running at full power. The pilot was notified of this by an amber warning light on the panel. If the light came on during takeoff, it usually meant the aircraft was seconds away from a catastrophic explosion.

Every aircraft has what is known as a "balanced field length" performance. This is the length of runway needed for the aircraft to stop in the event that the pilot must abort takeoff with the aircraft at flying speed. In most instances, there is not enough runway to stop; if so, takeoff is the only option. If a pilot experiences an emergency on takeoff, once he is airborne, the problems have a habit of multiplying. For instance, the T-33 can take off with a full load of fuel but cannot land; the shock to the landing gear is too great. If the pilot does manage to land without having the gear poke through the wings, the brakes will burn out before he can stop. Thus, he must burn off or vent hundreds of pounds of fuel before landing, and he must do this while in the middle of an emergency. Little wonder that when Day arrived at Moody, no T-33 pilot had ever survived a fire on takeoff. (In fact, shortly before Day arrived, World War II ace Don Gentile was killed in this fashion.) Even though the T-33 was the primary training aircraft for gunnery instruction and instrument training, and even though more aircraft and pilots would be lost because of this design flaw, it would be several more years before the problem was fixed.

One evening at the officers' club, Day and other pilots were talking about how to handle a fire on takeoff. There was nothing in the Dash-1 — the handbook for the T-33 — about this issue.

Day parsed the problem in a lawyer's fashion. "Here's what I would do," he said. "Airspeed is crucial. I think those guys who didn't make it pulled up trying to gain altitude for a go-around. The climb slowed them, the fire went into the sucker doors, and they lit up like a Christmas tree. If I caught on fire, I'd keep the nose down and build enough airspeed to close the doors."

Several days later, Day was to lead a flight of two aircraft — a two-shipper — to practice formation flying. They were taking off on the short runway at Moody. It was about five thousand feet long and had no overrun, and fifty-foot Georgia pines were off both ends. Day was Blue Lead. The other pilot was Blue Two. At about forty-feet altitude, Day's fire warning light popped on. No other light in the cockpit can get a pilot's attention so quickly.

"Blue Lead, you're siphoning fuel," radioed Day's wingman.

Before Day could respond, the fuel caught on fire and his aircraft looked like a Roman candle. Blue Two said, "Lead, you're on fire." He paused for a half second and added, "I'm sliding out to the side. No sense in both of us blowing up."

Because Day already knew the procedure he would follow, he did not have to think. "Moody tower, Blue Lead declaring emergency. Fire on takeoff."

"Roger that, Blue Lead. What are your intentions?"

Day pushed the nose down, staying low, barely clearing the pine trees as he built airspeed. An eternity of seconds crawled by. The airspeed reached 130 and the sucker doors slammed shut. The fire was blown out by the airspeed.

Day proceeded to burn off some fuel before returning to base. When he landed, the aft end of the aircraft was black from the flames. An examination revealed the fire had badly burned the control cables. Had Day made one hard movement, the cables would have snapped and he would have had to eject at low altitude — not a pleasant prospect in the T-33, as the cockpit was so cramped that pilots often broke their legs during ejection. And the parachutes of 1952 were not made for low-level bailouts.

As far as can be determined, Day was the first and only Air Force pilot to survive a fire on takeoff in a T-33. Just as he said in the officers' club, airspeed was crucial. Had he done the intuitive thing and pulled the nose up, he would have bled off enough airspeed that the fire would have gone into the engine and the aircraft would have exploded. Word of the young lieutenant's experience quickly made the rounds in the Air Force. Fighter pilots all over the country played and replayed what this guy Bud Day had done down at Moody.

That was the first time the Air Force heard the name Bud Day.

The next incident was not far away.

It is said that the military always refights the last war. That was certainly true in Korea. Within the relatively new USAF, the Strategic Air Command (SAC) reigned supreme. Should a full-scale war break out with the Soviet Union, it would be SAC's job to fly bombers loaded with nuclear weapons into the heart of the Russian motherland.

Korea was SAC's first war, and it was not going well because its fighting doctrine was based on big bombing raids like those conducted by the 8th Air Force over Europe during World War II. In Korea, however, a combination of adverse weather and enemy defenses exacted such a heavy toll on those raids that they were discontinued and the war became a fighter pilot's war. The star of the air-to-air war was the F-86 Sabre Jet, and almost all bombing was taken over by single-engine, single-seat fighter-bombers such as the F-80 and the F-84. When the war thus shifted, units flying those smaller aircraft back in the States were caught in the turmoil. Suddenly nothing was certain about assignments, about missions, about anything.

Day discovered this in November 1952, after he received his green card and was ordered to Tyndall AFB near Panama City, Florida, for a two-week transition course into the F-94. But there were no F-94s, and the backup F-89s had been grounded. Operation Fair Play was canceled and, with it, Day's surefire ticket to combat. Devastated, he concluded that not being able to fly combat and being forced to live in the Florida panhandle were the two worst things that had ever happened to him.

Doris agreed. Her vision of Florida had been palm trees, gentle breezes, and soft surf. They rented a small concrete-block house in Mexico Beach, a fishing village about twenty miles east of Panama City. Space heaters could not warm the house, so they were always cold. The white powdery sand from the beach was everywhere, all through the house. Doris believed in keeping a clean house, and — as it had been in Texas — the sand was a constant annoyance. This was their second Christmas away from Sioux City, and the only decoration on the Christmas tree was a string of colored eggshells. Doris was miserable the entire time Day was at Tyndall.

So was he. Bud and Doris had grown up in the clean fresh air of Siouxland and could never adjust to the pervasive stench of nearby paper mills. When Bud or Doris complained, the locals shook their heads and said, "That's the smell of money." The acrid, stinging odor of the paper mills was in their clothes and in their house. It could not be escaped.

On weekends, to get away from the stench, Bud and Doris drove east or northeast. They never ventured west along the panhandle; there was nothing there but a series of nondescript little towns.

The only good news at Tyndall was that in December 1952, Day was promoted to first lieutenant. His base pay was about $280 per month. Following the promotion came an assignment to Bergstrom AFB near Austin, Texas. Bergstrom was a SAC base where he could fly the F-84.

When Bud and Doris left Florida for what they hoped would be the last time, they saw what they considered a beautiful sight: Panama City in the rearview mirror. "Thank God we're leaving that place," Day said to Doris. "We will never come back."

Bergstrom was Day's first operational assignment. Flying a fighter, he drew an additional $200 per month. He made a vow that as long as he was on flying status, most of this would go to his parents back in Riverside. Clerks who handled the paperwork talked of this, and the word quickly got out among Day's fellow pilots at Bergstrom. They chided Day, telling him he was under no obligation to his parents.

"Yes, I am," he said. He also sent his parents extra money at Christmas.

Though the pay was an improvement and Panama City far away, Bergstrom was far from heaven. SAC was stultifying in the extreme, especially to a young officer. Micromanagement kept pilots under tight control, and the general attitude was "If you haven't been there, you can't go. If it hasn't been done before, we can't do it."

Day found it hard to reconcile the narrow bureaucratic attitude with the fact that the Bergstrom cadre was peopled with legends: fighter aces, men who had flown against Rommel in North Africa, men who had flown in the Italian campaign and even in Germany. They were some of the most colorful men ever to don flying suits;

one of them, a married man, flew his girlfriend around in a military aircraft. They were majors and lieutenant colonels and even full colonels who, at the officers' club, behaved like rambunctious second lieutenants.

Bud had much professional admiration for these men. But he and Doris had grown up in a different world with different values. They rarely went to the officers' club; now that Bud had settled down, it was too wild for them. Because an officer's social life revolved around the club, however, Bud and Doris had few friends at Bergstrom. They were slightly prudish, their solid Midwestern values firmly imbedded. Doubtless, some laughed at them.

SAC used so much of its budget to support big bombers that little was left over for young pilots flying fighters. The Air Force did not even provide flight suits; Day bought his from Navy surplus and Doris patched it so many times it looked like a worn quilt. He bought his flying boots from an outdoor-supply store and his gloves at a sporting-goods shop.

SAC also had a dismissive attitude toward young pilots such as Day — "newbies," they were called. The feeling was that the World War II pilots and the pilots who had been recalled would be doing the flying in Korea and that the newbies would never be of any use in the war. The danger of that attitude became abundantly clear to Day on a training mission when, for the second time, he narrowly escaped death.

Part of the reason for his mishap involved the flying characteristics of the F-84. A popular Air Force song of the time best describes the most treacherous and dangerous attribute of the aircraft.

> *Don't give me an F-84, she's just a ground-loving whore.*
> *She'll whine, moan, and wheeze, then clobber the trees.*
> *Don't give me an F-84.*

This inelegant verse was based on the well-known fact that the F-84 was so sluggish that, on a strafing run, the pilot pulled back on the stick to begin the climb-out the instant he fired his guns. Older pilots knew this from experience. But Day had never made a gun pass in an F-84 until one morning when he tagged along with three recalled pilots who wanted to go to the range and shoot.

The weather was marginal, but weather gurus said the low overcast would break up by midmorning. It did not, and while the pilots circled in anticipation, the four aircraft were burning JP-4 at prodigious rates. The flight had to shoot or return to base. The leader checked in with the range and was told the bottoms of the clouds were at five hundred feet, the tops at eight hundred feet.

Day shook his head. He had a green card and could handle almost any weather. But popping out of a cloud only five hundred feet above the ground in a jet aircraft was foolhardy. This mission should be canceled.

However, he was the newbie who was here to learn, the man whose opinions meant nothing. So he pressed on.

Targets were on a thirty-foot-high berm. The front side of the artificial ridge where the targets were located was almost vertical. The rear was sloped and descended into a declivity formed when bulldozers scraped up dirt to build the berm.

The range officer who controlled the aircraft was in a fifteen-foot-tall tower located about fifty yards from the target. He had an unobstructed view of the berm and, once they poked through the low overcast, of each aircraft as it rolled in at about four hundred knots on its strafing run.

Day pushed through the low clouds. He was to fire his guns at about twelve hundred feet from the target. But he was too far out, too flat and too low, dragging the aircraft toward the target. When he was closer, he pushed the nose over, fired, and pulled back on the stick. But nothing happened. The F-84 mushed toward the ground. Day applied full power, but the aircraft continued to mush. He narrowly missed the berm and disappeared into the declivity.

The range officer was horrified. A crash and fatality would mean days of paperwork. If an inquiry decided the accident was his fault, that he had not exercised the leadership expected of a range officer, his career could end.

The F-84 wallowed out of the declivity and began climbing.

The range officer's voice was shaking when he radioed Day. "Get off this range and do not ever come back."

"Roger that," Day replied in an equally shaky voice.

Once on the ground, the flight leader said Day was unsafe and not worth the trust of fellow pilots.

Day could only nod and say, "Yes, sir." But he knew the flight should never have gone up that day. No one was shooting to qualify; it was only to fill a square on paperwork, only to say they had been to the range. Day left the ramp as mistrustful of his fellow pilots as they were of him. And he was aware that, for the second time in his brief Air Force career, he had almost killed himself.

Day's first ER at Bergstrom, the first of his flying career, was mediocre. The most favorable thing it said about Day was that he "willingly accepts any assignment given him and carries it out to the finish."

His second ER also was ho-hum. Day received high marks for his legal advice to his squadron commander. This might sound good, but Day's job was as a pilot and not as a legal adviser; he was being praised for something outside his job. The ER said that Day would make a good staff officer — again not his job — and that he was qualified to "instruct in a civilian institution." Day's boss assigned him to act as defense counsel in military courts and said, "The results were outstanding as far as his clients were concerned." Another ER said that Day would do well in the JAGC (Judge Advocate General's Corps) or as squadron legal officer but that his flying ability was "average." SAC considered Day a lawyer more than a pilot. Things were moving in the wrong direction.

NEVERTHELESS, Day soon realized the dream of every fighter pilot: an overseas deployment. He was ordered to Chitose, Japan, for six months. Doris decided to go home to Sioux City while he was gone. Before Day left, he opened the first checking account he and Doris ever had. He told Doris that he wanted her to begin taking care of all family finances "in case something ever happens to me."

At Chitose, Day flew the F-84 on tracking missions along the border of the Soviet Union. It was perhaps the most dangerous mission of the Cold War. Soviet bombers often violated Japanese airspace by cutting across the corner of Hokkaido. U.S. fighters were cleared to shoot them down. When Day took off, his guns were loaded.

Besides eliminating any Soviet interlopers, the Americans had another aim. Sometimes the F-84s flew toward Soviet airspace as if they were conducting a mass attack. The purpose was to test Soviet response time.

The Soviets were not the only trespassers: American aircraft were flying deep into the Soviet Union to photograph military installations. When they returned, they were often being chased by Soviet fighters. Additional American aircraft waited at the Japanese border and hoped the Soviets would cross the line. And if Americans were in trouble, Day and his fellow pilots might assist in a rescue. During his deployment, a B-29 was shot down over Vladivostok Bay, and he was part of the flight that "capped" it — flew air cover until the crew was rescued. Through it all, America was shooting down Soviet aircraft and the Soviets were shooting down American aircraft. The Soviets did not complain because to do so would be an admission that their borders had been penetrated. And the United States did not want to acknowledge that American pilots were being shot down.

Once, Day was returning from a mission and ran short of fuel. He landed in Korea, where a squadron of the glamorous F-86 Sabre Jets was based. Day knew he would be on the base overnight and walked into the officers' club. Moments later, Lieutenant Colonel Robert Dixon, the squadron commander, entered the club and in a tone of disgust said, "Who's flying that hog on the ramp?"

Day's pugnacious nature, fueled by the pride every pilot feels in his aircraft, surfaced. It did not matter that he was a first lieutenant talking to a lieutenant colonel. "I am. You want to step outside and discuss it?"

Dixon declined the offer. It would be almost two decades before he and Day met again. And that meeting would be even less cordial.

UPON Day's return to the States, he went to "nuke school," where he learned the theory and the delivery of nuclear weapons. He attended Squadron Officer School — a program that teaches officers the first level of command — and then was ordered back to Moody to learn how to be an instructor in instrument flying. Afterward, he returned to Bergstrom. There, he found things were still moving in the wrong direction.

Day's next ER emphasized his personality and character, damning him with faint praise in irrelevant matters. He was a "good-natured, cooperative individual" who tackled his work "energetically and wholeheartedly." He had a "keen logical mind" and "responds favorably to constructive criticism." He would be "best utilized in a staff or administrative position at squadron level." His flying abilities were "average" — an outrageous conclusion given his green-card status and his time as an instructor.

One possible reason for the poor ER is that Day was surrounded by men who could do nothing but fly. Perhaps Day's SAC superiors were a bit intimidated by a lawyer-pilot with a college degree. When assigned as defense counsel to miscreants, he was a vigorous advocate who almost always saw his clients exonerated. He was far from the typical SAC pilot, and he never fit in at Bergstrom.

A year after returning to Bergstrom, Day again was deployed to Japan. Doris remained at Bergstrom this time. She was an Air Force wife, and it was her job to stay home and mind the house. To keep her company while he was gone, Bud bought her a dog: a Weimaraner named Copper. Unfortunately, while Day was gone, Copper jumped for a clothespin hanging on a line, got entangled, and hung himself. When Day returned, he wanted to buy Doris another dog. Money was so tight that he stopped smoking and used the cash he would have spent on cigarettes to buy another Weimaraner, this one named Smoky.

Day was still deployed to Japan when the Korean armistice was signed in 1953. He came home, and the Days, who were unsuccessful at efforts to have children, began discussing adoption. Both agreed that they wanted several children.

By 1955 Day decided to resign his commission and return to Sioux City. One of his fundamental beliefs was that hard work and diligence paid off with promotion. But that clearly was not true in SAC, or at least it would not be possible until a lot of senior people died. Day believed the best he would ever get in SAC was maybe to become a flight commander — a captain's billet — leading six pilots. That was not enough. He wanted to lead a fighter squadron in combat.

So many fighter pilots wanted out of SAC that headquarters was inundated with transfer requests. But SAC did not release its pilots, and if a pilot somehow wrangled a back-channel transfer, headquarters blocked it.

So Day was astonished when he put in for a transfer to England and it was approved. He received orders transferring him to the 55th Squadron of the 20th Fighter Bomber Wing at Wethersfield. This exceptional move may have indicated just how much his superiors at Bergstrom disliked him.

SHORTLY after Day received his orders, Doris was invited to attend a meeting of the Officers' Wives Club. She did not even know there was such a club. Once there, Doris found a very formal group with ritualized rules. At teas, the wives wore white gloves, and inside their homes, near the front door, was a guest book along with a silver tray, upon which people left their calling cards. The wives thought Doris had just arrived at Bergstrom. "I've been here more than two years," she confessed. "We are leaving. We have orders sending us to England."

She made a vow that she would join the Officers' Wives Club as soon as she got to England. And she would become part of the welcoming committee and would seek out and greet newcomers as soon as they arrived.

Every career military officer, when he retires and looks back over his years of service, has a favorite duty station. For Bud and Doris, that would be England. It also would be the place where Day's name became known throughout the Air Force for an incident that a half century later would still cause people's jaws to drop when they heard of it.

5

Sporty Flying

WETHERSFIELD was a former RAF base, one of the old bomber-recovery bases from World War II, located on the North Sea about forty-five miles northeast of London. The job of the 55th was to deliver nuclear bombs to Eastern Europe in the event the Soviet Union attacked through the Fulda Gap. Doing so would blow a hole through Communist defenses and allow SAC bombers an open door for their thrust to the heart of Russia.

Day arrived in England at a propitious time. Several senior officers were scheduled to return to the States, and the wing was in the process of converting from the straight-wing F-84G to the swept-wing F-84F, an aircraft in which he was already checked out.

Day's almost obsessive desire for increasing his skills in every area began to show results immediately. He was hardly on the ground before he began training to be a bomb commander, a job which calls for navigation and bombing skills far above those of other fighter pilots. It also meant that Day would be qualified to conduct a single-airplane flight carrying a nuclear weapon on a suicide mission to Eastern Europe should war break out.

Usually junior officers spend most of their spare time studying highly classified reports on the weapons and tactics of the enemy. But Day was given the job of "trial observer" — sitting in on British courts in matters involving Air Force personnel — on top of his other duties. The added load made no difference: Day was free from the politics and insecurities of Bergstrom, and his strengths not only shone through but became part of the official record. His first ER in England covered the period from June 1, 1955, to January 31, 1956, and said that his ability as a pilot "is well above average," that his appearance and military bearing "reflect great credit upon the Air Force," and that his "coolness and clear, precise decisions under favorable and unfavorable conditions are not usually found in a pilot or officer of his experience." The ER also stated that Day never complained about being a trial observer, even when that extra job kept him from flying. It ended by saying that Day had "unlimited growth potential" and should be promoted to captain. He was.

ELEVATED in rank, Day became the assistant standards and evaluation officer for the wing. A "stan-eval" pilot checked out other pilots and made sure they maintained their combat-ready flying proficiency. A few months after Day arrived, his boss rotated back to the States, and Day became the ranking stan-eval officer for the wing, a job usually held by a senior captain or a major. For a very junior captain, it was a splendid job. Subsequently, he was given the additional job of wing gunnery officer, which meant he wrote the procedures and was in charge of training other pilots on how to deliver nuclear weapons.

Life was very good for him and Doris. They lived in a centuries-old house in the village of Finchingfield. Day played golf frequently. Doris began to blossom as a military wife, demonstrating leadership qualities equal to those of her husband. She joined the Officers' Wives Club and ran for president against a colonel's wife. In the military, the status of a wife is determined by the rank of her husband, and it was almost heretical for the wife of a captain to run against the wife of a colonel. Doris, oblivious of tradition, won the race. She then set up procedures whereby members welcomed new wives and brought them into club activities as soon as they arrived. Soon she had members doing volunteer work at the base hospital. These changes were, within the ossified culture of the base, revolutionary.

As Doris and Bud were coming into their own, her dad's health began failing, so Sonwald turned his business over to Stanley, one of his sons, who lacked his father's acumen. The business foundered. As a result, in addition to supporting his own parents, Day began sending money to Doris's father every month.

Doris decided to press ahead with the decision made back at Bergstrom to adopt. She and Bud wanted a child around four years old, the age their child would have been if Doris had become pregnant a year or so after they were married. The age was their only requirement; the Days did not stipulate boy or girl or even race. Because they were not specific, their request was put at the top of the list. In the summer of 1957, they were told that an orphanage in Germany had a young boy eligible for adoption.

Klaus was a blue-eyed boy who was two years and three months old. The age wasn't quite right, but everything else that mattered was. One of the first things Day did was to change the child's name to Steven Michael Day. The "Steven" was for a friend from Bud's Marine Corps days, and "Michael" was in honor of Day's squadron commander.

The Days were ecstatic. At last they were beginning to expand their family.

IT was a slow process for the still relatively new Air Force to drop one by one the practices inherited from the Army Air Forces and to create new procedures. Therefore, it was not until the mid-1950s — almost ten years after the Air Force was created — that pilot survival training became a serious issue. Day was sent to a training program in Germany where pilots were blindfolded, trussed tightly, tossed into the back of a truck, and hauled into the Alps. There they were untied and told to find their way back. The route led through territory occupied by military units whose sole job was to capture the "escapees." The training was rigged so that every pilot was captured and interrogated. Shortly after Day was pushed into his cell, he overpowered the guard, took his weapon, and escaped. When he was recaptured, his arms were taped together. He broke his bonds and had his cell mate fake an epileptic seizure. When the guard came in to investigate, Day and his cell mate overpowered him, ripped out the floor of the building, and escaped — the only members of their class and among the very few in the hundreds of students who had been through the school ever to do so. Survival-school officials chewed Day out for tearing up the floor — destruction of U.S. government property, they called it. Day said that he was told the training was to be as realistic as possible and that he had only used the ingenuity and initiative expected of an Air Force officer.

A little more than a decade later, Day would have the opportunity to put his survival training into practice. And it would not be a training exercise.

FLYING duties at Wethersfield were among the most hazardous in the Air Force. Commencing a typical flight, Day would load his F-84F with two 450-gallon drop tanks, charge his .50-caliber guns, and check the "bluke" bolted to the belly of the aircraft. (The "bluke" was a blue concrete bomb the size and weight of the nuclear weapon he would carry in wartime.)

He was so heavily loaded that for takeoff he had to use Jet Assisted Take Off (JATO) bottles, attached to the fuselage, that would be jettisoned over the English Channel. He flew a "high-low profile" — that is, after takeoff he climbed to high altitude, where jets are more fuel efficient. By the time he reached the French coast, he was climbing through 34,000 feet.

As he approached Germany, he would let down until he was on the deck — around 100 feet — and make a simulated bomb run on a target. He would be at treetop level and 450 knots, executing turns at precise spots and on a split-second schedule, oftentimes in the full instrument conditions common in Europe. Arriving over the target at a precise time, he would execute a simulated "over-the-shoulder" delivery of a nuclear bomb. Then Day would make a high-speed low-altitude exit before climbing back to altitude. He did not practice air-to-air refueling on the return flight because, in wartime, his target would be behind the Iron Curtain and he would have run out of fuel about the time he reached Holland. He also flew missions in England, where wood and coal fires filled the air with soot and smoke, a combination that, when combined with cool moist air off the North Sea, often resulted in low clouds and fog.

To get down at very low altitude and go ripping across England and much of Europe was a fighter pilot's dream. And the Air Force had permission for low-level flights in the United Kingdom, Holland, Belgium, France, Italy, Spain, Turkey, and part of Morocco. When a pilot flew at 450 knots and less than 100 feet of altitude, a microsecond of inattention would turn him into a fireball. A fighter pilot had more chances to get killed in the space of two or three minutes than most people experience in a lifetime. The flying was fun and it was dangerous, a combination beloved by fighter pilots — "sporty flying," they called it. But jet aircraft were primitive by today's standards. The pilots often returned from missions in a critical fuel state or with flight-threatening mechanical problems. Ambulances ("meat wagons") and fire trucks screaming across the tarmac were a common sight at Wethersfield.

Day seemed to have more than his share of sporty flying. One night he took off for Étain, northeast of Paris, to pick up a small aircraft part. Captain Billy Moore, a wing staff officer who needed the night flying time, came along for the ride. Day was flying in the front seat of a T-33. Moore was in the rear. The weather was solid instrument conditions: low ceiling, limited visibility, and very cold, though the forecast called for improvement.

Day had a gnawing feeling about this flight; an inner voice was telling him not to take off. He went to base operations and asked what the weather was like along the route. He was told it was marginal.

The plan was for Moore to make the takeoff and landing. Day would fly the return flight.

As they crossed the English Channel, Moore asked for the current weather at Étain. The voice on the radio said that weather had deteriorated rapidly and that all of Europe was socked in: every runway within range was well below minimums.

Wethersfield, their home base, was zero-zero — no ceiling and no visibility.

"Billy, we're in deep shit," Day told Moore.

Moore wanted to fly on to Wiesbaden, easy to find because it was located on a big curve in the Rhine River. Day disagreed. "If we're going to bust our ass," he said, "let's go back to a place we know. Our friends can plow through the wreckage." Day told Moore to reverse course and fly the ground-controlled approach (GCA) while he watched from the front seat. When Day saw the runway lights, he would say, "I got it," take control, and land. It was a risky strategy. The shift from instrument flying to visual flying takes several seconds, and in zero-zero conditions, pilots rarely have more than a brief moment to make the transition.

Moore slowed the airplane, nailed down the airspeed, and locked onto a three-degree glide slope. At three hundred altitude feet, they saw nothing. At two hundred feet, nothing. One hundred feet came and went, and still Day could see nothing. They continued to descend. About ten feet from the ground, Day suddenly saw the runway lights. But the aircraft was slightly off course and too low to make a correction without digging a wingtip into the ground. "Take it around," Day said.

In these weather conditions and under these circumstances, the Air Force considered a bailout the proper procedure. If Day attempted another landing and banged up the airplane, he would face a board of inquiry.

He decided to make one more attempt. If they could not land, they would fly east of Wethersfield, bail out over open meadows, and hope he and Moore did not land in water, electrical lines, or trees.

"Faint heart never fucked a pig," he mumbled as the aircraft rolled in on final.

The approach was perfect, corrections no more than one degree and airspeed nailed. The rate of descent was also textbook perfect. Moore reached a hundred feet — maximum pucker point. Day was holding the canopy rails so tightly that his hands hurt. The aircraft descended through fifty feet and there was nothing. At thirty feet they were still on solid instruments.

"I got it," Day said. He pulled back slightly on the stick and felt the thunk of his tires on the runway. Unable to see the runway, he kept his eye on the compass and maintained his heading. He rolled to a stop, kept the aircraft lights on, and called for a tug to tow the aircraft off the runway.

A high degree of proficiency, combined with an equal amount of luck, had just enabled Day to do what was considered impossible. "I think we may be the only two guys to ever make a zero-zero landing in a jet aircraft," Day told Moore. He probably was correct. Once again, Day survived an experience that had killed numerous other pilots.

Day's second ER in England, covering 1956, was extraordinary. The squadron commander said Day had an "unusual aptitude for command" and an "extremely high standard of character and leadership." The wing commander added that Day was "one of the most outstanding leaders in this wing" and among "the upper 5 percent of all officers of like rank known to me." The ER said that Day "has proved himself to be not only the most popular among those he works with, but those he works for." Apparently word had gotten out about the fighter pilot who was also an aggressive lawyer, because a number of enlisted men had gone to Day for help rather than going to JAG lawyers. The ER noted that each time Day was sought out, he performed "in an outstanding manner." Day was also praised for calculating the first accurate figures on fuel consumption and range for the new F-84Fs, an accomplishment the reviewing officer said made the difference in aircraft returning from missions safely or running out of fuel.

The ER also said that pilots under Day's command "are far better supervised than any others in the squadron" and are so proficient that "they are always the first ones chosen for a particularly hard or difficult mission." Day himself was picked to be the first to check out in the F-100, which was replacing the F-84.

WHEN a wing converts to a new aircraft, the accident rate almost always goes up. This is particularly true in temperamental high-performance jets such as the F-100. Outfits transferring to the F-100 often tripled their accident rate, and one-quarter of the F-100s manufactured were lost in training accidents. But when the 20th Wing, under Day's supervision, converted to F-100s, there was a *decline* in the accident rate. Day revised the pilot handbook for the F-100, and the 20th Wing was commended and recognized as having the best standardization program of any Air Force unit in Europe.

IN 1953, some 3,600 American POWs came home from Korea, and America learned that a number of them had collaborated with the enemy. The collaboration had come after physical and psychological torture, and a new term, "brainwashed," was added to the lexicon. The novel and later the 1962 movie *The Manchurian Candidate* were inspired by stories of North Korean mind-control efforts. The military was extremely alarmed about the poor showing its members made as POWs and set about codifying a few guiding principles for the future. In 1955, President Dwight Eisenhower signed an executive order approving this new Code of Conduct. Members of the military assumed that since the code came from the president, it had the force of law.

On the surface, the code was a simple document of six articles:

1. I am an American fighting man. I serve in the forces which guard my country and our way of life. I am prepared to give my life in their defense.

2. I will never surrender of my own free will. If in command, I will never surrender my men while they still have the means to resist.

3. If I am captured, I will continue to resist by all means available. I will make every effort to escape and aid others to escape. I will accept neither parole nor special favors from the enemy.

4. If I become a prisoner of war, I will keep faith with my fellow prisoners. I will give no information nor take part in any action which might be harmful to my comrades. If I am senior, I will take command. If not, I will obey the lawful orders of those appointed over me and will back them up in every way.

5. When questioned, should I become a prisoner of war, I am required to give only name, rank, service number, and date of birth. I will evade answering further questions to the utmost of my ability. I will make no oral or written statements disloyal to my country and its allies or harmful to their cause.

6. I will never forget that I am an American fighting man, responsible for my actions, and dedicated to the principles which made my country free. I will trust in my God and in the United States of America.

The code was printed on wallet-size cards and given to all members of the armed services, who were also required to memorize it. Day studied the code and parsed every sentence from the standpoint of a lawyer. To him, the document was clear and unequivocal; it said what it meant and it meant what it said.

DAY'S work took him away from the base more than two hundred days each year, but he was climbing the ladder of responsibility, becoming known in the Air Force as a man who took his work seriously and who eagerly assumed responsibility beyond his rank. Some of these trips took him out of Europe. The Air Force had a base near Casablanca in North Africa, and because its weather was good for more than three hundred days a year, Day conducted many check rides and stan-eval flights there. (In an F-100, he could reach Casablanca in slightly more than two hours.)

It was on a flight out of Casablanca that Day had his fourth brush with death. The beginning of the flight was uneventful, but later in a violent thunderstorm the aircraft's electrical system failed. His backseater lost control of the aircraft and Day barely recovered in time to clear the tops of the Pyrenees. When he landed at Bordeaux, France, his tip tanks were dry and only three gallons of fuel were left in the main tank. Another few seconds and he would have crashed.

THROUGH all this, Day was a reservist, but in 1957 he became a member of the regular Air Force. Now he was a "lifer." Day continued with his job as stan-eval officer and flew not only out of Wethersfield but out of other bases around England.

On June 10, 1957, he went to the officers' club at Wethersfield to cash a check. Day was flying over to Woodbridge to conduct a stan-eval flight and thought he might need some cash. At the club he heard, "Hello, Judge. What are you doing here during the day?"

Day looked up when he heard "Judge" — his call sign. The man addressing him was Flight Surgeon Hap Hansen, a good friend. Doc Hansen said he was about to leave on temporary duty for a day or so, and Day said he was about to do the same. Neither said where he was going.

The next morning Day climbed into an F-84 with the name ATOM BUM printed on the fuselage. The aircraft was known as a hangar queen, a maintenance hog with a long history of mechanical problems. But it had been in the shop for weeks, and the maintenance officer had signed off on it as being in good condition. Day flew from Wethersfield to Woodbridge. It was one of those rare English days when the weather was clean and clear, and visibility was unlimited — a great day for flying. Once on the ground, Day listened as the other pilot conducted a briefing of the proposed check flight. Then the two men climbed aboard their F-84s.

Stan-eval flights were a complicated mix of high and low altitude, of navigational problems and checkpoints that the pilots had to hit with only a few seconds' variation permitted. These were simulated combat missions and were conducted under wartime rules of radio silence. Pilots communicated by hand signals.

The two pilots took off, Day in trail, and flew west over the Atlantic, then turned, dropped to the deck, and came back across the coast of England, brushing through the treetops, clicking off checkpoints, and simulating an over-the-shoulder toss of a nuclear weapon on a target north of Cambridge. Then the two aircraft headed back to Woodbridge at about three hundred feet altitude. As Cambridge passed under their wings and they saw the racetrack at Newmarket, Day suddenly smelled JP-4.

Anytime the pilot of a fighter aircraft smells fuel, chances are he is about to either burn or explode. The danger was compounded by the extremely low altitude.

He had to land immediately.

RAF Bentwaters was only a few minutes away. But when Day tried to call Bentwaters for emergency-landing clearance, his radio did not work.

Day took the lead, hand signaled to the other pilot to call the tower, and scrambled for seven thousand feet, the "flameout altitude," or the altitude from which an F-84 could be flown to a dead-stick landing. Day hoped to hold at seven thousand feet until he was over Bentwaters, then drop down and land. But a huge cloud — the only cloud in the sky in any direction — hung over the approach end of the runway. He turned slightly to circumvent the obscurity and saw two fighters coming at him on a collision course. He banked sharply. Then he saw two more fighters on the runway, rolling for takeoff.

Bentwaters was out as a landing site.

Woodbridge was only a few miles farther, the two bases separated by some fifteen thousand acres of Rendlesham Forest. Day raced for it, and seconds later, the field was in sight and he began his descent for landing.

As Day backed off on the power, the engine began coming apart. Suddenly explosion after explosion racked the F-84. Pieces of the engine were being blasted through the fuselage. Even with an oxygen mask on, Day found that the smell of vaporized JP-4 was so strong he was instantly nauseated. He rolled out on a runway heading, looked down, and saw he was over base housing. It was not far to the runway. At about three hundred feet, he blew the canopy, a necessary step before ejecting.

"Stay cool. Stay cool," he said to himself. "Just hold this heading another few seconds."

Then every light on the panel lit up. Day dropped the gear and flaps and nudged up the power. The engine did not respond. The aircraft shuddered violently and Day knew he could not make the final half mile. He was going to have to punch out.

On the ground, hundreds of people had heard the explosions racking the F-84 and looked up, watching in fascinated horror as the aircraft trailed fire and smoke.

At Woodbridge, Lieutenant John Pardo was serving as the mobile control officer. It is the job of whatever pilot holds this rotating job to sit in a vehicle at the end of the runway and make sure that all incoming aircraft have their landing gear down.

(More than a decade later, Pardo would be flying an F-4 Phantom in Vietnam. When another F-4 was shot up, he had the pilot drop the tail hook. Pardo maneuvered his F-4 until his canopy was against the tail hook and then he pushed the wounded F-4 until it was over Laos and the crew could bail out and be rescued. "Pardo's Push" became one of the great flying stories of the Vietnam War.)

Suddenly Day's radio, which had not worked for the past few minutes, cut in and he heard Pardo shout, "Eject! Eject! You are on fire! Eject!"

The transmission was also heard in the tower, in base operations, in the squadron commander's and wing commander's offices, and in ready rooms. Pilots from all over the base ran outside and looked skyward.

Day, hearing Pardo's announcement that he was on fire, muttered, "Like I don't know it?" The controls locked and Day pulled the ejection handle. As he separated from the seat, the aircraft rolled and exploded.

Because he was below three hundred feet and because the ejection and the spectacular explosion were almost simultaneous, all eyes followed the burning jet as it hit the trees and erupted into a tremendous fireball and column of black smoke.

By now Day should have been descending gently beneath a parachute. Instead he was at about a hundred feet, upside down, following the trajectory of the crashed aircraft. After watching his aircraft crash and explode, he took a quick look over his shoulder and saw the chute had not opened. He put his feet together, bent his knees, and said, "I am about to bust my ass."

Then he was in the trees. For a split second he heard the sound of snapping branches. Then he heard nothing.

Across the base, an alarm went off in the hospital. The flight surgeon, who was there on temporary duty covering for someone else, heard the siren. His first thought was *Thank God this is one pilot I won't know.* He lit a cigar and jumped into the right front seat of the ambulance. When the ambulance and rescue personnel arrived at the crash site, firemen climbed over the wreckage to pull the pilot's body to safety. But there was no pilot.

Day regained consciousness, hearing the burning of his aircraft and the sound of .50-caliber ammunition cooking off. Through the trees he saw the fire trucks and emergency vehicles around his aircraft and wondered why they were there instead of with him. He also wondered if he would be hit by his own ammunition.

Day pulled himself to a sitting position. Now he could hear the rescue personnel. They had found no pilot in the wreckage and were wondering how they could have missed seeing his parachute. They were whistling and shouting. He put his fingers in his mouth and whistled.

A few moments later a flight surgeon was bending over him.

"Judge?"

Day looked up and said, "Doc?"

"Bud?"

"Hap?"

It was Hap Hansen.

Day laughed. "I thought I was dead. But now I know I'm alive because you would never make it to heaven."

Day was in great pain. His right ankle was smashed, and X-rays would later reveal a hairline fracture of his lowest lumbar vertebra, the L-5. From head to toe he was covered with bruises. But considering he had just become the first man in the history of the U.S. Air Force to eject from a jet aircraft with no parachute and survive, his injuries seemed almost incidental.

Day was taken to surgery. The next morning the surgeon came into Day's room and shut the door. He was very sober.

"Captain Day, I hope you are a Christian," he began.

"Not a very good one," Day said.

"Then you better pray."

"Why?"

"Because you will never fly again. Your ankle was powdered. I see no way we can fix it. You will have a stiff ankle for the rest of your life. You have to face that reality." He looked at Day and repeated, "You will never fly again."

"Well, I'm gonna try," Day said.

Day's squadron commander, Major Michael McCarthy, also visited.

He stood by the bed, stared at Day, and said, "Bud, by all accounts you should have died out there." He shook his head. "There is not enough luck in the world to attribute your survival to luck. You . . . survived . . . a . . . no-chute . . . bailout." McCarthy was a devout Catholic with thirteen children. He paused again. "God must be saving you for something special."

Day thought about all the times he had cheated death: the fire on takeoff at Moody, the near crash at Matagorda, the zero-zero landing in England, landing with three gallons of gas in France. And now the most improbable of all.

The idea that, as Major McCarthy first suggested, God was saving him for something special would become a bone-deep and fundamental belief of Bud Day. And out of that belief would come great strength and the calm assurance that no matter what happened to him in life, he would prevail. Until he had performed his appointed task, he would be safe from all harm.

But what was the task?

WHEN a fighter crashes, the details are sent to the Pentagon, and from there to Air Force bases around the world, the purpose being twofold: first, to determine the cause of the crash so preventive measures can be taken to avoid another crash for the same reason, and second, to point out what the pilot did right and what he did wrong so other pilots facing similar circumstances might profit.

Within days, almost every pilot in the Air Force learned that a Captain George Day had jumped out of a jet aircraft and survived. The British newspapers filled with stories about the American bloke who ejected from a jet with no parachute and lived to tell about it. The consensus among both journalists and generals was that no pilot could eject from a jet, have a failed parachute, and survive. Many in the Air Force said that Day must have had a streamer — a partially opened chute that slowed his descent — or that his chute blossomed at the moment of impact and saved his life. But a lone witness was discovered: a lieutenant colonel (who later became a three-star general) who had been in the tower that day confirmed the simple fact that the chute never deployed.

The failure was no mystery. The Air Force had found that high-speed ejections from jet aircraft blew the panels out of parachutes that were designed for bailing out of propeller-driven aircraft. A new parachute designed for high-speed bailouts had been introduced, and Day had been wearing one of these. The new chute had powerful rubber bands around it so as to deploy slowly at high speed. But the bands were so strong that at low speeds the chute would not deploy at all.

Day wrote a long message to the Air Force flight safety officer, and his wing went back to the old parachute.

While Day recuperated from surgery, he revised the wing's tactical doctrine — the bible for wartime deployment. Fourteen weeks after the no-chute bailout, to the astonishment of his doctor and against all conventional medical wisdom, he passed a flight physical.

He was back in the cockpit.

For years afterward, Day would meet Air Force people and introduce himself, only to hear, "Are you the same Bud Day who survived a no-chute bailout in England back in 1957?"

He would clap them on the shoulder, smile, and say, "Yes, I am. How you doing, pal?"

The person would stare in amazement. "How did you walk away from a no-chute bailout?"

Day would laugh and throw his hands wide as if he were as mystified as everyone else. He would have to tell the story again and again, and in the end his questioner would look at Day as if he were some exotic specimen better found in a museum. People just don't jump out of jet aircraft without a parachute and live to tell the story.

DURING the 1950s, the Air Force held annual gunnery meets at Nellis AFB near Las Vegas. There, pilots from throughout the Air Force competed in all phases of aerial combat. The 1958 meet was particularly important because it was the first all–F-100 competition. Day was ordered to Nellis to be a judge in the bombing competition. A highlight of the trip was his meeting legendary Air Force officer Robinson Risner, who had been an ace in Korea.

Day and Risner would meet again.

One night Bud and a group of pilots went into Las Vegas and visited a club where an entertainer played a song called "Misty" on his xylophone. The song was introduced by the Erroll Garner Trio in 1954 but languished. In late 1959 Johnny Mathis would take the tune to number twelve on the *Billboard* charts, where it would stay for seventeen weeks.

When Day first heard the melody, there were about five seconds of silence before the room erupted in prolonged applause. Then the entertainer played the song on the piano, and the applause was even greater. People in the room — including Day — simply could not get enough of "Misty." Bud bought a dozen records of the song to take back to England. For years afterward, he walked around humming the song or singing snatches of it.

In Day's ER covering the period from April to October 1958, the reviewing officer said Day was "one of the most highly qualified young Air Force officers I have known." Air Force headquarters in Europe used tests developed by Day to measure the combat effectiveness of other tactical fighter units across Europe. Day was ranked "one of the best F-100 pilots" in the wing.

The wing commander endorsed the ER by saying that Day "is one of the most capable and proficient officers I have ever known" and that he "maintains a Marine Corps officer standard of discipline and military bearing." The wing commander added that he had sent Day to represent the wing at conferences in Europe and back in the States because Day's briefings were the caliber of those delivered by full colonels. He ended by recommending that Day be promoted to major ahead of his contemporaries.

But not all was good news. In December 1958, Doris's father died. In February 1959, Day's mother died, followed by his father in April. He did not attend any of the funerals.

The adoption process for Steven had dragged on for months and now was in a critical stage. Day felt he could not leave England until the Germans approved the adoption.

Much of the delay had to do with the extreme — and sometimes bizarre — diligence of German bureaucrats. Since Day's last stateside assignment had been at Bergstrom AFB, he was considered a Texas resident. But Day had been born in Iowa and had just been given orders sending him to St. Louis, Missouri. Somehow this utterly confused the adoption agency. In addition, Doris was of Norwegian descent, and postwar Norway was not known for its affection toward Germans. A German judge sent some staff to Iowa to investigate Doris's family and to ensure Steven would have the same rights and privileges in America as those enjoyed by American children.

Making sure that everything about the adoption proceeded smoothly became an obsession with Day. "God spared my life in the no-chute bailout," he told Doris. "I think it was because we are supposed to get Steve."

Day's superiors reminded him of his orders to St. Louis and said that he had to go back to the States.

"No, I don't," Day replied. "I'm not leaving until this is fixed."

Eventually, high-ranking Air Force officers and the father of one of Day's law-school friends who was a U.S. senator from South Dakota interceded for Day with German officials. The logjam broken, in June 1959, the new family of Captain George "Bud" Day, Doris Day, and Steve Day left England. For Day there would be two months of training at Maxwell AFB in Montgomery, Alabama, and then, in September, he would report for duty at Saint Louis University as an assistant professor of air science in the ROTC program.

Day, as would any fighter pilot, considered the assignment not only an undesirable one but one that would take away any chance of promotion. ROTC jobs usually were held by nonrated staff weenies — an officer's last assignment before retirement. Plus, this was what was known as a "hard assignment," which meant he could not be transferred early. For the next four years he would be out of the cockpit and out of the operational Air Force, lost in the Missouri backwaters.

Whatever God was saving him for would not be found in St. Louis.

6

Building Time

DAY had learned from his father to accept whatever came his way, not to complain, and to always do the best possible job. So he decided to make the most of the St. Louis assignment. "Maybe what God has in mind for me is raising this little Kraut, raising a great family," he told Doris. "I still have a lot of hunting and fishing to do. I still have a lot of flying to do."

Anyone who knew Air Force culture of that time would have had considerable doubt.

In 1959, the U.S. Air Force turned twelve years old and was going through enormous changes. Ten tactical fighter wings had been deactivated in the years after Korea. These cutbacks meant there were far more fighter pilots than there were available flying slots. SAC dominated the Air Force, and SAC believed bombers were the only aircraft that mattered. Fighter pilots said the tactical side of the Air Force had been "SAC-umcised."

That an officer with Day's education and performance could be sidetracked into an ROTC assignment is proof of this. But at St. Louis, Day was to turn conventional wisdom on its head. In a purely bureaucratic sense, his accomplishments there were nothing short of phenomenal. And those accomplishments were possible not because Day knew how to operate inside a bureaucracy but because he did what Midwesterners do: he worked hard.

Saint Louis University, while not well known, is a sound school, a Jesuit school that is very demanding of its students. Day considered it comparable to one of the military academies, in that competition among students is fierce and demands of professors are high.

Day was one of the most educated pilots in the Air Force. But he could never forget what he learned as a caddy: educated people drive bigger cars, wear nicer clothes, and have leisure time to play golf. Their conversations usually are loftier, their manners are better, and they just *know* things. As a result, upon his arrival, he began taking night classes for a master's degree in international law.

When Day is asked about the people who most influenced his life, he quickly responds with the names of two academics: Marshall McKusick, dean of the law school at the University of South Dakota, and Kurt von Schuschnigg at the University of Saint Louis. Von Schuschnigg was a man of considerable reputation. He was a former chancellor of Austria who, in World War II, had been imprisoned by Hitler. He had been a judge on the World Court and had written a definitive text on international law.

Von Schuschnigg's influence on the young pilot could be seen clearly in Day's choice of topic for his master's thesis.

On May 1, 1960, Francis Gary Powers, a contract pilot for the CIA, was shot down while flying a clandestine spy mission over the Soviet Union. The shoot-down led to one of the more serious international incidents of the Eisenhower administration. The prevailing opinion among legal experts was that since America and the Soviet Union were not at war, the spy flight clearly violated international law.

Von Schuschnigg disagreed with that line of thought and so did Bud Day. When a prominent academician wrote an article titled "The Illegality of the U-2 Flight," Day decided to rebut it with a thesis titled "The Legality of the U-2 Flight."

Day's choice of topic shows not only von Schuschnigg's influence but Day's contrarian nature. (He would eventually publish an abstract of his thesis in the same journal in which the academician had published his anti–U-2 article.) But more important, Day's thesis made him an expert on a matter in the mainstream of military and government thinking. And it sharpened his passion for politics.

The first 16 pages of the 102-page document are an exegesis of the nature of Communism. These pages lay the groundwork for Day's position that America and the Soviet Union were not at peace but rather that "an undeclared war" existed between the two countries. Day claimed that "the long history of evil deeds by the Soviet Union clearly entitled the United States to justify the flights as a reprisal." He noted that numerous acts of the Soviet Union "clearly amounted to aggression" and that the United States, in sending an unarmed U-2 aircraft on a spy mission, "actually exercised great restraint." The U-2 flights over the Soviet Union were an effort to get vital information, "to prepare our defenses against the calamity of a nuclear surprise attack." Those who said the flights violated international law could do so only by ignoring international realities. Punches were being thrown; it no longer mattered if the bell announcing the start of the round had not been rung.

Day's reasons for choosing the topic aside, the document is important because it reveals much about his deep antipathy toward the Communist model of government. A few years later, he would fight desperately to keep the thesis a secret.

Another reason Day's tour in St. Louis is important is that he turned a nonflying dead-end job into one of the best flying billets in the Air Force. And he did it while teaching a full load of courses and studying as a graduate student.

In St. Louis, Day chose not to live near the university but instead some twenty-five miles away in O'Fallon, Illinois, only a mile or so from Scott AFB. Not long after arriving, he went to the base to locate the commissary and check out the base hospital.

A clerk saw his wings and asked, "Are you a jet pilot?"

"Yes."

"Do you fly the T-33?"

"Yes."

"Are you current?"

"Yes."

In fact, because Day had been the stan-eval officer at a combat-ready fighter wing in England, he was a high-time and highly qualified pilot — better qualified than the instructor pilots (IPs) at Scott. The clerk's face lit up. He summoned an officer, who asked Day for a favor. The base was converting to jets and setting up a conversion school. The school was primarily to train the old Military Air Transport Service (MATS) pilots, and it offered these old heads the chance to convert to jet fighters. Could he pick up a new airplane and ferry it back to Scott?

Day's boss in St. Louis said his job did not require his presence forty hours every week; Day could have Fridays off to fly.

He went home humming "Misty."

Day flew 209 hours the first three months he was at St. Louis. To put this in perspective, a pilot assigned to a fighter squadron at the time flew about fifteen hours a month. Ground duties and training took up the remainder of his time.

In addition to teaching ROTC students; flying on Fridays, weekends, and some nights during the week; and taking graduate courses, Bud started a new business with Doris. Day had read a book that explained how to turn $1,000 into a fortune by investing in real estate. Day knew better than most that flying jet aircraft was a dangerous business. He and Doris were looking to adopt another child, maybe several more. And while he believed that God was saving him for a special job, he also was a Midwesterner suffused with common sense. And if something happened, he did not want his wife and children dependent on his pension or government insurance. Bud and Doris set up the Armed Forces Land Corporation, intending to buy old run-down houses, fix them up, sell them, and reinvest in more real estate. Their first purchase was Day's old home place back in Riverside: 2222 Riverside Boulevard. Day paid the state $1,500 for the house, then fixed it up and rented it. He then bought a seven-unit apartment building, followed by an old house that he divided into four apartments. All of the real estate investments were back in Sioux City. The plan was to retire there, manage his by then extensive real estate portfolio, and take the state bar exam.

But he was not the only one with plans. In St. Louis, Doris had begun having intimations that someday something might happen to Bud. Determined that she must be able to support herself and the children, Doris learned to be a milliner and soon was turning out not only hats but something called a "whimsy" — a veil to cover the hair. Pink was her favorite color, so everything was pink. Her business was so successful that she began buying material in bulk and storing it in the garage. Soon her income matched Bud's salary.

In St. Louis, Bud and Doris adopted their second child. Steven now was seven years old, a handsome blond who was never anything but ideal, a "good boy" in every way: smart, obedient, and loving toward his parents.

As they did with every major decision, Bud and Doris prayed long and hard before filing the adoption papers. Secretly, both wanted a girl. If the state of Illinois sent them a boy, they decided, that would be a sign from God that they should later adopt still another child. If Illinois sent them a girl, then they would know their family was complete. Their desire for a girl was not evident in the adoption papers. As before, they listed no particulars about sex or race. They knew they would find the baby they were meant to have.

In early 1963, Bud and Doris learned that a friend was having an out-of-wedlock baby, what at the time was called a "gray baby," and the mother wanted to put the child up for adoption as soon as it was born. On February 27, 1963, Doris received a call saying a baby boy had been born. Doris did not want to meet the mother. Plus she was deeply fearful that the mother might change her mind at the last minute. She asked Bud to fly to California to pick up the baby.

While Doris anxiously rearranged diapers and bottles and baby clothes and the dozens of other necessities for a new baby, Day left for Los Angeles. The mother carried the baby to the door of the hospital and handed the child over to him. She also gave him a bag of diapers and bottles. Day cradled the baby, juggled the bag of supplies, walked back to the rental car, and returned to the airport. Years later Doris would say, "Bud didn't even count the fingers and toes."

"When you get a baby like this, you take what you get," Day said.

The trip across country must have been challenging. From Los Angeles to St. Louis was about three hours in the new Boeing 707. Add in the drive to the Los Angeles International Airport and the time spent waiting for the flight, and Day had the infant for some six hours before he arrived in St. Louis. He had never before cared for a baby. All he could do was occasionally stick a bottle into the child's mouth. When he did, the baby cried in apparent discomfort. Day noticed a flight attendant watching him and said, "I don't know much about this."

"I can tell," she said and leaned over to help.

She showed Day how to burp the baby, which stopped his crying for a while.

Day fed the infant, looked at him, and thought about a name. He also decided to begin a family record, to buy a camera and begin taking movies of the two boys.

Beth and Charlie Hubbs, the Days' best friends, met Day at the airport and bought him home, where Doris was waiting.

When Doris opened the door, Day held up the boy and said, "Doris, meet our new son."

She reached out with a big smile and asked, "What is our son's name?"

"Meet George Everette Day Jr."

Day's birthday was February 24 and the new baby had been born on February 27. The birthdays were so close that Day figured the new boy was meant to be a junior.

Doris looked at Bud and said, "God doesn't figure our family is complete."

"Doris, let's not adopt a girl until this one is potty trained."

DAY's job title was assistant professor of air science, prosaic in the extreme, and his first ER notes that "his involuntary assignment to this duty was not in accord with his career objectives," but that he "consistently exerted a maximum effort with enthusiasm." As usual, if he saw something he considered wrong, it was his nature to correct it. He was on campus only a few weeks when he saw someone walking across the university grounds in an Air Force uniform bearing the insignia of both an officer and an enlisted man. Day stopped the man and questioned him. The man apparently resented the questions, and moments later the two were duking it out. Day knocked the man to the ground as several ROTC students rushed to help. They held the man down while a university employee called the FBI. It turned out that the man was an ex-convict who planned to ransack the dormitories. Day received a commendation from the university.

All of the Scott AFB pilots whom Day checked out in jets were of higher rank than he. But his ER notes that "Captain Day is always in complete charge" and able to supervise without friction, a rare gift considering the egos of fighter pilots.

Reading between the lines of the ERs, one could see a foreshadowing of the combat leader Day would become. He was all business. Very demanding. Very professional. But he never forgot his manners. When he crawled out of the cockpit after checking out a pilot, he said, "I enjoyed flying with you." He complimented his subordinates. He was a soft-spoken and kind man, with elaborate, almost Victorian manners.

Day's second ER covers the period from April 1, 1960, to March 31, 1961, and falls into the water-walker category. He rewrote and streamlined ROTC operating procedures. He changed the way ROTC students were selected and made ROTC participation a highly competitive and highly desired program among students.

The reviewing officer said Day was the best judge of men he had ever known and was the best jet instructor at Scott. The endorsing officer noted that Day was so popular among students that they adjusted their schedules to take his classes. And though he was the most recent ROTC officer to arrive on campus, he was selected over all others to be commandant of cadets. An additional review from the major general who commanded all Air Force ROTC units said Day was among the top five officers assigned to the twenty-six colleges and universities in the entire ROTC program.

The ER covering the period from April 1, 1961, to March 31, 1962, was even better. Day's reviewing officer said that his performance exceeded the previous year's; that he had established a way to control drill attendance "that had completely eluded his predecessors"; and that he forced a decision-making process on cadet leaders that "so enhanced their prestige and self-confidence that it has been observed and favorably commented on by the dean of the college." The ER said Day's ability to identify and nurture leadership among students was "outstanding." Esprit de corps in the cadets was higher than it had ever been. ROTC applications increased from 22 percent to 50 percent.

The next five-month rating period ended August 31, 1962, and said that Day had lowered the absent-from-drill rate to 4 percent — less than the university's sickness rate. One of the key measuring points of an ROTC program is how many sophomores apply to take advanced ROTC, a step that almost certainly signifies that upon graduation they plan to go on active duty. Applications for advanced ROTC went from 125 the previous year to 430. The endorsing officer said that because of Day the entire campus looked upon Air Force ROTC students as a "prestige outfit." It is little wonder that while at St. Louis, Day was promoted to major "below the zone" — that is, ahead of his contemporaries.

But it kept getting better. The ER covering the period between September 1, 1962, and July 26, 1963, included a checked block that said Day was "outstanding, almost never equaled," a ranking that requires justification and several endorsements from senior officers. The ER said that under Major Day, the ROTC program at Saint Louis University had shown a marked increase in the production of highly qualified pilot-oriented Air Force officers. Of twenty-three ROTC graduates, fifteen went into pilot training. The Reverend Martin Hastings, dean of the College of American Studies at the university, declared Day as a "superior example of an Air Force officer." Another endorsement noted that Day had received his master's degree in international law and was among the "most highly qualified, dedicated, and distinguished officers I have known." The commandant of all Air Force ROTC programs said Day was in the "top five of forty-seven majors in his area."

It is little wonder that when Day left St. Louis, he was assigned to the Armed Forces Staff College in Norfolk, Virginia. This is a school an officer must attend before he is considered for promotion to higher levels of command. On January 17, 1964, Day graduated and was judged "outstanding" in every category. Among those who had made a big impression on him while he was in Norfolk was one of the guest lecturers, Navy Admiral John S. McCain.

As a graduate of the Staff College, a major promoted below the zone, and a man with astonishing efficiency reports, Day applied for and thought he would get an assignment in the tactical Air Force. He wanted back in the cockpit. If this thing going on in Vietnam turned into a full-scale war, he hoped to be there, but for that to happen he needed to be in a tactical unit.

Three jobs were available. The first was advising the 107th Tactical Fighter Group, an Air National Guard unit in Niagara Falls, New York, that flew F-100s. Most Air Force officers considered such assignments right down there with ROTC assignments. Day made a few phone calls and found that the 107th was so short of pilots that it could not achieve a "combat-ready" rating, and the Air Force was considering disbanding it.

The second possibility was a staff job in the Pentagon. But going to the Pentagon meant he would become a staff weenie, so he summarily turned that job down. There was a spot as an exchange officer, flying an F-8 Crusader with the Marine Corps. Day wanted to fly with his beloved Marines, but he did not want the six-month tour at sea that was part of the assignment.

The Air Guard unit in Niagara Falls was the only choice.

Day took a deep breath and decided he was going to make the Guard unit a combat-ready outfit.

ONE day in 1965, Bud heard that Robinson Risner — the famed Korean War ace he had met at Nellis back in 1958 — had been shot down in Vietnam but had been rescued. Later, in September, Day taxied in from a flight, and before he could alight from the aircraft, an officer came running up and said, "Bud, they shot down Robbie again. This time they got him. He's MIA."

Bud shook his head in sympathy.

DAY's final ER at Niagara Falls tells the story of his three years there. The ER said Day had performed his duties "in an absolutely superior manner." Not only had he made the 107th combat ready but he survived one of the most-feared experiences of a commander: a no-notice operational readiness inspection (ORI). An ORI begins when a group of senior officers drops in unannounced and outlines a wartime scenario, and for almost a week the unit operates on a high-tempo wartime footing. Both active-duty and Guard units often flunk a no-notice ORI. But Day's group got through without a failure, downgrade, or makeup — the only Air National Guard unit in America that year to do so and get a combat-ready rating.

Day's ER recommended he be considered for command of a fighter squadron. The ER said Day, out of all officers assigned to the unit since its creation in 1948, "is by far the most effective."

For the three years he was at Niagara Falls, Day flew more than thirty hours per month as a test pilot, instructor pilot, and flight examiner. He accumulated almost five thousand flying hours. Very few pilots in the Air Force had as many hours of jet time as did Bud Day. Again, Day was rated "absolutely superior" — an almost never-bestowed evaluation. And the endorsing officer recommended that he be promoted "well ahead of contemporaries."

DESPITE all this, it seemed to Day that back-to-back dead-end jobs meant his career had stagnated. He and Doris had many long talks about this. After Niagara Falls, he would have the time and grade to be considered for promotion to lieutenant colonel. But the promotion would almost certainly include a dreaded Pentagon assignment or a staff job. With his time in the Marines added to his time in the Air Force, he could retire in 1968 with twenty years of service. Bud and Doris decided that once he could retire, he would. They would then return to Sioux City, build a two-story brick house on Country Club Drive, and spend the remainder of their days in the place where they grew up, worrying about their real estate investments and little more.

THE year 1966 was pivotal for Bud and Doris. His tour at Niagara Falls was coming to an end, the war in Vietnam was escalating, and many of Day's fellow fighter pilots had coveted combat assignments. That year Bud and Doris celebrated their seventeenth wedding anniversary. And in 1966 they again filed an adoption application. This time they were specific: they wanted a girl, preferably one about four years old, thus putting her between the ages of Steve and George.

Instead the adoption agency offered *two* girls — twins — who were sixteen months old. Bud and Doris named the girls Sonja Marie and Sandra Marie, "Marie" having been both the name of Doris's mother and the middle name of Bud's mother.

At last, the Day clan was complete. One son was born in Germany and another in California, and the two girls were from New York.

The parents were from America's heartland. In one sense, the Days were the perfect family of a professional Air Force officer.

Perhaps the one oddity was the name Doris Day, the same as a popular movie star of the time. Ever since they were married, people commented on her name. Now, if Doris called Bud's office and asked to have him paged and said her name was Doris Day, the switchboard operator often hung up. It was difficult for her to cash checks. She began asking her friends to call her Dorie.

During all this, opposition to the war in Vietnam was growing at home: antiwar protests had taken place the previous year at the United Nations and at Rutgers University. Now demonstrations were spreading. The antiwar feeling was so strong that military people who worked at the Pentagon were advised to wear civilian clothes to work. Public officials were speaking out against the war. None of this made sense to Bud Day. To a Midwesterner, politics stopped at the water's edge. America was at war, and it was the duty of every American to support the effort.

In early 1966 Day read an article in the *Air Force Times* saying there was a critical shortage of squadron commanders in Vietnam. He was a high-time pilot and a senior major who had been recommended for promotion below the zone to lieutenant colonel. He had years of glowing efficiency reports. He thought all this made him a prime candidate for a squadron commander slot in Vietnam. It could be his last assignment before retiring.

To a civilian, it seems bewildering at best, callous at worst, that a forty-one-year-old man with four children — three of them in diapers — would ask to go to war. But such is the nature of the warrior; a warrior rushes toward — not away from — the sound of the guns. Bud Day had volunteered for the Marine Corps in World War II and had volunteered for combat duty during the Korean War. Now he was volunteering again.

This time he would need no waivers.

This time he would find combat.

This time he would find everlasting glory.

Vietnam was his war.

* * *

Doris was not happy about Bud's volunteering for Vietnam. By now they had thirty-eight rental properties back in Sioux City, a tidy portfolio that was producing enough income that they were able to buy their first Cadillac. Doris was obsessed with the idea that one of the children might die. What if that happened while Bud was away?

And Doris had a premonition about Bud: something was coming, something big and maybe something terrible.

In December, Day flew to Fairchild AFB near Spokane, Washington, and went through survival school. Pilots were turned loose in the woods and told to make their way to a certain point. All were captured so they could be interrogated. Sleep deprivation gave pilots a hint of how disoriented they could become. But no matter how authentic the Air Force tried to make survival school, several underlying and self-evident facts kept the training from being too realistic: it cost the American taxpayer a half million dollars to train a combat pilot. If he was on the way to a war zone, it was expected that he should get there in top form. One could push, but only so hard.

Bud wasn't alone in wanting to change locales: Doris did not want to live in the cold and rain of Niagara for another year. At last, she hoped to take the children to a place that was hot and dry. So Day began flying all over the country, looking at communities near Air Force bases. He settled on Phoenix, Arizona, next door to Luke AFB.

Bud wanted to visit home one more time before he left for Vietnam, so he and Doris and the children drove from New York to Sioux City. They visited St. John Lutheran Church, where they had been married and where George and the twins had been baptized. When church members heard Bud was en route to Vietnam, they gave him a medallion that stated I AM A LUTHERAN. He hung the medallion around his neck with his dog tags.

He went out to Graceland Cemetery to his dad's grave and sat on the edge of the tombstone. As is the case with many sons who have troubles with their fathers, it was not until after his father's death that the perspective shifted and Bud began to see his father in a different light. Sitting there in Graceland, Bud talked to him about not being able to come to his funeral and about all the unresolved issues from his childhood. He knew that his father understood, that he would have believed the most important priority was to bring Steve into the family.

Once he "set things right with the old man," he was surprised how his perception changed. He remembered his dad fondly and with great respect. "He was a determined old bastard," Bud realized. "Events were not going to overwhelm him. He was going to overwhelm events."

In a few more years, men would say the same about Bud Day.

WHEN Bud and Doris arrived in Phoenix, Bud pointed and said, "Look at the mountains. Aren't they pretty?"

Doris glared. "Not as pretty as an Iowa cornfield."

If anyone wants to know how adaptable are professional military people and how quickly they make decisions, consider this: The Day family arrived in Phoenix on March 7, 1967. On March 8 they found and rented a house at 5238 West Lewis Avenue, a four-bedroom home with a fenced yard. The furniture arrived from Niagara Falls on March 9. By March 13, Steve was in school.

Accommodations and education settled, Day showed Doris the route to the nearest shopping center, grocery store, and beauty shop, and to Luke AFB. He gave her the names and phone numbers of two pilot friends at Luke; she was to call them if there was an emergency or if she needed anything. Day went out to Luke and asked what else he could do for his wife to help her while he was gone. "Get her a credit card," he was told. Day had never heard of a credit card. But he got one with a $500 spending limit, figuring that would be enough. He would, after all, be gone only a year.

Bud unloaded all of Doris's pink fabrics and materials for making hats and whimsies and arranged them just as she wanted. He collected the family's winter clothes and put them in storage. Next March when he returned, he would take them out of storage for eventual use in Sioux City. One morning he got up very early and spent all day grilling hamburgers and cooking roasts, enough to last the family several weeks. Every time Doris pulled one of these out of the freezer, she would say, "Your father cooked this for you before he left. He will be back home in . . . ," and she would tell the children how many months remained.

Day opened a closet in the new house and showed Doris his black lawyer's briefcase. He figured the worst thing that could happen to him in the next year was that he would be killed. If so, she would find everything she needed to know in the briefcase: a list of pallbearers, the location of their marriage license, his birth certificate, his military personnel file, a list of his life insurance policies and bank account numbers. Detailed instructions of every step she should take were in the briefcase. He thought he had covered every possible contingency.

On March 18, Bud took Doris and the children to Las Vegas; he wanted them to see all the bright lights, to see the place where he first heard "Misty." While they were there, Day went to the officers' club at Nellis and ran into an officer who told him a mutual friend had been shot down in Vietnam and was MIA.

As they left the club, Doris asked, "What does 'MIA' mean?"

"Missing in action."

That did not sink in. "What happens if you are missing?"

Day shrugged. No need for Doris to think about this. "You just pray they find you."

In the spring of 1967, America was preparing for what would go down in history as the Summer of Love — a summer of antiwar demonstrations, protest songs and marches, and sex, drugs, and rock and roll. It was midafternoon on Easter Sunday when Doris and the four children drove Bud to Luke AFB to see him off. At the airport, she looked at him for a long moment. She did not want to cry. Air Force wives don't cry when their husbands go to war.

Doris was nervous. She was still afraid one of the children might die. Her husband was going off to war and she was in a new town where she knew almost no one, and she was in charge of four children. Bud was more than her husband; he was her best friend. After the children went to bed every night, she and Bud sat up and chatted. And on Sunday afternoons after church, they went for long rides and talked. To her, Bud was an optimistic man who saw the bright side of everything. He would not tolerate gossip. He was a practical man, a courteous man, and he was understanding as are few men. He never criticized her. The closest he ever came was to say, "Doris, I don't think I would have done it that way." She thought of what a good and wonderful man and husband he was. His only flaw was that he got on her nerves with his incessant humming of "Misty." But now that did not seem so important. Almost in desperation she said, "Bud, just come back. Even if you are in a basket."

Bud put his hands on her shoulders, looked deep into her eyes, and said, "I will be back and I will be back whole."

He knew of her fear that one of the children might die, and he wanted to strengthen her. He squeezed her shoulders so hard that she flinched. "Doris, you are a good wife and a good mother. God gave us these four children, and it will be His will if He takes one of them back."

He dropped his hands from her shoulders, said, "I love you," and turned and walked toward the waiting airplane. His back was straight and his head was high and he took long steps. As is the nature of fighter pilots, he never looked back.

Steve held his mother's hand and wept. George, who was turning into a quiet and shy little boy, was mute. The twins tried to follow their dad to the airplane.

Day took off at 3:30 p.m., on schedule to the minute.

He flew to California and then to the Philippines for a week of jungle survival school. Officers from New York or Chicago or other big cities, men whose feet had rarely been off the concrete, found the jungle a terrifying place. They were particularly afraid of snakes. But back home, every time the Big Sioux flooded, Day's yard had become populated by poisonous snakes; he kept a hoe leaning against the house just to kill them. And he had spent so much time roaming the Loess Hills and hunting pheasants that the outdoors held no terror for him. His Marine Corps training had taught him of edible plants, how to live off the land, and of land navigation. About the only thing Day had actually learned at the Air Force jungle survival school was that if he was shot down and had to "escape and evade" (E & E), he should stay off the trails and make his way through the jungle.

As was true for every member of every branch of the military assigned to Vietnam, adherence to the Code of Conduct was drummed into Day. He was told that if he was captured, the code would sustain him through any interrogation: "Just remember the code and you will be okay." But Bud Day did not plan on getting captured.

7

Hit My Smoke

DAY arrived in Vietnam at the zenith of his career. He was a senior major who almost certainly would soon be promoted to lieutenant colonel. And he was about to be named a command pilot. He was widely known in the Air Force as a man with a curious reputation that combined macho and intellect. He was the guy who survived a no-chute bailout and whose gunnery and bombing scores were just about perfect. But he was also the guy who wrote the book on the delivery of nuclear weapons and on fuel management of fighter aircraft. He remained one of only two lawyer–fighter pilots in the Air Force, a fact that wrinkled many a brow.

On April 4, Day landed at Da Nang and the next day flew to a new base named Tuy Hoa. It took him only a few days to realize that the article in the *Air Force Times* was wrong: there was no shortage of squadron commanders in Vietnam; in fact, it was the opposite. Lieutenant colonels held every squadron commander job, and so many majors were running around that they were relegated to staff jobs.

Day's assignment was with the 309th Squadron, which flew F-100Ds in close-air-support missions. Every pilot has a ground job, and Day's was as a scheduler: the man who matched pilots and aircraft with assigned missions. Scheduling was a bookkeeping position usually held by a junior captain, thus it was a dead-end job for a senior major.

For the next two months, Day scheduled "monkey-killer missions," meaning bombing missions where the intelligence was so faulty or so out of date that what was said to be a "truck park" or an "enemy camp" was nothing but jungle. It was a frustrating assignment. Day knew this would be his last war, his last chance to lead men in combat, and he was chomping at the bit. He was forty-two and in the best physical condition of his life. He worked out daily and could do dozens of one-armed push-ups. At five foot nine and 152 pounds, he was the prototypical smallish wiry fighter pilot, a man who could fit comfortably into the cockpit of an F-100. His hair was close-cropped, even for a military officer. He was movie-star handsome, with a direct stare, an erect stance, and a professional no-nonsense demeanor. And even in a baggy flight suit, he was a squared-away officer.

Day liked the wing motto: "Return with Honor." But he was not doing what he imagined he would when he had volunteered to come to Vietnam. The only good thing about the assignment was that, once again, Day could schedule himself to fly as often as he wanted. And he did. He flew attack missions almost daily, sometimes two in one day, and by the end of May had flown seventy-two combat missions.

On one of those missions he came to the aid of an Army Special Forces camp that was about to be overrun by enemy soldiers. He laid his bombs down danger close, saved the Special Forces camp, racked up a body count of 143 enemy soldiers, and was recommended for a medal.

If Day thought he was qualified and ready for a bigger job, so did others. In late May, he was ordered to Saigon to meet with the director of operations for the 7th Air Force.

SEVERAL weeks earlier, two O-1 "Bird Dogs" had been flying a Forward Air Control (FAC) mission out of Da Nang. The Bird Dog is a small single-engine, propeller-driven "bug smasher" that crawls through the air at around a hundred miles per hour. FAC missions in South Vietnam were to locate and identify enemy-troop emplacements and then call in attack aircraft.

The two Bird Dogs were over the demilitarized zone (DMZ) when one was hit by a SAM and blown out of the sky. This was the first time SAMs had been utilized so far south, and the incident brought to a head what the 7th Air Force already knew: FACs had one of the highest mortality rates of any flying job in the war. Now that missiles were part of the equation, their mortality rate would climb higher.

Suppressing the SAMs was more than a tactical need; it had strategic implications in that the missiles themselves were supplied by the Soviet Union. The Cold War still loomed large in American military thinking. If war between these superpowers became a reality, the United States would use giant B-52 bombers to penetrate deep into the Soviet Union. The Soviets would use SAMs against the B-52s. The Soviets wanted to find out how effective their missiles were against the B-52s, and America wanted to find out if the electronic countermeasures were effective against the SAMs. Vietnam would be the proving ground.

Even better than testing countermeasures was eliminating the chance of being fired upon. Since President Lyndon Johnson would not then allow American pilots to attack Hanoi and Haiphong, where supply shipments to the South originated, the supplies would have to be interdicted before they reached the South.

America needed eyes in North Vietnam.

DAY's conversation with the director of operations was, as are most conversations between colonels and majors, somewhat one-sided.

"Major, we're cranking up a new outfit. It is called Operation Commando Sabre. It is top secret and you're the CO [commanding officer]. We're going to use F-100Fs as FACs."

That was a lot of information. Did he hear right? Majors don't command fighter squadrons in Vietnam. F-100s used as FACs?

The colonel pointed to a map on his wall. "You'll be attached to the 37th Tactical Fighter Wing. Officially you are Detachment One of the 416th Tactical Fighter Squadron [TFS] at Phu Cat. That's the closest F-100 base to North Vietnam. You'll be working up north in Route Pack One. All war supplies coming down the Ho Chi Minh Trail have to come through this area." He paused. "The area is heavily defended."

(The U.S. military divided North Vietnam into geographic areas called "Route Packs," with Route Pack One being the southernmost and Route Pack Six, the area that included Haiphong and Hanoi, the northernmost.)

The colonel pointed. "This is where the Ho Chi Minh Trail reenters Vietnam from Cambodia. Your AO [area of operations] includes the Mu Gia Pass, a real hot spot. The North Vietnamese are moving SAMs into Route Pack One, and that threat has to be eliminated."

Day wondered about the choice of aircraft. The F-100F is a two-seater, a training model used to check out new pilots. They were few in number; only 339 were manufactured.

Almost as if reading Day's mind, the colonel said, "The F model gives you an extra set of eyes. The aircraft will go in low and fast. One man flies the aircraft, the other looks for targets. We've assembled a few pilots and aircraft at Phu Cat. They're waiting on you. This sort of thing has never been done before, so you'll be developing doctrine and tactics as you go along."

The colonel paused. He knew from Day's personnel file that Day had flown across most countries in Europe at high speed and at about a hundred feet of altitude. "Major, what do you think of using F-100Fs as FACs?"

Day paused and looked at the map. He remembered that when he ripped across Europe, he could see church steeples and rivers but that was about it. Trying to locate, identify, and mark camouflaged targets as small as a AAA battery seemed impossible, especially if people on the ground were shooting at you.

"Sir, I think it's a very bad idea."

"Fine. Get up to Phu Cat, take charge, whip that group into shape, and go to work."

"Yes, sir."

THE distinction between flying "up north" and flying in South Vietnam may elude many today. But in 1967, North Vietnam was the most heavily defended real estate on earth, a place where pilots could walk on the flak and play tag with the SAMs, a place of highly lucrative targets such as truck parks, fuel depots, railroad stations, power plants, and enemy air bases. By contrast, South Vietnam was relatively safe, devoid of AAA and SAMs, boasting very few lucrative targets, and requiring mostly monkey bombing. So when a Vietnam-era fighter pilot says he flew up north, that means he ripped off the front gate of hell and flew into the deadliest air-defense system ever devised.

PHU Cat was a former Vietcong training base south of the DMZ, about twenty miles northwest of Qui Nhon and near the infamous Route 1, a road known around the world because of Bernard Fall's seminal work *Street Without Joy*.

When Day first came to Vietnam, he wrote almost daily letters to Doris and the children. Then he bought tape recorders — one for him and one for Doris — and began sending home taped messages. When he moved to Phu Cat, he sent Doris a tape that said, "I have a new job. I have the cake and the icing too."

He did not tell her that he was the commanding officer of a top secret unit, that he was flying up north, and that he had one of the most dangerous jobs in Vietnam. And she, being The Viking, knew better than to ask.

Commando Sabre "tasking" — to use the military term — was simple: stop the flow of supplies from north to south. To do this, pilots would locate and identify truck parks, fuel dumps, and enemy convoys, then call in strike aircraft — those carrying bombs — and direct the attacks against the targets.

There were no precedents, no history to draw upon. The Air Force had flown FAC missions in Korea. But that was fifteen years earlier, and now SAC domination of the Air Force meant there was no FAC doctrine. Thus, Day's job was not only to crank up the first jet FAC operation in history but to develop Air Force doctrine and tactics for the FAC mission. And he had to do so at a new base in an undeveloped country.

He had the outfit operational in two weeks.

For a few days the Commando Sabre group used the call sign of the 416th TFS. But this was a special outfit, and a special outfit needed its own call sign. The call signs of FAC units in 1967 and those that came later all reflected their aggressiveness in the face of great danger: Gunsmoke, Stormy, Wolf, Nail, Typhoon, Playboy, and Tiger.

In mid-June a new call sign was heard in the skies over North Vietnam.

Misty.

In the beginning, when the new guys began broadcasting their wussy call sign, there must have been a few snickers. If so, they didn't last long.

Other pilots quickly learned that the "Fast FACs" or "Super FACs" or "Misty FACs" were an aggressive bunch of bastards who pressed the fight; they got down in the weeds, trolled for trouble, and did things with an F-100 that had never been done before.

For most, "shit" is a one-dimensional expletive. But fighter pilots have a multifaceted usage of the word that might be confusing. For instance, if a pilot describes a fellow officer as a "shit" or a "real shit," then that officer is an unpleasant fellow. On the other hand, if that officer is described as a "good shit" or a "great shit," then he is a prince among men. No higher praise can be awarded a fighter pilot than to say he is "shit hot." (The phonetic version used in polite company is "Sierra Hotel.") Finally, if a pilot is being fired at by AAA, SAMs, machine guns, and rifles, and the Gomers are standing on hilltops throwing rocks at him, he is "in the shit." The Mistys flew only up north, and they were in the shit on every mission.

Earlier, when FACs found a target — or thought they had found a target — they launched marking rockets, then said, "Do you have my smoke?" The strike pilot then came back with "Roger that." The FAC would say something like, "Your target is fifty meters north of the smoke," or "Your target is twenty meters west of the smoke." When the strike aircraft attacked, they usually saw no signs that they had killed anything other than monkeys.

The Mistys came screaming in, fired their rockets, and asked, "Do you have my smoke?" When they got an affirmative, the Mistys said, "Hit my smoke." When Mistys called in a strike, often there were secondary explosions, indicating an ammunition supply or fuel dump had been hit. A truck park might be obliterated. The Mistys found targets that, when bombed, made things blow up; made the ground shake.

For about a week after Misty cranked up, it was just as Day had feared: targets were impossible to find. But after maybe a half dozen flights, the Mistys not only knew the AO intimately but began to see the hand of man against the jungle. They saw tracks on the road still glistening with water and knew a vehicle had recently passed. They saw faint condensation from a truck exhaust at dawn, anomalies in camouflage that revealed it was not real, or wilted leaves that stood out ever so slightly from the jungle. They could pick out the shape of a gun battery under the camouflage. They developed "Misty eyes": they could see what no other pilots could see.

"Hit my smoke" and high-value targets became the hallmarks of the Mistys. That and their aggressive nature. Indeed, everything about the Mistys was a reflection of Day's leadership. Tigers breed tigers. A candy-assed commander will have few tigers working for him. Each makes the other uncomfortable.

"Misty" would become a call sign of mythic proportions, one of the most famous of the Vietnam War.

* * *

IN the beginning, the Mistys were numbered according to the chain of command, and then according to when a pilot entered the group. As the first commander, Day was "Misty 1."

"Misty 2" was Bill Douglass, the operations officer and a laconic fellow who became famous for consistently neglecting marking rockets in favor of pointing the snout of his F-100 at a AAA battery and boring in with guns chattering.

The other pilots were lieutenants and captains, junior birdmen who, like the Flying Tigers or the Eagle Squadron or the Doolittle Raiders of World War II, were volunteers. And, as is often the case with elite outfits, they were in awe of their commanding officer. They had checked him out and knew he was qualified to fly almost every jet fighter built and that he had almost five thousand hours in the cockpit. He was the only squadron commander in Vietnam who was a major, so he had to be shit hot. Plus, he was a plainspoken man. Four decades later, when former Mistys were interviewed, they to a man spoke of Day's bluntness. "He called a spade a fucking spade," one said.

Phu Cat was a busy base, host to several fighter squadrons and numerous support groups. Transient pilots were always passing through. They wanted to know about Commando Sabre. Aircraft flying out of Phu Cat usually flew in flights of four or eight aircraft. These guys took off before dawn, seven days a week, and they flew alone. Who were they?

All questions were turned aside with "That outfit is top secret and you don't have the need to know."

But there is one thing that warriors always know: where the battle is. And the word got out among men who wanted to fly and fight: if you want to get in the shit, call Major Bud Day at Phu Cat.

Calls began coming in from Sierra Hotel fighter pilots at Nellis, Willy, Cannon, and Luke, fighter bases inhabited by warriors. And the warriors flocked to Bud Day. During the years of the Vietnam War, some three million Americans passed through Vietnam. Only 157 of those men served as Misty pilots. But those

157 men wrote history large. It would be difficult to find another outfit so small in number from which would spring so many legends, so many decorations for valor.

And so many shoot-downs.

Mistys had the only job in the Air Force whereby a pilot could strap on a fighter, not file a flight plan, and go where he wanted, at any altitude and at any speed. A typical mission was to take off, fly north, divert east over the Gulf of Tonkin, then drop down and take up a heading through Route Pack One, also known as the "Pack." The reference point for entering the Pack was often a big house on the banks of the Ben Hai River. The white house had a red roof and was called "Tara" or the "plantation."

Each F-100F had a pilot in the front seat and another in the back — "the pit" — who took photographs and wrote down the location of AAA or SAM sites on a map. The photographs were developed immediately upon landing, and sometimes the information was used in a "cross briefing" for the next Misty flight. Armament was minimal: two pods, each containing seven white phosphorus marking rockets, and two 20 mm cannon. The cannon had four hundred rounds of ammo and fired at three thousand rounds per minute, so the few seconds of cannon fire were to be used only if working a rescue and enemy forces were close. Nevertheless, these men were Mistys, and it was not unusual for them to point their aircraft at a gun emplacement and fire away.

Day had decreed that speed was good, so Mistys came in with a lot of smash — 450 or 500 mph — and at about four thousand feet. But four thousand feet is almost a mile high, and at 500 mph the landscape is a blur, so sometimes they flew slower and lower. The AAA fired at them had a muzzle velocity of about three thousand feet per second. This meant it took one second or less for the explosive rounds to reach their altitude. So the Mistys jinked — altered the flight path in an unpredictable manner — constantly. This was a tremendous workload on the pilot and — because he could not anticipate the jinking — gave a tremendous pounding to the guy in the pit.

Mistys worked the AO, looking for targets for about an hour before climbing out to the tanker to refuel. After another hour and a half down in the weeds, they tanked again and worked the AO another hour or so before returning to Phu Cat. The missions were so demanding that oil needed to be added to the engines after four hours of flying time. The average mission was five hours, but some lasted six or seven. In July, Day stepped up the pace and went to four sorties per day, which meant he had continuous coverage of the Pack for about twenty hours every day.

While Mistys often violated rules about speed and altitude, the one operating procedure they never violated was the order not to go over a target twice on one mission. Such a move was considered suicidal. And though the Mistys liked to say that when they went up north they were alone and unafraid, that was nonsense. They were terrified. When Day and the other Mistys returned from a mission, they sometimes had to be helped from the aircraft. They might have lost three or four pounds; their flight suits were sodden with perspiration and urine. They were so sweat-drenched that their boots squished when they walked. And they knew a marrow-deep fatigue that came from being shot at hundreds of times in the past five hours. Indeed, Mistys were shot at from the time they entered the Pack until they exited. It was not unusual for a Misty departing North Vietnam airspace to look down and see the next Misty flight entering the AO. And it was not uncommon that the entering aircraft trailed behind it, like a series of airborne farts, puff after puff of smoke from exploding AAA.

From the beginning, Mistys came home with holes in the wings and fuselage. By mid-August, Day had taken hits on three missions and was considered — in Misty lingo — a "magnet ass." In one of his tapes to Doris, he told her about being hit and added, "Remember, Doris, that's the name of the game."

In Vietnam, Day developed and wrote Air Force doctrine for jet FACs. But several other things mark Day's leadership of the Mistys. The most important speaks to the issue of character and integrity, traits noted in many of his ERs. He was more concerned with the welfare of his men than with his own advancement, a rare trait in the Air Force and a sign of a great leader. But this was something he learned in the Marine Corps, where taking care of subordinates is almost a religion. The trait was best illustrated by a story.

One morning Day took off before dawn and found the AO covered with patchy fog and a low cloud deck — a recipe for disaster. A gunner needs to know the course, altitude, and speed of his target. The course of an aircraft is obvious. A gunner could look through the patchy fog and estimate with considerable accuracy the altitude of the cloud bottoms. Had a Misty come in skimming the bottoms of the clouds, the gunner would know his altitude within a hundred feet or so. AAA gunners in North Vietnam were some of the most experienced in the world. Thus, low clouds and fog sandwiched an aircraft into a narrow zone from which it would be almost impossible to escape.

Plus, a Misty would not see AAA or missiles until they popped through the fog. And by then it was too late to maneuver.

Day returned to Phu Cat and postponed the outgoing flight until the fog lifted.

A few minutes later, the vice wing commander, a full colonel, banged open the door of the Misty office, accosted Day, and said, "I have frag orders for Route Pack One." ("Frag orders" are fragmentary orders, a brief outline of a mission.)

"I just came from up there," Day said. "The weather is too low."

The colonel raised his voice. "You don't get it, Major. That's a Seventh Air Force TOT [time on target] and you have to meet it. Get that aircraft in the air."

Bill Douglass and several other Mistys were in the room and moved away. But they listened.

Day moved so close to the colonel that their noses were about four inches apart. "YOU don't get it, Colonel. I don't care what Seventh Air Force says. My men are not going."

The colonel stomped out. Douglass and the young pilots looked at one another. They had a boss who would risk his career for his men. The incident became part of the legend of Misty 1.

About that same time, Day decided that the Mistys' intelligence officer, a lieutenant colonel assigned from the wing, was not up to unit standards. He fired the colonel, another risky career move and one that so angered the brass that, to get even, they replaced the colonel with a first lieutenant. The replacement, Ray Bevivino, was an Air Force Academy graduate who believed he could win the war by himself. He worked so many weeks without a break that Day had to order him to take a day off. Using information that was as close to real time as then was possible, Bevivino developed the best intelligence system of any Air Force unit in Vietnam.

Another part of Day's Misty legend concerned his greatest flaw as a leader: he flew too much, six or seven days a week. When Bill Douglass talked him into taking a day off, Day used the time to fly missions in South Vietnam.

One of the most amazing facts about Day's time as leader of the Mistys, and for at least four months afterward, is that no Misty ever aborted a mission for mechanical reasons. This is remarkable. First, aborts were common at every F-4 and F-105 outfit in the theater. Numerous fighter pilots were not as committed to combat as they might have been; many were in Vietnam only to get a ticket punched, and they lacked the warrior ethos. Some of them dropped their bombs far from the target. Second, a jet fighter is a complex and temperamental piece of equipment. It is relatively rare for a fighter to be fully mission capable (FMC), that is, every aircraft system — radio, engine, mechanical, electrical, weapons — works as advertised. Oil pressure may be down a bit. The exhaust temp might be a few degrees too hot. A radio might be scratchy. A pilot, if he so desires, can always find a reason to abort. And third, Day had only seven aircraft for a mission that called for twenty-hours-per-day operation at high speeds, frequent use of the afterburner, and almost always high-G maneuvers.

But Mistys were warriors, and warriors don't look for reasons to abort; they look for reasons to fly. If a Misty had ammo in his guns and the afterburner worked, he launched.

A cornerstone of the Misty legend concerns some sporty flying performed by Bud Day during an early August mission. He was snooping and pooping when his Misty eyes detected an anomaly; perhaps it was a few wilted leaves, maybe the hint of a shape under a tree, maybe the glint of sunlight on AAA barrels, something so subliminal Day would have found it difficult to explain. He backed off and called in a strike force of F-105 "Thuds." Then a jeep broke out of the jungle and went racing down the road. Day could see the local road network and knew there was only one way the jeep could go. He racked his aircraft around, and as the truck turned a 90-degree corner, Day was down low, coming straight at it. He launched a rocket that went through the windshield and blew the jeep to smithereens.

When the Thuds arrived on scene, Day muttered to himself, "I'm going to light these bastards up."

He pointed the F-100 at the anomaly and fired a marking rocket.

All hell broke loose.

His rocket exploded a fuel dump and set off a chain of twenty-eight secondary explosions. For a Misty, happiness was a secondary explosion, especially when, as in this case, the explosions ripped the camouflage off a large truck park.

More strike aircraft were called in. They did not have to ask for directions, as the column of smoke was visible for miles. One of the strike aircraft hit a SAM site, and the explosion cooked off several missiles.

It was a wildly successful day for the Mistys.

By mid-August the Mistys were having a measurable impact on the flow of war equipment into the South, in locating SAM sites, and in controlling rescue efforts for downed pilots. The Pentagon wanted to know more about this outfit, top generals craving good news that they could give to a Congress increasingly restive about the war. So Day was ordered to Japan to brief the vice chief of staff of the Air Force.

The briefing went well, and Day was feeling good on the flight back to South Vietnam. He had bought a new $10 watch (a Seiko that had become the official squadron watch of the Mistys) and a case of Johnnie Walker to stash under his bunk. On September 11, less than three weeks away, he was flying to Hawaii to meet Doris for ten days of R & R — rest and recuperation. Doris already had reservations at the Reef Hotel on Waikiki, a standard room for $14 per day.

On the morning of August 26, Day got up early and taped a message to Doris and the children. Then he did what he had never done before: he taped a second cassette, put both in the outgoing mail, and then, after a 4 a.m. breakfast, went to the ramp to watch the first Misty flight take off.

He was flying the second flight, checking out a twenty-six-year-old Air Force Academy graduate named Corwin Kippenhan. "Kip," as he was called, was Misty 13.

Day grimaced when he saw they were flying an aircraft numbered 954. Every fighter has its idiosyncrasies, and 954 had a bad shoulder harness in the backseat. The harness could not be cinched down tightly, and no one seemed able to repair or replace it. Kip was flying in the front seat, and Day knew that when Kip began banking and yanking, he would be battered. It was going to be a rough flight.

Day and Kip were crawling into the cockpit when an Air Force corporate jet landed. These little "Scatbacks" usually carried senior generals. Every commander at Phu Cat had a frisson of trepidation when this particular aircraft landed: it was from 7th Air Force, which was commanded by General William "Spike" Momyer, a man famous for flying onto a base and firing commanders. Momyer had fired so many colonels, men whose insignia of rank is an eagle, that he was known as the "bird killer."

But when the door of the aircraft opened, there was no frenzy of saluting: it was not Momyer. Instead it was a group of intelligence officers with photographs of an SA-2 missile site containing three SAMs in the launchers. B-52s were conducting frequent bombing missions in the area, so this site had to be destroyed.

The intelligence officers drove across the ramp and showed Day the photographs. He recognized the area immediately. It was in what Mistys called the "Fruit Orchard" west of "Fingers Lake," one of the most dangerous parts of the Pack. Strike pilots had been shot down here and never heard from again. No one knew if they were prisoners in Hanoi or if, as fighter pilots said, "They woke up on the wrong side of the grass."

This could be a day of sporty flying.

A half hour later, Kip and Day were down in the weeds and ripping along at almost five hundred miles per hour, banking and yanking, grunting hard from the Gs. When they were a mile from the target, it seemed as if Hades had opened up and the residents were throwing fireballs at the sky. Day had never seen so much AAA. He and Kip flew through the barrage, and it was a miracle they were not hit. Day thought he saw a SAM, but he was not sure enough to call in a strike.

Day and Kip worked another part of the AO, hit the tanker, and dove for the deck. This was Day's sixty-seventh penetration of North Vietnamese airspace in about nine weeks. It was around 1:30 p.m. Maybe if they came in again on a different heading, they could find the SAM.

"Let's make one more pass," he told Kip.

Hey, faint heart never fucked a pig.

This time they came in from the west, low over a karst outcropping. The weather was hazy, with about three miles visibility. Kip dropped down to about a thousand feet and "cobbed it"; he was traveling at 575 mph, depending on speed and hoping for surprise.

But enemy gunners were on alert, and a wall of flak greeted the aircraft. Kip pressed on, jinking hard as fireballs from 37 mm cannon filled the air. Kip and Day were hammered by almost continuous explosions.

Then Day saw the missile. No doubt about it, this was a SAM site. At that moment, the aircraft took a direct hit in the aft end, lurched, shuddered, and seemed to stop in midair. Every warning light on the panel came on. This bird was going down.

"I have the aircraft," Day said, taking control.

Day had written the procedures for such an emergency. He knew what to do: light the burner, scramble for sky, and turn for the coast. The ocean was about ten miles away, maybe ninety seconds of flying time, but at three thousand feet the aircraft lost hydraulic pressure, the controls locked, and the aircraft nosed over. The flight path was describing the outside of a circle and placing heavy negative Gs on Day and Kip. Day's head and shoulders were jammed against the canopy. Papers, maps, the camera, a water bottle, dust, and dirt filled the air. The aircraft was pointed at the ground and about three seconds from crashing.

"Eject! Eject! Eject!" Day ordered. He pulled the ejection lever. (In an F-100F, the backseater goes first, followed a second later by the frontseater.)

When Kip's chute opened, two panels blew out, and as he descended rapidly he noticed two things: The F-100 had crashed and exploded. And Major Day was maybe a quarter of a mile away, limp in the chute, clearly unconscious and descending so rapidly that he *passed* Kip.

When Day and Kip ejected, automatic radios — "beepers" — on their parachute harnesses began broadcasting on the emergency frequency. A rescue helicopter was scrambled, and it homed in on the beepers.

Misty 1 was down.

It was the beginning of one of the most incredible sagas of the Vietnam War.

8

South Toward Freedom

PAIN brought him back from unconsciousness.

His right arm was wrecked. The ulna was broken about four inches below his elbow and was sticking through the skin. The humerus was broken midway between his elbow and shoulder. His left knee was dislocated and already beginning to swell. He could not see out of his right eye.

The broken arm and dislocated knee were the results of ejecting at 575 mph while pressed against the canopy. His flailing arm and leg apparently had hit something. But the eye — how did that happen? The only thing he could figure was that when he bailed out, his oxygen mask did not separate properly and slammed him.

He had to call in the rescue helicopters, the Jolly Green Giants; he had to get out of here. He was down near Vinh Linh in one of the most heavily bombed areas of North Vietnam. Every time a Misty was shot at, Ray Bevivino marked the AAA site on his maps. This area was the most heavily marked part of the Pack. The local population would not look with favor upon a downed American airman, so this was going to be a race between the Jollys and the Gomers. And he was the prize.

Day tried to reach into his flight suit to pull out his radio, but his right arm wouldn't move. He switched to his left, placed the radio on the ground, and slowly extended the antenna. Then he picked up the radio and took a quick look around. He was on the edge of the jungle, only a hundred yards from a Vietnamese village.

Someone was running toward him, threshing through the bushes.

Day looked up. A boy — he could not have been more than fourteen years old — was pointing a rusty bolt-action rifle at him. The boy's finger was on the trigger, and he was shaking from fear and excitement. Day froze.

The boy tossed Day's survival radio aside, then snatched the new Seiko off his wrist.

Little bastard.

All the time the boy was shouting, doubtless telling his comrades he had found the American pilot. He tried to snatch Day's pilot-school ring. Day jerked his arm away. (Pilots don't wear wedding rings when flying over enemy territory, so his was back in Phoenix.)

The boy grabbed Day's survival knife and began slicing the parachute harness with such reckless abandon that Day feared he might be cut by the sharp six-inch blade. By now the boy's friends had arrived, and they were having a field day. Souvenirs from a downed American pilot were highly prized. One boy pulled at Day's boots, another stripped him of his flight suit. In seconds, Day was down to his shorts.

By now his plight was beginning to sink in. Just moments earlier he had been flying one of the most technologically advanced aircraft of his time, master of an almost limitless domain, with the might of the U.S. military behind him. Now he was badly injured, on the ground in one of the most dangerous parts of North Vietnam, almost naked and surrounded by panicky souvenir-grabbing teenage boys who were very anxious to get him away from the parachute. They knew that the beeper in his parachute harness had been transmitting since he ejected and that a rescue helicopter could be on the scene in minutes.

If they wanted to keep him, they had to move him.

The boys hammered him with their gun butts and prodded him with the muzzles. Day's knee injury was so painful it was almost impossible for him to stand. He balanced on one leg, tottering, then began to limp along, his captors dancing about, looking over their shoulders. The little party had gone only a few steps when it seemed half the AAA guns in North Vietnam erupted around him. The *splatting* muzzle blasts of the 37 mm cannon told him the guns — which were in revetments — were depressed to the lowest level; they were firing almost straight across the ground.

Then he heard the rapid *whomp, whomp, whomp* of helicopter blades. A Jolly was inbound, pressing hard into the face of the guns, homing in on the beacon in Day's parachute. The helicopter was so low his wheels were dragging through the trees. The AAA fire increased; the sound was horrendous, and Day realized the gunners were hoping an air burst would down the chopper. But still the Jolly pressed on, weaving, swerving, the pilot ignoring the flak bursting above him and the countless AK-47s being fired at him. He was determined to find the downed pilot. Now that big beautiful chopper was so close that Day could see a man with a rifle in his hand standing in the open door. He did not know it, but the figure was Corwin Kippenhan, who had been rescued within minutes after landing. "We've got to find my buddy," he told the crew. A crew member had handed him an M16 and said, "We're going in. Shoot anything that shoots at us."

Procedures dictate that a rescue chopper doesn't land unless the crew is talking to the downed pilot. Over the noise of the chopper, Kip could hear shouts and then long bursts from AK-47s. From the sound of it, he thought Day had been shot.

Day saw the Jolly approach his parachute, pause a half second, then twist and dip and swing left. Had the chopper turned right, it would have flown over Day and, he believed, panicked his young captors and enabled him to escape. But it did not.

The boys around Day were euphoric that the chopper had been driven off. They laughed and jumped about and waved their rifles in the air.

Every second increased Day's awareness of what a serious condition he was in — not just the fact that he had been shot down and captured by the enemy but the nature of his injuries.

Fighter pilots are control freaks. They have to be in charge. But Day was not in charge, and he had no control over what was happening.

His right arm hurt so much he wanted to scream. And his left knee hurt so badly he could not bear to put his weight on it. But his young captors were oblivious to his injuries. Slamming him hard in the back with their rifle butts, they forced him toward the nearby village of Vinh Linh, a place virtually destroyed by American bombing. There he was met by a village elder, who shouted out what Day thought was a list of America's sins against Vietnam. Then the women and children of the village fell upon Day, beating and kicking and pulling and pinching. When he was beaten to the ground, they lifted him by his ears and the beating resumed.

In retrospect, it is a miracle Day survived his first few hours on the ground. Other pilots and crew members shot down in this area had been summarily executed with bullets in the head.

Day's hell march continued through several villages until, about dusk, he entered a small camp. He had marched about four miles and was in shock. Day was pushed into a hole that had been shoveled out from the side of a bunker. It was about six feet long and maybe two feet wide, and he thought of it as being the size of a coffin. Over his head was a log roof covered by dirt.

His left hand — his good hand — was wrapped in wire and tied to the logs. His legs were bound with rope, about thirty feet of clothesline with maybe a dozen granny knots, amateurish but effective. Day looked on in amazement, almost as if he were a dispassionate spectator, when locals paraded by his hole in the bunker. He did not understand Vietnamese, but it was not difficult to figure out what the locals were talking about as they stared at the broken bone protruding from his arm, chattered about the peculiar angle at which his right arm hung from his body, looked with astonishment on his left knee, which now was purple and about the size of a football, and pointed at his right eye. He did not know it, but his right eye was solid red from ruptured blood vessels and was a fearsome sight. Dozens of flies and insects buzzed about

Day's head and crawled across the broken skin of his arm. A guard handed him a bowl of watery soup and a handful of rice.

Most people in Day's condition would have thought only of getting some kind of medical attention. Day thought only of escape. E & E was his duty, dictated by the Code of Conduct. The code said nothing about the nature of injuries, nothing about the risk of being shot, and nothing about the risk of making his wife a widow or making his children fatherless. It was very simple and straightforward: if an American fighting man is captured, it is his duty to make every effort to escape. Bud Day knew exactly what he had to do.

The Vietnamese looked at Day and believed he was immobile. Day reinforced the belief by defecating and urinating and remaining in his own waste.

Guards jabbed him hard with the muzzle of their rifles. He groaned and wondered how long he would be able to endure his injuries and the beatings without sustaining further damage. But he did not move. He lay in his filth and plotted his escape. It had to be soon. Survival school taught that escape during the first few days when in the hands of ill-trained militia is much easier than escaping from battle-hardened soldiers.

But that night the area was hammered by bad weather, the terrible and ferocious thunderstorms of Southeast Asia, some of the most violent on earth. Lightning and thunder and winds and prodigious rains lashed the landscape and made escape impossible.

The next morning the guards unwrapped the wire from his left arm, and that evening they did not retie it. When they wrapped his legs with rope, he offered no resistance. He lay there and moaned.

Three days after his shoot-down, Day's first English-speaking interrogator arrived. His English was rudimentary at best, mostly a collection of nouns and pronouns. But his intent was clear: he wanted military information from the downed pilot. Day moaned and did not answer.

Then came a French-speaking Vietnamese doctor to repair Day's arm. Because of Day's numerous visits to Casablanca, he knew enough French that the two could almost carry on a conversation.

The doctor sat Day on a bench and had a guard sit beside him, put an arm around Day's neck, and hold tightly. The doctor washed Day's arm with plain water; he had no soap and used no disinfectant. Then the doctor seized Day's right hand and pulled hard, causing bones from the fractures to slide and pull apart. Day screamed. The guard laughed. It was going to be impossible to set the multiple fractures without anesthetic. The doctor pulled out what Day called a "horse needle" and injected novocaine into the broken arm. The guard wrapped his legs around Day's waist and pulled hard on Day's neck while the doctor braced himself and yanked on the pilot's hand. The doctor pulled, massaged the bones around, then folded the arm at the elbow. Day knew this was not a proper orthopedic procedure. The bones were not aligned. A nurse prepared a plaster cast that went from the top of Day's shoulder, down his arm, and over the knuckles. She used a rag to fashion a sling to support the cast. After the cast was applied, Day was flung back into the casketlike hole in the ground, weaker than ever.

For the first time in his life, Day knew real fear. This is understandable. The survival schools were broader than they were deep. A big part of the training regarding how to resist interrogation was more intellectual than practical. Day was taught to resist as much as possible, to lie, mislead, misinform, alter the facts, and dodge questions. That was what he was trying to do. But they were beating the hell out of him and — except for the primitive cast — refusing him medical attention.

At Phu Cat he had prayed every night for the safety of Doris and the children. And he prayed for the safety of the men under his command. He knew in an intellectual sense that death was always very close. But now he needed more than the once-a-day prayers. He needed help on a minute-to-minute basis. There was an urgency to his prayers that had never been there before.

* * *

THE rescue helicopter had taken Kip to the hospital at Da Nang. He turned out to be okay, one of the few pilots to go through a high-speed ejection without injuries, and hours later he was back in the Misty command post at Phu Cat.

The mood was somber. Misty 1 was down, and Kip believed Day had been killed. The news brought home to the Mistys what a deadly business they were in. For the next three or four days, every Misty flight flew through the hell of the Fingers Lake looking for their boss, trying unsuccessfully to raise him on the emergency radio frequency. Kippenhan suffered such a classic case of survivor guilt that he soon left the Mistys and finished his tour with another outfit. He did not want to fly again, so he became a scheduler. A few years later he resigned his commission and became an airline pilot. For the rest of his life, he never got over the fact that he was rescued and Day was not. Decades later, he said, "When two guys go out and one comes back, that's not a good deal."

By now Day's boy-guards were disgusted with the odor of stale urine and old fecal matter that clung to him. They were tired of repeated trips to bring him water. They filled a canteen and left it in his den.

Day tried to keep track of time. On what he calculated was the fourth day after his shoot-down, two guards came and motioned for him to get out of the hole. He refused and was dragged out and marched a few yards away to a young man in civilian clothes who the interpreter said was a colonel. When Day refused to answer military questions — the name of his outfit, the type of aircraft he flew, where he was based, his mission — the guards beat him with rifle butts. The young colonel snapped and unsnapped his holster, pulled out his pistol, and pointed it at Day as the interpreter warned Day he would be shot if he did not answer questions.

"Drop dead, kid," Day said.

The colonel pressed the pistol against Day's head. Day pretended to faint. The guards beat him with gun butts and kicked him. But he would not talk. It grew dark and he was taken back to his hole.

Day knew it was only a matter of time before soldiers arrived to take charge. In the meantime, it would be a real coup for the ill-trained militia to wrangle information from him. He suspected their methods would grow more harsh.

He was right. Early the next morning the interrogation resumed in an open A-frame hut with exposed beams. When Day refused to talk, a rope was tied around his ankles and the other end thrown over a beam. He was hoisted into the air and hung there, head down, feeling the bones in his broken arm being pulled apart, then forced together, then pulled apart. In agony, he was left for hours as flies and mosquitoes crawled on his exposed skin, as sweat coursed down his body onto his face and into his nose and mouth. The hemp rope stretched, and after a while Day's head touched the ground. For the next hour or so he thought his neck would break as the full weight of his body pushed down on his head. Then the rope stretched more, his shoulders took more of his weight, and the pain was relieved. At dusk he was untied and shoved, kicked, and dragged back to his hole.

Day knew there would be more torture. And he knew he did not have the strength for such an ordeal. Every session would leave him weaker. He had to escape. Soon.

The next evening, after another day of beatings, he made his move.

The jungle was only a few miles from the camp. He had flown over this part of North Vietnam so many times that he could have drawn a detailed map of the surrounding countryside. The jungle was safety. He had to reach the jungle.

As they had for the past several nights, the guards did not bother to wire Day's good hand to the rafter, and there was only a big granny knot holding the rope on his legs. Day's eyes never left the guards, who stood on the nearby road, laughing and carrying on a loud boisterous conversation as he unwound the rope from his legs. He grabbed his canteen and whispered, "Help me, Father."

As he slithered out of the hole and crawled around the bunker, he prayed he would not be shot in the back. He elbowed his way over the edge of the rice paddy and stood up. His foot slipped in the mud and he fell on his broken arm, causing more pain than he had ever known. He gritted his teeth to avoid screaming. He noticed that his shorts were almost torn from him. Now there was little left except for the elastic waistband and the pouch — rather like an athletic supporter.

Day listened. Silence. He took a quick glance skyward to where the Milky Way pointed south toward freedom and he was gone, limping and lurching and staggering across the rice paddy. He was virtually naked and with injuries that would have put a man in the intensive care ward. But he was on the move, following the code.
Escape and evade.

Day was about two miles from the camp when he heard the loud gongs and urgent whistles that signified his escape had been discovered. He was beyond the rice paddies now, and the ground that looked so smooth and level from the air was in fact bumpy and irregular. Every hobbling step was agony. His broken arm pulsated with pain. Because the cast was bound to his body, he could not use his arm for balance. And since he was blind in his right eye, he had no peripheral vision and very little depth of field. He seemed always off balance, always lurching, always in danger of falling. The lack of food, the pain of his injuries, and the soreness from the beatings, combined with the tension of being a hunted man, were draining his energy reserves. He was on the edge of sliding into shock.

He remembered that no American pilot had ever escaped from North Vietnam into South Vietnam, and at some level he knew the very idea of escape was ludicrous. He did not exactly blend in with the indigenous personnel: a bare-assed American, seriously injured, with no food, attempting to cross some thirty miles of enemy territory. One sighting of him, even from a distance, and he would be recaptured.

He lurched on into the night, now guided by a giant thunderstorm far to the south. By the first hint of dawn, Day figured he had walked about six miles. He saw that the jungle where he hoped to find sanctuary was a thin and wispy forest. A lake was between him and this forest. On one edge of the lake were numerous artillery emplacements used to shell American bases just beyond the DMZ. He decided to walk around the other side of the lake. Finding a place to hide and to rest would be almost impossible in the scraggly copse of trees that was his destination. Nevertheless, that was the only sanctuary.

Suddenly, from the skies overhead, he heard a long shriek, then another, and another, and bombs began exploding less than a mile away. One of the most frightening and devastating experiences of the Vietnam War was an attack by B-52s, dropping bombs from so high that the aircraft are neither seen nor heard. The only indication of their presence was horrendous explosions that marched across the landscape, shredding the jungle and blowing great craters in the earth. The devastation caused by a single B-52 is about a block wide and can be a mile long.

Such an attack was known as an Arc Light, and Bud Day was caught in one.

The explosions came closer, tossing tons of mud and dirt into the air. Day clasped his hands over his ears and crouched in pain. Every seventh or eighth bomb was caught in the burst of the previous bomb and exploded about a hundred feet above the ground. These airbursts had the effect of "daisy cutter" devices, blasting vegetation in a wide radius, blowing down trees, uprooting bushes, and sending red-hot shrapnel flying in all directions. The very earth writhed in pain. It was like Armageddon.

The strike seemed to go on forever. Dozens of bombs were dropped, the last one landing about a hundred yards away from Bud. Had the strike begun one second later, Day would have been killed.

Then there was silence. Day was alive but overwhelmed with fatigue. His feet were lacerated and bleeding. For the past week he had eaten only a watery soup, and he was losing weight rapidly. He needed food for the march south. But there was no food.

Every North Vietnamese for miles around was awakened, and now they would be moving, checking for damage. Then the gun emplacements on the lake, the ones not damaged by the bombs, began firing. It was almost daylight when Day crawled under a bush to hide. Only yards away, children were moving around and adults were carrying food to the gun crews. Day's body cried for sleep. But if he went to sleep he might snore and someone would hear him. Instead he peeped out of the bush and planned his escape route for that evening. It would be through the area just bombed — not the safest path because of the danger of unexploded bombs but the most direct route. He was in a free-fire zone — anything that moved was fired upon. This was an area of heavy enemy activity, and he knew this part of North Vietnam was subject to artillery barrages. Sometimes pilots who had been flying farther north dropped unexpended ordinance here. He was traversing one of the most dangerous parts of North Vietnam. All day long he drifted in and out of consciousness, fatigue pulling him toward blessed sleep, pain and the fear of capture keeping him awake.

Evening came and the activity around him slowed. No moon was out and the darkness was palpable. But the stars were visible, pointing the way south toward freedom.

As Day limped and lurched his way through the area where the bombs had exploded, he wondered if he had made a good decision. Bomb blasts had fused the substrata of sand into sharp glassy material that made walking almost impossible. His feet were leaving a bloody trail.

Clouds moved in and obscured the stars and brought the torrential unrestrained rains for which Vietnam is renowned. Day could find no shelter. The cast on his arm grew soggy.

Eventually the rain slacked but the clouds remained and he could not see the stars. Which way was south? He would stop and wait for the weather to clear.

Day did not realize it, but the first signs of disorientation were wrapping their loving arms around him. He had pushed to the edge of his physical and mental limits. He found a bush, lay down, and went to sleep, so utterly exhausted that he could not swipe at the clouds of mosquitoes chewing on his bare body. Rest. Blessed rest. Tomorrow would be a better day.

He did not know how long he slept or whether it was the middle of the night or dawn when either a bomb or an artillery shell exploded nearby. One moment he was asleep, the next minute he was flying through the air, vomit streaming from his mouth and blood cascading from his nose and ears. He landed in a sprawl, and the most sickening nausea he had ever known swept over him. His ears were ringing. His body was racked with convulsions.

The dry heaves continued long after his stomach had emptied. Now his sense of balance was gone. He crawled aimlessly like a wounded animal, searching for safety.

After a while, he settled down and took stock. He was dehydrated from vomiting, so he took a slow and deliberate drink of water from his canteen. The water kicked off another round of uncontrollable vomiting. Eventually, he collapsed into a troubled sleep.

Doris was fidgety all day Saturday. She was troubled and did not know why. She cleaned the house and ironed clothes. She had prepared enough food for the children to last the ten days she would be in Hawaii. She had hired a babysitter to stay with the children. She had lost weight in preparation for the trip and was down from 122 pounds to 105 pounds. She wanted to look her best when she met Bud.

Saturday afternoon she decided to iron more clothes. She reached for a can of spray starch but accidentally picked up a can of oven cleaner. She pressed the button on the aerosol can. The can was empty and made a hissing *pssssst, pssssst*. The sound was like a knife to her heart; in that moment she knew something had happened to Bud.

She uttered a silent prayer. Then she made a pot of coffee and sat down and waited for the phone call.

Bud Day as a Marine in World War II. His children would later refer to this as the "Elvis picture."

me — King Cole

Bud sparring with a fellow Marine, circa 1943.

Summer of 1948. Doris and Bud on the fender of his 1940 Ford coupe. Doris's father was so upset that Bud was not wearing a shirt that he sent him home.

College student Bud Day with his parents at the house on Riverside Boulevard.

May 28, 1949, wedding picture. Bud's parents are to his right. Doris's father and stepmother are to her left.

Captain George Day in the cockpit of an F-84F in 1956.

Bud, Steve, George, and Doris while stationed at Niagara Falls, 1964.

The first group of Misty pilots, June 1967. Bud Day, "Misty 1," is kneeling center. Corwin "Kip" Kippenhan, standing, second from left. Bill Douglass, standing, far right.

Misty 1, a few days before he was shot down in August 1967.

Colonel Day shortly after his release from prison, March 1973.

Mike McGrath, a former POW, drew this sketch of an American officer "in the ropes." Day was tortured numerous times in this fashion. *U.S. Naval Institute*

The letter written by John McCain, signed by Bud Day, and carried from Hanoi to America by Norris Overly.

Doris and Bud were reunited at March AFB in California on March 17, 1973—after he had spent five years, seven months, and thirteen days as a POW.

Misty reunion, June 1973, at Luke AFB. Ray Bevivino (left) and Bill Douglass pour champagne for Misty 1.

Retirement photo of Colonel George E. Day. *USAF photo*

President Gerald Ford awards the Medal of Honor to Admiral James Stockdale, Colonel George Day, and Navy SEAL Tom Norris.

James Stockdale and Bud Day on the steps of the U.S. Capitol, September 1998, lobbying Congress to "Keep the Promise" of free health care for military retirees. *U.S. Naval Institute*

Day's statue, now in front of an airport in Sioux City, Iowa.

Orson Swindle and Bud Day with Senator and Mrs. John McCain in front of the "Straight Talk Express," McCain's campaign bus during the 2000 presidential elections.

The message arrived at Luke AFB about 1:30 a.m. Sunday saying Day had been shot down. But the duty officer decided to let Doris sleep through the night. He knew there would be no sleep after the message was delivered.

The knock on the door came at 7 a.m. Sunday.

Her first thought was one of annoyance. The knocking might awaken the children. She threw on a robe and opened the door and saw two men in Air Force uniforms and a woman. She knew who they were: the "notifying officer," a chaplain, and a woman from Family Services.

Her hand flew to her throat. "Oh, no. Not me too," she said.

"Mrs. Day, he's just missing," the chaplain said. "He had a good chute and we heard his beeper."

"Then he's okay if he had a good chute," Doris said. She wondered what a beeper was and made a mental note to call a friend and ask.

She looked at the chaplain and smiled. "They really got themselves a tiger this time."

The notifying officer said, "Major Day was in an aircraft with another pilot who was rescued. There was a strong chance Major Day also was rescued. If so, we will be notified within the next few hours." He showed her the note saying Major George E. Day had been shot down over North Vietnam.

Doris looked up. "North Vietnam? I didn't know he was flying up there. I thought he was in South Vietnam."

She called Charlie Hubbs, the family friend she and Bud met at Niagara Falls, and told him what happened. "Charlie, what's a beeper?" she asked.

He told her and then said Bud Day was either a POW or on the move, pushing through the jungle toward South Vietnam. "We call it 'escape and evading,' " he said.

Doris awakened Steve and said, "Stevie, Dad's been shot down. They're looking for him but can't find him." Then she called her stepmother and her sister and said, "Bud has been shot down in North Vietnam. He is listed as missing. They haven't found him yet. Please pray for him."

All day long Doris waited for a message saying Bud had been rescued. It never came. That night when she went to bed, her Air Force status had changed. Now Doris was an "MIA wife," a wife whose husband is missing in action. It would be six months before she had another word about her husband. And in that time she would not know if she was a wife or a widow.

WITH dawn came the most severe headache Bud Day had ever known. His skull was bursting with pain. The constant ringing in his ears told him his eardrums were ruptured. Blood from his nose and ears had crusted on his face and neck. Vision in his one good eye was blurred. But worst of all, he had lost a night of travel. He had to move south. His goal was to find Tara and from there cross the DMZ to the Marine outpost at Con Thien.

It is a measure of the man that in this most desperate of moments, his thoughts were not of despair. For Bud Day the glass was half full. Years later, in an autobiography, he would describe this moment, writing that he mumbled, "Count your blessings. It isn't all bad. At least you're out of the hole and free." The recent storms had washed the air, and the air was sweet. It was a glorious day.

But every time he tried to stand, nausea overwhelmed him. He could not walk. He collapsed and fell into a deep sleep and slept through the day and all through the night, letting his body rest.

It was midmorning when he awakened, and the growling in his stomach reminded him he had not eaten in four days. He looked around and saw he was in an area of scrubby bushes. It was another clear and beautiful day, a good day for a walk.

Almost reluctantly he sipped from the canteen, wondering if the debilitating nausea would overcome him again. But it did not. He put the morning sun to his left, which meant south was straight ahead. He stooped so his head would not stick above the bushes and began limping south.

After three or four steps he collapsed.

It would have been easy to give way to self-pity, to be captured. But Bud Day subscribed to the idea that if he put his mind to a task, he could do it. Obstacles did not matter. His dad taught him that the job at hand was everything. As he later wrote, if he believed there were things he couldn't do, he would still be working at the meatpacking plant in Sioux City.

Propelled by pure willpower, he stood up and pressed on. But the side effects of the bomb blast, the pain of his numerous injuries, the weakness from lack of food, the growing disorientation, all compounded, and sometime in midafternoon he realized he had been blundering along, as he said, with the "blind staggers" and taking no steps to avoid capture.

The growing disorientation manifested itself in brief and disconnected flashbacks, quick slices of memory. He was near the breaking point; he was becoming delusional.

He discovered a new pain in his lower right leg. A piece of metal was sticking out of the skin — shrapnel from the bomb blast. If it wasn't already, Day's leg, he knew, would soon become infected.

He found a large banana tree whose leaves were filled with water and replenished his canteen, drank his fill, then replenished the canteen again.

Rapid mood swings were overtaking him. Now, having drunk a great deal of water that alleviated his hunger pangs, he found that his spirits climbed. *I survived the explosion,* he said to himself. *It has to be all downhill from here. I'm going to make it.*

A few moments later a thought hit him. *I wonder who is drinking that case of scotch I stashed under my bed.*

His mind was rambling.

What did they do with my pictures of Taiwan and Japan?

What is that quote from Teddy Roosevelt I had on my wall? Something about war. This war is . . . I can't remember.

Yea, though I walk through the valley of the shadow of death, I will fear no evil. Because I am the meanest son of a bitch in the valley.

Which Misty will send my things home to Doris?

Finally he fell into a fitful sleep.

On the morning of the fifth day, he guessed he was about fifteen miles from the Ben Hai, the broad river that runs down the middle of the DMZ. He had to have food. But he was crossing a strange land of stubby trees broken by bomb blasts; remnants of napalm tanks and large bomb craters; war-crust over the ancient mud of Vietnam. He climbed through a trench filled with the unmistakable, never-to-be-forgotten smell of rotting corpses. He was moving across a land peopled by the dead. And there were many more miles ahead of him before he could reach freedom.

He approached a thick stretch of jungle and remembered what the instructors said at survival school in the Philippines: Stay off the trails. Make your own trail. Keep to the jungle.

Whoever put that bit of wisdom into the curriculum had never tried to make his own trail through a jungle in Vietnam. The jungle was almost impenetrable — heavy going that sapped his energy after only a few yards. Day rested and after a while returned to the trail and hoped he did not meet any enemy soldiers. He prayed fervently and then was embarrassed by his prayers, feeling like a hypocrite because his heavy drinking back at Phu Cat seemed out of sync with his present religious fervor.

As dusk came, he climbed a knoll, took stock of his landmarks, and realized that the day had been spent walking in a circle. He was back almost where he had begun that morning.

Henceforth he would stay on the north-south trails used by enemy soldiers. He would be very quiet and would listen carefully.

He knew his condition was deteriorating. Even his good leg was unsteady, and the cuts on his feet were swollen and pursed outward from infection. Vomit and blood streaked his torso. He was badly sunburned. His body odor repelled him. Except for the cast on his arm, he wore only what amounted to a loincloth. He was stumbling through a garden of evil and growing more delusional.

He prayed for strength.

9

North Toward Hell

THE bush had purple berries.

Day was taught at survival school not to eat purple berries, as they are often poisonous. But he was too hungry and too weak to care. He grabbed a handful of the small shrunken berries and jammed them into his mouth. The berries were sweet and nourishing, with no touch of the nausea that would have accompanied toxic fruit. The blend of sugar and acid gave him an energy boost, took away the growling pangs in his stomach, and calmed him enough that he could assess his situation.

It was dusk — time for the debrief.

Debriefing after every flight had been a ritual since flight school, and the habits of sixteen years are not easily cast aside. Day slumped to the ground, replayed the past hours, and knew he had not performed well. It had been, to use his words, a "pathetic day."

He knew that the energy boost was temporary, that he was running out of steam. He had to have food. And he badly needed medical attention.

Off to the south he heard the booming of artillery — American artillery — almost certainly coming from "Leatherneck Square," the four Marine bases between Route 9 and the DMZ, the U.S. bases closest to North Vietnam. Tomorrow he would walk — as always — toward the sound of the guns.

By dawn on the sixth day, he was in thick jungle and walking down a wide, heavily packed trail that clearly received a great deal of use by enemy soldiers. The clear sky soon changed to an overcast, and then a steady drizzle began that dampened the jungle sounds.

Suddenly Day felt a premonition. He limped off the trail and eased into the thick jungle, dropped, and hid under a bush. Seconds later a North Vietnamese soldier loped up the trail.

After the soldier passed, Day waited awhile, then lurched back onto the trail and continued south. A few hours later he saw a small frog in a puddle. Instructors at survival school said frogs were excellent sources of protein. Day wasn't sure he had the strength to kill the frog. He leaned over, reached out with his left hand, and slapped at the water several times before he caught the mud-covered and slippery little frog. Then he pushed it headfirst down his throat, chewing hard. He crunched and pushed, crunched and pushed, then — after the frog stopped twitching — chewed for a long time.

It was a long way from eating frog legs back in Sioux City. Tears sprang to his eyes as he remembered those once-a-month restaurant visits with Doris. Those frog legs had been cleaned and dipped in egg, then dredged in flour and spices and fried in butter. What a delicacy. A mud-covered live and squirming Vietnamese frog is another matter. Day found a bit more sustenance when he stumbled upon a bush bearing a single orangelike fruit that had a sweet and tasty pulp.

Now he was picking his way across a big open area where signs of war were everywhere: broken trees, shell holes, a moonscape of utter desolation. He often heard artillery, and occasionally rounds landed within sight. The U.S. Marines were firing H & I — harassment and interdiction — rounds into North Vietnam. American fighter aircraft frequently roared overhead. Day had flown over this area almost daily and knew he was close to the plantation. He was without concealment as he crossed the bleak landscape, a limping, mud-covered wraith, and every moment he was afraid of being seen.

After he crossed the dangerous area and sat down to rest his bloody feet, he realized his emotions were on a roller coaster. One hour he was almost euphoric at the progress he had made and at his proximity to the Marines. The next he was despondent over his bloody feet, the pain in his arm and leg, the lack of balance from using one eye and from having his arm lashed to his body, the thought of being virtually naked in a strange land, surrounded by enemy forces.

At dusk he crawled under a bush, did a quick debrief, said his prayers, and went to sleep.

By midafternoon the next day, he was at a bluff overlooking the Ben Hai River, which ran down the middle of the DMZ. There was the house with the red roof — the plantation.

The dark gray waters of the Ben Hai looked to be some seventy-five yards wide, about the size of the Missouri. But this river was moving much faster than its American counterpart. And the clay banks were vertical: there was a drop of at least ten feet to the water.

From the plantation it was only three or four miles downriver to the "Freedom Bridge," the span used by those in the North fleeing to sanctuary in South Vietnam. Except for that one day when he had wandered in a circle, his navigation had been precise. The plantation had been his goal from the moment he escaped. After a week, guided only by a few mountain peaks, stars, and the sound of artillery fire, he was exactly where he wanted to be — at a landmark he had flown over many times. He nodded in approval. That long-ago Marine Corps training in land navigation had served him well. He took a long drink from his canteen and settled down to wait.

At dusk he approached the house. Suddenly three North Vietnamese soldiers rounded a turn in the path and were walking toward him. They were relaxed, joking and not paying attention to their surroundings. Day faded into the underbrush as they walked past.

Then he heard the noises of a big camp and knew dozens, perhaps hundreds, of enemy soldiers were quite near. They were preparing for the evening meal. He skirted the camp and took shelter in the woods, wondering if American forces knew of the big enemy camp in the DMZ.

All he had to do was cross the river and walk a few more miles. But he must not attempt the crossing at night — it was too dangerous. Mosquitoes chewed on his emaciated body, but they could not pierce his elation. Tomorrow he would be free.

Day smiled and relaxed.

Suddenly out of the blackness came the shriek of an inbound artillery shell. Day knew it might land within lethal range and pushed his body into the earth. The shell landed about seventy-five yards away, and shrapnel ripped through the bushes — U.S. Marines at work again. Day remembered how Marines went about firing H & I rounds: first, an introductory round, then either up one click in elevation or one click on the azimuth, then another round, then repeat. Day pushed his body deeper into the earth. The second round landed to the left. Had the Marines elevated the gun a notch rather than changing the azimuth, it would have landed on top of him.

The Marines returned the artillery piece to the original setting. Day knew from the sound that this one had his name on it. He tried to disappear into the hard earth.

The round landed twenty feet away.

A dud.

Then came eight more rounds on the same setting, all landing twenty, thirty, or forty feet away. With each inbound shriek, he hunkered down, praying for Doris and the children. He knew he was about to die.

All eight rounds were duds.

Day lay shivering, wondering if the rounds had delayed fuses that might go off any second. Then he remembered that small rounds explode on impact.

His first thought was one of anger. Some goddamn defense contractor had supplied shoddy goods to the U.S. Marine Corps. Then he was grateful for the shoddy goods.

Even so, if he ever had the chance, he was going to have words with the contractor.

Once again Bud Day had escaped certain death. Nine consecutive duds from the Marine Corps. Such things did not happen. His belief that God was saving him for a special task had never been stronger.

But Day knew he had to get away from the artillery shells and find a place to hide. He wanted to be in the river, drifting downstream, by first light. He slid out of concealment and limped toward the river. As he neared the water, the mosquitoes grew bigger and more voracious, but most of his head and neck was a crusty scab of hardened blood and body fluids, and there was little for mosquitoes to chew on.

The sound of the insects, coupled with the adrenaline surge that came with knowing tomorrow was freedom day, made it difficult to sleep. But he had to — he would need strength for tomorrow's final push. Day set his mental alarm clock for 3:30 a.m. and drifted into a fitful slumber.

At what he knew was only a few minutes from that time, Day awakened and shook his head to clear the cobwebs. Almost immediately, he heard the banshee wail of falling bombs. Another B-52 strike. This one was going to be close.

The target was the enemy camp about a hundred yards away. This answered his question about whether or not U.S. forces knew about the enemy stronghold in the DMZ.

As the bombs began falling, shrapnel, dirt, and tree limbs ripped over Day's head. Numerous secondary explosions sent flames high into the air. It seemed the bombs would never stop falling. Occasional airbursts rocked the earth and thunderous shock waves hammered the ground. Day counted around two hundred bombs before the devastation ceased.

He was still alive.

He thanked God for once again saving his life.

Day knew that enemy troops from throughout the area would rush toward the camp. He had to take advantage of the confusion and make his move. He sneaked past the plantation and down to the banks of the river.

THE front page of the August 31, 1967, issue of the *Phoenix Gazette* included a long article about the war in Vietnam. Deep in the story were several lines about yet another U.S. aircraft being shot down several days earlier; the 666th U.S. aircraft lost in the past three years. This one had been an Air Force jet with a two-man crew. Doris underlined the reference and wrote to the side, "Bud's aircraft."

DAY found a big piece of bamboo, ideal for him to hang on to and float down the river. But he needed something to break up his silhouette and hide his shape. He tried to pull up several bushes but was too weak, so he broke off a few small branches and hoped they would do the job.

Daylight was hurrying, and he was out in the open on the high riverbank. He slung the canteen over his shoulder, seized the piece of bamboo and the small branches to his chest, crouched, and tried to ease down the precipitous bank. Day slipped in the mud and skidded down the embankment, bamboo and limbs flying. The pain in his arm and knee was almost unbearable. He hit the water with a splash and grabbed the bamboo.

The current was far faster than he imagined, maybe four or five knots, and quickly washed much of the mud from his cast. It was a startling white. He kicked with one leg, trying to move toward the middle of the river. The speed at which he was swept downstream frightened him. He paddled hard for the opposite shore.

In seconds he was swept past the plantation. An enemy soldier stood on the landing, looking across the river. Day tried to drop lower behind the piece of bamboo. The soldier stared for a moment, then lifted his rifle and aimed at Day. At this range, the soldier could not miss. Then he slowly lowered his rifle but continued staring at the bamboo. Whatever the soldier's reason for not shooting, Day, once again, was saved from almost certain death.

Now he had other things to worry about. The Freedom Bridge was only a mile or so downriver, and enemy soldiers would be camped there to stop defectors. The light was coming on fast and he would not again be confused for driftwood. He had to cross the river and be out of the water before he reached the bridge.

But how? The current was pulling him downstream at a fearful pace.

He closed his eyes and muttered a quick prayer.

Then he saw a deep crevice cut out of the south bank of the river. The current swept him into the eddy, where he seized a broken log. He was in a South Vietnamese emplacement that had taken a direct hit and was surrounded by a jumble of broken logs and rotting human body parts. The sweet coppery odor nauseated him. He pulled himself onto the bank. Ammunition belts, rifles, supplies, and a hodgepodge of military equipment were all around. He wrapped an ammunition belt around each of his bloody feet to serve as makeshift sandals. A loaded AK-47 was on the riverbank, but he was too weak to carry it.

Now he was on the south bank and in South Vietnam. He was so near to freedom — to a hospital, food, and an airplane ride home to Doris and the children.

He lay on the bank, exhausted. His mind was wandering.

This part of Vietnam was a meat grinder that resembled the barren battlefields of World War I, where every tree was leveled by artillery and where rotting corpses littered the landscape. Fumes from the ceaseless artillery barrages were so intense that few bugs lived there. This was a moonscape, a no-man's-land, barren and bleak and covered with the smell of death. Already the buildup for what would be the 1968 Tet Offensive was beginning, and the area was filled with at least three divisions of North Vietnamese regulars.

Day found a cache of discarded food rations. Marines from Con Thien had eaten at this very spot. Judging from the condition of their waste, they had been here recently, maybe yesterday. But every bit of food was spoiled. The Marines did not want the enemy to use the food and had stuck bayonets into every can they had not eaten. In the blistering heat, the contents spoiled within hours.

As hungry as he was, Day felt immense pride at the battle discipline of the Marines who had passed this way.

Day pressed on, skulking from bush to bush. Far off in the edges of consciousness, he knew he should hide until dark. But he could not afford to waste this day; he was too near the end of his endurance. He had to press on.

Suddenly an atavistic survival sense surfaced, and he knew enemy troops were close. He ducked under a bush, and a second later more than a dozen North Vietnamese soldiers appeared, loaded with heavy packs and moving south on the trail. The weight of their loads bent them forward. Had one of them looked a few feet to the side, Day would have been sighted, a skeletal mud-covered wretch, kept alive only by a burning spirit and a sense of duty.

The soldiers passed. Day waited a moment and gathered his strength. But just as he was about to limp across the trail, another group of soldiers appeared. They too were carrying heavy packs, bent over, staring at the trail. Day slumped to the ground and watched the feet of the soldiers pass by inches from his head.

Day eased from under the bush and limped south. Several hours later, he captured another frog and pushed it down his gullet. The immediate surge of energy told him how very weak he was.

He had to reach Con Thien soon. He had to.

Night came and he collapsed in the underbrush. Day tried to go through his debrief and to say his evening prayers, but he couldn't concentrate; his mind was wandering. He figured he had lost around forty pounds since his shoot-down.

The sun was well up when Day awakened. His first thought was of food. His second thought was that everything he could see and sense was trying to kill him: the jungle, enemy soldiers, B-52s, Marine Corps artillery, starvation. For every second of the past . . . how many days? Twelve? Fourteen? Judging by the length of his beard, it may have been as much as three weeks, and every moment of that time he had been only a step away from capture. He had faint intimations that his ability to think clearly had all but disappeared. And he realized he might unknowingly make a mistake that would result in his capture. A great pressure not to do anything stupid nagged at him. He knew he was only a day, maybe a day and a half, from Con Thien.

Sometime that morning, Day slipped into a netherworld between sanity and insanity, between life and death. He heard a voice that prayed loudly and thanked God for bringing someone so far and with such an unfailing sense of direction. The voice went on for three or four minutes, and then Day realized it was his own. He grimaced in anguish. An enemy soldier could hear him for a hundred yards. He bit his lip and resolved to keep silent. But it was not long before he again heard the voice and widened his eyes in wonder as he listened. Such an impassioned prayer. Then, again, he came back into the world and realized it was his voice.

American fighter aircraft and spotter aircraft were close — sometimes the jets went over his head, and he frequently heard bombs falling.

The shrapnel wound on his right leg had caused his leg to swell to twice its normal size. The skin was taut and angry. His left knee was still grotesquely swollen. He lurched from side to side as he walked, and every step was excruciating. Day was making his way down a steep hill into a bombed-out area when he heard a Bird Dog — a slow, single-engine FAC aircraft — coming toward him. The thick jungle canopy prevented him from seeing the aircraft. The Bird Dog circled overhead, and Day realized the pilot was looking for an enemy camp.

A little Bird Dog would not be out snooping and pooping unless the pilot was acting on information from intelligence. If that assumption was correct, Day could be in the middle of a heavy concentration of enemy soldiers. If there was only some way to get the Bird Dog's attention, the pilot would radio for a rescue helicopter, and within minutes the close-air-support aircraft would be strafing the jungle and a Jolly Green would come in and snatch him.

He lurched out of the jungle and stood on the edge of a bomb crater. Now the Bird Dog was approaching from the southwest on a course that would take him directly overhead. Day waved frantically. But the Bird Dog went into a shallow bank, and Day was blanked out by the bottom of the aircraft. Had the pilot been fifty yards either left or right, he almost certainly would have seen Day.

Then the Bird Dog pilot reversed course. Again Day leaped about, waving his good arm. But for a second time the pilot banked and could not see Day.

The pilot had come over the same area twice, a very dangerous maneuver. Clearly something on the ground was attracting his interest. It could only be enemy soldiers.

Day was still playing out in his mind the details of a helicopter rescue as the sound of the Bird Dog softened, then disappeared. He slipped into a crushing and abysmal depression. Twice he had been within only a few feet, a few seconds, of being rescued. He knew he was no more than a ten-minute helicopter flight from Con Thien.

Day lurched back into the jungle, back onto the heavily used trail, moving slowly, staying near the bushes, ready to duck into the undergrowth at the slightest sound. Several hours later he found a small stream and stopped to soak his feet. He sat silently for blissful moments. Then he drank as much water as he could hold and was refilling his canteen when he saw a sight that galvanized him: a thick, heavy land crab about three feet away. Food!

Day stooped to seize the crab when he heard a chilling sound: someone was chopping wood no more than fifteen feet away. Day was afraid to blink for fear he would be seen. Slowly he raised his head and stared at the back of an enemy soldier.

The crab was forgotten as Day crawled off the trail into the bushes. Seconds later a dozen soldiers appeared. Day had walked into the middle of the camp that the Bird Dog pilot had been searching for.

Machetes were hacking away all around him, cutting camouflage. He was surrounded by soldiers who were setting up an ambush for the next Marine patrol that came this way.

About noon the chopping slackened, and Day realized it was time for the siesta that was so popular in Vietnam. He waited and listened, and when he was sure that the camp was asleep and that no guard could see him, he crept onto the trail and limped south.

He fought to hold on to sanity. The voice had returned, that loud voice that talked to Doris or prayed. He clamped his mouth shut, but a moment later the voice returned.

Day knew he was losing his grip on sanity. That voice might cry out at the wrong time. He had counted how many enemy patrols? Thirty? Next time he might not hear the soldiers before they saw him. And there seemed to be no way he could control what was going on in his mind. He was seized by a great fear.

Suddenly a large artillery piece fired from only a few feet away. He jumped in fright as round after round was fired south toward the Marines at Con Thien. Between explosions he heard the sound of running feet. *Slap! Slap! Slap!*

He lurched off the trail and collapsed into the thick jungle.

Day watched the bare legs of the soldiers pass by and knew he had used up all the luck any one person could have.

He eased back onto the trail and several times in the next hour narrowly avoided more patrols — he doesn't remember how many — but he either heard them a second before they appeared or moved off the trail when an inner voice told him to seek cover.

He saw the Bird Dog again and then saw two Marine Corps helicopters, one holding high and providing cover for the one that was landing and replenishing supplies.

He was in South Vietnam.

He had made it.

Up ahead, very close now, was the Marine Corps firebase. All he had to do was walk into the camp — slowly, with hands held high — tell them who he was, and within hours he would be in a hospital. They would take care of his injuries and feed him and put him on an airplane that would take him to a military hospital in America, where Doris and the children could visit. It was only a matter of hours.

He pushed down the trail toward where the helicopter had landed. It was dusk when he rounded a corner of the trail and found himself looking at the back of an enemy soldier who was washing clothes in a stream. Day was caught out in the open; moving backward was as dangerous as moving forward.

Slowly and very carefully he walked around the soldier, not making a sound. It took an eternity of seconds. Then he was around a corner in the trail and out of the soldier's sight. It was almost dark and he was exhausted. He had to sleep.

He lay down under a bush and said his prayers. His last thought before he fell asleep was that tomorrow he would be with the Marines. When he told them he had been a Marine in World War II, there would be handshakes and backslapping and *Semper Fi*. They would lay out the best meal they had for him and would summon a chopper to return him to the Air Force.

The next day was cloudy and overcast — ominous and threatening. Day continued south. He heard helicopters. Jets flew overhead. He heard Marine artillery. Freedom was close. Euphoria swept over him, and he could almost taste the hot chow at Con Thien. He could almost feel the hot soapy water. He welcomed the operating room and the surgery he would have to have in order to heal his broken body.

It was only a matter of an hour. Maybe two. "I got it made," he said.

Then there was an angry shout behind him. He looked over his shoulder and saw two Vietnamese boys — they could not have been more than fourteen or fifteen — holding AK-47s.

His first thought was *I didn't come this far to surrender to these sons of bitches*. He ran. Or tried to run. He was lurching and stumbling, an easy target even for excitable boys. Bullets struck him in the left thigh and left hand. Still he struggled on, into the jungle, trailing blood, and rolled under a bush. A second later a stream of automatic rifle fire shredded the leaves over his head. The boys circled, looking, and then one of them stopped no more than a foot away. He kicked Day and called to his friend.

Day was back in the hands of the enemy.

The boys turned Day over to their superiors, a group of battle-hardened soldiers who had set up an ambush for Marine patrols. The soldiers were twenty or thirty yards farther up the trail to spring the trap. Day had walked into the back side of the ambush.

Day's captors were brusque and businesslike but without the brutality he had earlier experienced. When Day refused to give more than his name and serial number, the officer nodded and walked away to talk with a radio operator. A few moments later he returned, staring at Day with open curiosity. Day knew that whoever was on the other side of the radio transmission had identified him as the pilot who had escaped from Vinh Linh.

The officer gave Day a ball of rice and a small container of nuoc mam, a highly flavored fish sauce, to pour over it. It was a feast.

The cast on his arm was shredded and falling apart. A combat medic examined the ring finger of Day's left hand. The fingertip was attached by little more than a thread of skin. The medic sprinkled the gunshot wound with powder and wrapped it. He took a long look at the festering shrapnel wound Day had received a week or ten days earlier and inserted a bamboo sliver into the wound. There was a copious discharge, and then the medic pulled the piece of shrapnel from Day's leg.

A soldier asked Day how long it had been since he had eaten a full meal. He wrinkled his brow. "I don't know. I think it was about two weeks. Maybe more." The enemy soldiers were as tough as any soldiers who ever took to a battlefield. But they could not go two weeks without food and still be on the march as had this American. They could not hike some twenty-five miles through enemy territory with nothing but a canteen of water — not in the condition that this man was in. They stared in wonderment. It was good for them that not all Americans were cut from this bolt of cloth.

Then five large Vietnamese appeared with a sling under a bamboo pole. One pointed for Day to get into the sling. Once Day was in the sling, he was blindfolded. The bearers took off at an effortless ground-eating trot. When Day — already thinking about escape — moved the blindfold to have a look, one of the bearers kicked him in the head. He continued to adjust the blindfold. Each time, he was kicked in the head.

By evening Day was back at the banks of the Ben Hai, where he was dumped into a small boat and taken across the river. The bearers carried him all the next day, always north, and around evening stopped in a small village. The soldiers began laughing and celebrating, and Day knew he was back in North Vietnam.

Early the next morning the bearers ordered Day back into the sling and they were off, miles disappearing beneath their feet. Then they stopped and one of the bearers snatched the blindfold from Day's eyes. The bearer was smiling. Day didn't understand why until he looked around and realized he had been returned to the camp at Vinh Linh from which he had escaped.

He was ordered out of the sling. Since he had escaped by walking out of the camp, he was going to return by walking into the same camp.

At every step he was kicked and jabbed and poked by local villagers. Had he not been accompanied by soldiers, it is likely the local populace would have killed him. The procession stopped. Standing in front of Day were the guards from whom he had escaped. It was bad enough to have lost a prisoner. But this prisoner had a broken arm and a swollen leg, and was blind in one eye. They had lost much face.

One of the guards pointed to the same hole from which Day had escaped and ordered him inside. An angry guard jerked Day's feet together and bound them tightly. Then the guard used wire to tie Day's left hand to an overhead beam. All the while the guard was muttering, and punching and kicking Day. Once Day was securely bound, an officer pulled his pistol and jammed the barrel between Day's eyes. He paused, then viciously pistol-whipped Day on each side of his head.

The two guards who had been on duty the night Day escaped appeared, and one used all his strength to punch Day in the face and stomach. He continued the beating until he was soaked in perspiration and gasping for breath.

Then other guards got into the act. Day could not move; all he could do was absorb the beating. His one good eye was almost swollen shut. He desperately needed to urinate, but the guards would not take him outside. So he urinated on himself, something he would do many times in the years ahead.

Another group of soldiers appeared. When it was dark they returned Day's flying boots and ordered him to put them on. The boots had no laces and were supported with a single strand of wire around his ankles. Within minutes, Day's staggering pace resulted in dirt and small rocks collecting in the boot tops. The debris was trapped by the wire, and soon his ankles were a bloody pulp. Every time he stopped, his captors slammed him in the back with rifle butts. He had to keep marching.

The captors marched Day from village to village, always northward, his boots filling with blood. That night he was thrown into another coffinlike hole, kicked and punched, and then tied to a beam with a piece of wire. Out of anger and pain and frustration and defiance, he shouted, "You miserable cocksuckers! You sons of bitches!"

His captors did not understand the words, but they understood the tone. They beat him until he was unconscious.

The next morning Day had his first real meal in three weeks: rice and potatoes and peanuts. This was followed by a bowl of rice with gravy. Embarrassed by his near nakedness, his captors gave him a cloth to wrap around his waist.

After breakfast he was led from the village. The locals beat him and kicked him and spit on him, a pattern repeated in every village on the route.

Day was concerned that he might contract blood poisoning in the gunshot wound on his left hand. He urinated on it frequently to keep it clean, an act that disgusted his captors, and each time he did so, they beat him.

After about two days he arrived in Vinh, a city near the coast on the old railroad route from Saigon to Hanoi and a collection point for downed American airmen. The old railroad tracks had been torn out and the bed used as a road; it was one of the better roads in North Vietnam and a road often seen from the air by U.S. pilots. Over the course of the war, dozens of those pilots would later travel by small vehicle up that same road. They would find that they preferred the view from the air.

Day was dumped in a bamboo building, where guards wrapped a chain around his ankles and secured it with two locks. He had escaped once; they were making sure he did not do so again.

Early the next morning guards unlocked Day's chains, and he was blindfolded and marched perhaps fifty yards away. Guards removed the blindfold, and Day found he was in a small pagoda, one of the few religious structures left standing in North Vietnam. He would remember the pagoda for the rest of his life because it was here that he would experience his first real interrogation.

The session began slowly and easily, as do most effective interrogations.

"Have you ever heard of Riner Robson?"

"Who?"

"Riner Robson."

Day realized his interrogator was asking about Robinson "Robbie" Risner.

"No, I don't know anyone named Riner Robson."

A rapid series of questions followed: "What aircraft do you fly?" "What is your unit?" "What was your mission?" "What was your job?" "What are the names of other people in your unit?"

Each time he answered with his name, rank, serial number, and date of birth and said he expected to be treated in accordance with the provisions of the Geneva convention.

The interrogator laughed, and Day heard for the first time a litany he would hear often during coming years: "The Geneva convention applies to war. Your country never declared war on my country. The Geneva convention does not apply to you. You are a criminal, a Yankee air pirate."

Day stared in amazement.

The interrogator continued, "You escaped from the people. Your attitude is very bad. You are the blackest of criminals."

Then came a long lecture about Vietnam's history of overcoming foreign invaders. Day responded by demanding medical attention.

"The Vietnamese people are very short of medical supplies," Day remembers his captor saying. "We don't have to use it on criminals. Your medical treatment will depend on your attitude. You could help yourself by showing a cooperative attitude toward the people. Then the people would be humane and lenient."

Again came the questions regarding military information.

"I don't understand," Day answered.

He was returned to his cubicle with an uneasy feeling. He heard a noise down the hall and sensed another American officer was there. "This is Air Force major George Day and I need to go to the toilet!" he shouted.

Down the hall, the other person cleared his throat, acknowledgment that Day had been heard. The guards also heard. One pounded Day to the ground. Day lay there, eyes closed, gathering his strength against a great unknown. The guard continued on down the hall, and after a moment Day heard a hammering sound — what he later would learn were the sounds of shackles being put on or taken off — and then deep moaning, the sound of a man in great pain.

The sound came from Air Force major Norris Overly, a pilot shot down September 11 on a night mission. Overly had an enormous hematoma on his lower back, an injury that arose when he ejected and was dragged across the ground by his parachute. The infection caused him great discomfort, especially when he was forced to lie on his back.

That night Day slept fitfully, caught between sleep and apprehension. The morning began with another interrogation. To any question beyond the "Big Four" — name, rank, serial number, and date of birth — Day answered, "I don't remember."

The interrogator became increasingly angry and finally paused and stared at Day a long moment. "I will teach you to remember," he said. "I will make you a cripple."

He made a motion with his hand, and two burly guards seized Day and jerked his arms behind his back, causing the cast to dig into his shoulder and send searing streaks of pain through the broken arm. The guards looped a rope over the cast and then around the left arm and jerked hard, lashing Day's wrists together. They moved the ropes up to his elbows and again cinched down hard. Now his arms were tied together from wrist to elbow. As the guards knotted the rope, they occasionally jerked upward, pushing Day's elbows toward his shoulder blades and causing him to believe his chest was being pulled apart and his shoulders were being yanked from their sockets. A pain he did not know existed swept over him.

"What was your unit?"

To talk would both give the North Vietnamese information about a top secret and highly effective unit that they did not know existed and lead to countermeasures that could result in the death of his Misty pilots. Day knew that a POW's military unit is a fundamental bit of intelligence for captors; he would be asked this question many times. But he would never talk of the Mistys. Never.

"I was hurt in the bailout. I don't remember."

"I will make you remember."

The interrogator nodded, and one of the guards put a stick into the ropes at Day's elbows and twisted, winching the ropes tighter, yanking Day's elbows higher and higher. He felt his shoulders dislocating. Circulation in both arms was cut off, and his arms began swelling and turning purple. Tendons in his chest separated from his sternum, and it felt as if his chest were being ripped apart.

He moaned. He knew the guard wanted him to scream, and he swore he would not give them that satisfaction. Nevertheless, sounds came from him that he did not recognize.

Whoever wrote the Code of Conduct had never experienced this sort of pain. Day wondered how long he could hold out.

The interrogation continued. To each question Day said, "I don't remember."

"I will teach you to remember."

Day would find later that his adversary had softened up many pilots. The interrogator knew from experience that he could reduce a proud American fighter pilot to a sniveling, crying, pleading baby in a matter of minutes. If this one wanted to resist, okay.

He nodded and the guards twisted the rope tighter.

Day had always heard that when a person is subjected to sustained and severe pain, after a while the neurological mechanism that reports pain to the brain shuts down and the pain lessens. He found that was not true. The pain did not lessen; it increased. Minute by minute it increased. And after several hours, when the ropes were untied, the stinging as blood returned to his arms was as severe as the torture. The fingers on his right hand now curved into a feral claw. He could not move his fingers and he could not open his hand. He knew the nerves in his arm had been severely damaged. Day looked at his crippled hands in horror and disbelief.

His interrogator smiled. "I told you I would make you a cripple."

"You miserable son of a bitch. You did."

The guards punched and kicked Day as they carried him back to his room.

Down the hall, Major Norris Overly had been returned to his room with no beating. He was allowed a bath and given a generous meal.

That evening the door to Day's room opened. His interrogator introduced the camp commander, a man who appeared to be about twenty years old. A guard handed the commander a small green stick, an innocuous little stick rather like a baton. Day ignored it.

"What organization are you from?" the young man asked.

"I was injured in the ejection. I have no recall of that."

Whap!

The commander struck Day across the face, and Day realized that a small green stick could deliver enormous pain.

"What base you fly from?"

"I don't remember."

Whap!

"What airplane you fly?"

"I don't remember."

Whap!

After a few slices across the face, Day heard an inner voice begging for relief, begging for anything that would stop the pain. Every blow further disoriented him.

The same questions elicited the same answer for the next two hours. Before long, Day's face was swollen and bleeding, and he could barely see from his one good eye. But he could perceive one thing with the utmost clarity: the blood and the pain from that sustained beating hardened the cement of his hatred for Communism. During the torture session he told himself that if he gave the enemy soldiers any military information, he would be a traitor. He was a career military man and he had certain standards that were inviolate, higher standards than most civilians could ever imagine. If he did not abide by the Code of Conduct, if he did not keep the faith, he could not live with himself. He could not face Doris, whose cousins had been imprisoned and tortured by the Germans in World War II. It would be better to die a bitter and miserable death in a Vietnamese village than to break the faith. And every blow made Day more determined to resist. Every blow increased his hatred for his captors.

The interrogation ended when Day's face became so swollen he could not move his lips to say, "I don't remember." The camp commander was exhausted. His shirt was soaked with perspiration and he did not bother to hide his frustration.

The commander had an ominous last word. "Tomorrow you pay. Tomorrow you tell me many things." The commander paused and repeated the camp mantra. "If you do not, I will turn you into a cripple."

There was something about the way he said it that told Day tomorrow would indeed be different. But how could it possibly be worse?

It was barely daylight the next morning when Day was frog-marched back to the pagoda. A half dozen Vietnamese officers sat against the wall, spectators for the coming event, their faces betraying their anticipation at what was about to happen to the Yankee air pirate.

Day knew vaguely that the concept of "face" was very important in Vietnam. He was about to discover just how important. The camp commander was plying his trade in front of witnesses; he had to have results or the shame would be tremendous.

Day's arms were trussed behind his back, locked together from wrist to elbow. Because of the rigidity of the cast, his body was twisted into a pretzel shape that, even before the torture began, was immensely painful. He gritted his teeth when he saw the guards pick up the piece of wood to twist the ropes tighter.

But this time it was different. A rope dangled from a rafter. A chair stood under the rope.

The interrogator turned to Day. "If you not immediately answer all questions, I turn you into cripple."

Day remembered from survival school in the Philippines that each enemy interrogator would have his own style of questioning.

Apparently the repertoire of the commander was limited to the threat of turning a pilot into a cripple. The North Vietnamese wanted intelligence, but so too did Bud — and now he knew something about his antagonist.

Because Vinh was a collection point for American POWs before they were shipped north, the local commander's job appeared to be to soften up the Americans, to give them a shock treatment of brutal torture that would get their minds right and show them what to expect if they did not cooperate. And the commander took his job seriously. Day was to discover later that the commander had made many men remember and that he had crippled many American pilots.

The commander pointed to the building where Day was being held prisoner. "The other man told us everything," he said. "There no need for you take this punishment." He nodded and one of the guards pushed Day up onto the chair. Day did not move fast enough, and the guard delivered a brutal kick to his injured right leg, causing Day to scream in pain.

Then the guard took the rope dangling from the rafter and tied one end to Day's wrists. He pulled hard on the other end, jerking Day's arms high behind his back. Day had thought the session would begin with questions. But today the commander was getting right down to business.

The commander looked at Day and said, "Now you pay." He jerked the chair away and the guard pulled hard on the rope. Day thought his arms would rip from his body. The big cast on his right arm was forced against his chin. As he swung from the rafters, perspiration dripped down his face and fell from his nose and chin. He could feel blood vessels bursting in his arms. His chest bulged like a pigeon's breast and he heard his body making wretched sounds as pieces were pulled apart. To blot out the pain, he began counting, thinking that if he resisted long enough the enemy would become discouraged and give up. He prayed. Hours passed and the pain only grew. He dangled before the curious eyes of the seated Vietnamese men.

He had sworn that he would not scream again. But then, from somewhere deep inside, came long warbling primal wails.

The guards stared impassively. To amuse the men seated against the wall, the interrogator occasionally walked over and spun Day on the rope.

About 10:30 a.m. the interrogator smiled and asked, "Now you remember?"

Day could not speak. He shook his head. One of the observers stood up and walked away. Nothing was happening. The spectators were becoming bored. The commander had to seize the initiative. He could not let the Yankee air pirate cause him to lose face. He motioned toward one of the guards. With one hand the guard seized the cast on Day's arm; with the other he seized Day's wrist and twisted hard. Day heard his arm snap and he felt the shards of freshly broken bones grinding against his skin. What he described as a "blue-black sea of pain" washed over him, and somewhere he heard a high, shrill scream, a sound that could not be human.

A cascade of perspiration appeared on his face. His eyes bulged. He vomited. His bowels loosened. Urine streamed from his body.

After a moment the interrogator spoke calmly. "Now I have broken your arm. I am prepared to break the other arm. When you come down you will be a cripple. You will never work again. You will never feed your family again. You will be double cripple."

Day looked at the man's eyes and knew he was speaking the truth. Day wondered what it would be like to spend years captive with two broken arms. How would he feed himself? How would he bathe himself and take care of bodily functions? Could he even survive?

"Take me down. I'll answer your questions."

"No!" shouted his interrogator. "I not take you down until you answer question."

Above all else, Day had to be released from the rope. He felt as if his shoulders were being pulled from the joints. He had to have relief. Somehow he found the strength to insist on being taken down.

"I will not answer any questions as long as I am hanging here." Even as he said it, he thought, *That's not me talking.* All he wanted was relief, so why had he defied the interrogator?

The guard lowered Day to the chair. Day smelled urine and excrement. Blood and pus covered his right leg, and he realized that the guard's kick must have ruptured his wound again. Around his wrists were rope scars that would be visible for the remainder of his life.

The interrogator smiled. "I told you I would cripple you."

"You son of a bitch. I think you did."

Day was frightened. Both hands were locked into claws, with fingers curled against the palm. His left wrist was twisted inward. His right hand had no feeling, and he could not make it move at all. It was only with extreme difficulty that he could move his arms.

The commander stepped in front of Day, hooked his thumbs over his belt, bent forward, and asked harshly, "What political party your family?"

The first thought through Day's mind was *Damn, I got my arm broken for that?* Then he said, "In America, military men are not allowed to participate in partisan politics."

"What unit you from?"

Day invented the name of a unit and fabricated the name of an Air Force base. When asked for the names of fellow pilots, he paused a moment. "Charles Lindbergh. Wiley Post." The interrogation lasted only a few minutes. The purpose was not so much to get information as it was to get Day talking, to start a process, to create a precedent so the next time it would be easier.

In the pagoda at Vinh, Day learned a truth not taught in survival school. American training assumed that interrogators spoke reasonably proficient English, that they were educated and sophisticated, that they had some basic knowledge of a POW's country and of his military structure. But in many countries, interrogators might be not only young but uneducated, even not very bright. Their English might be rudimentary. Such young men can display unimaginable cruelty. Their limited facility with English makes them even more ominous, distant, remote, implacable — and dangerous.

Day was also to learn from bitter experience another truth: always tell lies you can remember. Interrogators keep detailed notes of every interrogation and instantly pounce on any inconsistency.

Day was blindfolded and marched back to his room. He counted his paces across the small compound and, when he passed Overly's room, said, "The rotten sons of bitches rebroke my arm."

Overly cleared his throat, signifying he heard and understood.

The next morning the commander told Day that he and the other criminal would be taken to Hanoi. "If you talk to him, you will be shot."

That evening Day was hauled onto the back of a small truck. The truck had transported war materials into South Vietnam and was returning to Hanoi. There were no gas stations along the way, so the truck carried extra fuel in a fifty-five-gallon drum. In an obscene embrace, Day's arms and legs were tied around the leaking and malodorous drum. Overly was tied to another drum. A guard climbed aboard and sat in the back. Ordinarily a pilot as severely injured as Day would have been tied down and the guard would have sat in relative comfort in the cab. But Day had escaped, remained at large more than two weeks, and made it into South Vietnam. He was a high-risk criminal and must be watched vigilantly.

The truck lurched into the night. Frequently the sound of a low-flying American jet was heard, and each time the truck slammed to a stop and the driver and guard jumped out and ran for the jungle. If the truck had been bombed — and trucks were favored targets to attack — it is easy to imagine what would have happened. During those times when the guard ran for the trees, Day tried to draw out Overly.

But Overly would not talk. He believed the threat about being shot.

Early in the morning of the third day, the decrepit truck entered the outskirts of Hanoi and labored through the labyrinthine streets before coming to a stop in front of a foreboding structure: four-teen-foot-high walls topped with broken glass. The gate opened and the truck eased inside.

Day had entered Hoa Lo, one of the most infamous prisons in the world, a place American POWs called the "Hanoi Hilton."

10

The Bug

In the brotherhood of the military, no act of bravery is an isolated event. Each generation of American military men stands on the shoulders of those who have gone before and is at one with warriors yet unborn. Valorous deeds, heroism, and selflessness, along with pain, suffering, and deprivation, all are part of a continuum that began when George Washington entered Valley Forge in the bitter winter of 1777; pressed on through the heat and hardships of the Mexican-American War; was bound tightly by the fratricidal Civil War; was raised to a new level in the trenches of World War I; and was immortalized on Omaha Beach and Iwo Jima. By the time the Vietnam War began, the blood of American men at arms had soaked the soil of their native land, the sands of a dozen Pacific islands and half the countries in Europe, and the snows of Korea. Thousands of American warriors were buried under simple white crosses in cemeteries around the world.

The gates of Hoa Lo opened and embraced a new generation of Americans.

These new POWs were acutely aware that under those simple white crosses, the spirits of American patriots were stirring restlessly. These new prisoners were mostly pilots. Many were strutting, boastful, independent, and over-the-top prima donnas, self-centered and egotistical men who fought their wars at five hundred miles per hour and, after their missions — at least in the Air Force — drank scotch and ate steak in the officers' club and then slept in air-conditioned comfort.

No American POWs in history would be subjected to such institutionalized brutal and prolonged torture sessions as were the men in Hoa Lo.

Did these men have the strength and the character of their brothers who had fought in the mud and who had given what Lincoln called "the last full measure of devotion"? Were these pilots as tough as the infantrymen who had fought in Europe? As tough as the Marines who had fought in the Pacific? Would they uphold all that is noble about the U.S. military? All that is noble about America? Or would they break the proud continuum?

THERE were no good times to enter Hoa Lo. But Bud Day arrived at a particularly bad time and under a particularly bad set of circumstances.

The French built Hoa Lo in 1901. "Maison Centrale" was the original name, but over the years the prison became known by the street on which it was located. The purpose of the prison was to incarcerate, torture, and execute the Vietnamese who opposed French colonialism. Until 1954, when the French were defeated at Dien Bien Phu and left Vietnam, thousands of Vietnamese, including some who now were national leaders, lived a subhuman existence within the walls of Hoa Lo. Earlier inmates knew first-hand that to mount any sort of resistance, prisoners must have two things: a strong military structure and good communications. In 1966, North Vietnamese guards discovered that the American POWs were tightly organized according to rank and had established a very effective communications system. The guards had reacted with a prolonged and violent purge. When Day arrived in late 1967, the prisoners remained subdued and the guards remained brutal.

The guards had been waiting for Day. Because of his escape, he was a notorious and unrepentant "air pirate" and "criminal" with a "bad attitude" who had to be "punished." (Prison officials never used the word "torture"; they favored instead "punishment.")

The initial interrogation of new prisoners took place near the front gate in a building known as "New Guy Village." The idea was to take a POW who probably was injured during his ejection, who may have sustained wounds from the local militia after he was shot down, who was exhausted and confused by the arduous nighttime travel and apprehensive about his future, and immediately subject him to torture. It was a sound and effective method of interrogation designed to break the spirit and force a "surrender" and then a "confession" of his crimes. Many a fighter pilot found that in the space of a half hour he was crying and screaming, pissing all over himself, and pleading for mercy.

The North Vietnamese Army had lost much face because a severely injured Bud Day not only had escaped but had been on the loose some three weeks in an area teeming with their soldiers. Thus, when Day arrived in late October 1967, it was imperative that the North Vietnamese regain face — a process that is always out of proportion to the original offense.

A guard jerked Day and Overly off the rear of the truck and hustled them in different directions: Overly into a solitary cell about six feet by six feet, and Day into Room 18. The room had knobby plaster walls to muffle screams, and the floor was splattered with blood.

There Bud Day met the Bug.

Because American prisoners did not speak Vietnamese and because the names and ranks of their captors were a closely guarded secret, POWs assigned each jailer a nickname, usually based on a physical characteristic. The Bug was about five foot three and plump. He was probably in his early thirties. He got his nickname because his right eye was cloudy and drifted up and to the right, which reminded some of a wandering bug's. When he worked himself into a rage, which was frequently, he waved his arms and contorted his face and jumped about in an irrational manner.

The Bug was the most vicious and feared of all the interrogators in Hoa Lo.

Day was barely in the interrogation room before his legs were clamped in rusty irons and he was pushed to his knees and ordered to hold his left hand high overhead. Usually a prisoner on his knees held both hands high over his head. But Day's right arm was in a cast and could not be straightened.

For those of you who do not understand how being on your knees can be considered torture, you can try a simple experiment. Get to your knees, preferably on a concrete floor, and reach high overhead. Set yourself a goal, say twenty minutes. Very quickly, a sharp lancing pain begins to radiate from the knees. Do not stand when the pain becomes great. Imagine that a guard is nearby and that if you move, you will be jabbed with his bayonet. And know that your knees will not become numb: your pain will only increase over the hours.

Day was on his knees for several hours. While the Bug shouted questions, two guards kicked him in the back and the leg. One vicious kick to his right leg again broke open the infected shrapnel wound and sent blood and pus oozing down his body. The guards slapped open hands over his ears and slammed him with heavy blows to the back of his head. The Bug was particularly incensed about Day's earlier escape. Every question about the escape brought particularly vicious kicks and slaps.

Several hours later one of the Bug's assistants jerked Day upright, twisted his right wrist in the cast, and pushed hard on his right shoulder to force the cast up high enough that his wrist could be pulled behind his back. They trussed his arms tightly behind him.

Bud Day was going in the ropes.

There were many forms of torture at Hoa Lo, but the most feared, the most painful, the most productive, and the one that left truly permanent side effects was going in the ropes. Unlike other new arrivals, Day had experienced the ropes and was fearful of revisiting that particular corner of hell. Already both arms were devoid of feeling and his hands were clenched and useless. He could not eat, drink, go to the bathroom, tie the string on his pajama pants, take the lid off a water pot, or unfold his blankets without help from a guard. He was so weak from hunger that he could barely stand. He had lost about fifty pounds. His injuries were severe. At a deep primal level he realized he might not come out of this alive.

The two guards forced Day's arms behind his back and turned them until the backs of his hands were together. They tied the limbs tightly and then began pushing his bound hands over the top of his head.

"What is your military unit?" the Bug screamed.

"I was injured when I ejected from my aircraft," Day said. "I don't remember."

"Give me the names of your fellow pilots!" the Bug shouted. "What is the next target in Hanoi that you were to bomb?"

The Bug smiled and nodded as his two assistants used all their strength to force Day's arms up over his head. Still the American would not answer.

Years later, Day recalled that he "began to pray for strength. It was clear it would be useless to pray for mercy."

Several hours later Day was a piss-covered, shit-streaked, vomit- and sweat-sodden wreck. The air was filled with the odor of the discharge from his infected leg. The Bug asked Day, "How do you think of your treatment by the Vietnamese people?"

"I think my treatment is savage and barbaric."

He was thrown into solitary — "solo," the POWs called it. The room was dark and dank and dirty. The window and a ventilation hole were covered with a bamboo mat. Day's narrow cell contained two concrete beds, each equipped with rusty iron stocks that could be operated from outside the room. Big rats ran freely through the cell. Day was placed in the stocks and handcuffs.

The stocks used in Hoa Lo, like the handcuffs — screw-down "hell cuffs" — were made by the French for small-boned Vietnamese prisoners and were not big enough for Americans. Sometimes it took two guards, using all their strength, to force the hell cuffs and stocks shut over the wrists or ankles of POWs. Swelling and discoloration of the flesh began within minutes. Often the swelling was so severe it bulged out to cover the handcuffs or the stocks. The agony was indescribable.

During that long lonely first night in Hoa Lo, Day realized he was being singled out and that harsh times were ahead. But there were things the North Vietnamese must never discover. First, they must never know anything about the Mistys. To disclose the mission or tactics of the Mistys would mean that some of his young pilots would die. Second, the North Vietnamese must never know that he was a lawyer and had written a master's thesis on the legality of the U-2 flight. The Vietnamese must never know that he was qualified to deliver nuclear weapons, that he had been a college instructor and an instructor pilot, that he was squadron commander of a top secret squadron, that he knew about electronic surveillance in Europe, or that he was an expert on Communism. If the guards discovered any of this, he would be considered a propaganda prize of the first magnitude. He — probably more than any other POW — simply could not allow himself to be opened up.

The next morning Day was hauled back to the knobby room and ordered to bow and kneel with his left hand in the air. This was known as "holding up the ceiling."

A half hour later the Bug leaned down and shouted, "Tell me the names of pilots you flew with!"

"I can't remember."

The Bug nodded and his two assistants moved in. Day was put in the ropes.

And when he reached the limit of his endurance, when the pain became more than he could bear, Day gave in. He knew they would want more than he had given during the torture session at Vinh. When he was asked for the names of his squadron mates, he offered Charles Lindbergh and Wiley Post. When the Bug wanted more, he added Billy Mitchell and Will Rogers.

The Bug was pleased. The blackest of the criminals, the Yankee air pirate, had surrendered. He had shown a good attitude.

Day was despondent. He wondered if he would make it, if he would ever see Doris and the children again. He resolved that he would think of them only at night when he said his prayers, that his days would be devoted to staying alive.

He quickly learned the prison routine. A prisoner had to stand up and bow when a guard entered the room. Never mind that many of the guards were illiterate teenagers and that the POWs were officers. A fighter pilot thinks of himself as superior to all beings, especially to those unfortunate souls who are not pilots. To bow to a peasant boy was humiliating.

The POWs were also told that they should never speak unless spoken to. They especially must not communicate with their fellow criminals. If a POW was caught communicating, he was immediately tortured. Nevertheless, the POWs talked through the walls and under the doors and signaled through open windows. Communicating, perhaps more than anything else, sustained the Americans. Talking to their brothers was their life's blood.

Through whispered conversations under the doors, Day was briefed on the tap code used by prisoners. To understand the tap code, you must imagine a grid, five spaces across and five spaces down. The alphabet — minus the letter K (for which C is substituted) — is superimposed over the grid. The top line is the letters A through E, the second is F through J, etc. To communicate, a prisoner first tapped to indicate what row he was on and then again to indicate the letter. Almost everything was reduced to shorthand. The common sign-off was "God bless you," which was reduced to "GBU." POWs became so facile at the tap code that they could converse at the pace of normal conversations. The knuckles of good communicators were heavily calloused.

Prisoners were fed twice daily — around 10:30 a.m. and again around 4 p.m. — usually a watery cabbage soup. Often the soup contained rocks, glass, animal hair, dog skulls, and even fecal matter. Not surprisingly, Day found that the prison diet did little to help him regain weight. Cells were occupied by snakes, enormous spiders, scorpions, and most of all rats — big rats. Rats owned the night and scampered across sleeping POWs, scrounging for scraps of food. With summer would come hordes of voracious mosquitoes.

POWs relieved themselves in a bucket called a "bo," which they were allowed to empty every day or so into a trench that ran through the prison. The trench often became blocked, and POWs used a bamboo "shit stick" to push fecal matter on down the way. To Bud Day, the trench smelled almost as bad as the stockyards back in Sioux City. Most POWs had dysentery, which, combined with a paucity of toilet paper, made them stinking wretches. Cold-water baths were allowed maybe once a week.

After about ten days, the guards replaced the cast on Day's right arm. When he saw his arm, he winced. His bicep was no bigger than his wrist.

The guards, tired of taking care of Day, moved Overly into the cell. Overly shaved off Day's three-month beard, fed him, washed him, tended to his wounds as best he could, and ministered to him as would a nurse. "He was very kind to me," Day said. Indeed, he saved Day's life. And for that Bud would always be grateful.

Day learned that Overly was a B-57 pilot. When Day asked Overly what information the guards sought from him, Overly said, "They wanted to know about the airplane. I told them everything they wanted to know. It's an old airplane and I am not going to get tortured over an obsolete airplane."

When Overly began asking questions, Day pleaded fatigue. He was caught in a terrible quandary. He decided to reveal nothing of himself to his fellow American. He did not even tell Overly what aircraft he flew. The man had answered every question from his captors. He had not been tortured. Overly had been slammed around a few times by the guards, but he was not beaten and kicked; he did not go to his knees and hold up the ceiling and he did not go in the ropes. He had not been in shackles or hell cuffs.

He had been allowed to bathe and to receive medical attention for the hematoma.

Day and Overly promised each other that the first one out would visit the other's wife and children. Day knew that Doris was fine, that she could take care of the kids, and that with their Air Force friends and the proximity of Luke AFB, The Viking would be okay. He tried not to worry about her. She had her job and he had his. One day they would be reunited.

Overly was obsessed with getting out of jail and going home.

By now a cold, damp winter had descended upon Hanoi. Day and Overly slept on concrete beds covered with thin straw pads. A single cotton blanket gave little warmth. The POWs wore cotton pajamas and were always cold.

Decades later, Overly was asked if he was tortured. "There are many forms of torture," he replied.

True enough. But while Overly had spoken and justified doing so, Day would not even confirm to a jailer that the sun rose in the east. He was utterly contemptuous of his captors and had a visceral loathing of Communism. He would give his captors nothing until he was near the point of permanent disfigurement or death. And then he would lie and mislead.

Thus, a wall came down between Day and the man who had saved his life. Day talked about growing up in Sioux City, about Doris and the children, but shrugged off all but the most innocuous questions about his military career. He never mentioned the Mistys. He did not even tell Overly that he flew an F-100.

Day learned that Robbie Risner, whose face had recently been on the cover of *Time* magazine, was also a prisoner at Hoa Lo. So was James Stockdale, the cerebral and charismatic Navy pilot. Both of these men were senior to Day and were respected leaders. But to the guards, Day's escape made him the most notorious and unrepentant of all the men at Hoa Lo. Rank did not matter; face did. As a result, Day went to torture sessions almost daily. At each session he spent several hours holding up the ceiling, or was beaten and kicked, or was put in the ropes. And through it all, he did not surrender.

One day Overly returned from an interrogation session — POWs called them a "quiz" — and said, "We're about to get a roommate."

A few hours later the Bug made it official. He swaggered up to Day and said, "Now you are nothing. We have the crown prince."

Day was relieved to be nothing. He wondered who the new guy was and why he was being placed in the cell with him and Overly.

The next morning the cell door opened, and a wreck of a man was carried inside on a stretcher and dumped onto the floor. He was in worse shape than Day. Both arms were broken. His leg was broken. A shoulder had been smashed by a rifle butt. He had been stabbed with a bayonet. He was the most severely injured of all the American POWs to enter Hoa Lo. He was near death.

Trying to cheer this shell of a man, Day smiled. "I'm Bud Day." He pointed. "This is Norris Overly." He paused. "Welcome to the Hilton."

With eyes burning bright with fever, the thin, white-haired young pilot looked up from his stretcher and told his fellow prisoners his rank and name. The rank was lieutenant commander, U.S. Navy. The name was John McCain.

McCAIN had been shot down in late October. Because he would answer no questions, the North Vietnamese initially refused him medical attention. He was about to die when the guards saw a newspaper story that said the son of Admiral John McCain had been shot down. Admiral McCain was about to become the senior military officer in the Pacific Theater, commander of all American forces fighting in Vietnam. Once North Vietnamese officials realized their prisoner was a celebrity, they hospitalized him, performed surgery, and gave him medications. A constant stream of high-ranking North Vietnamese officers visited him in the hospital. Even Vo

Nguyen Giap, the most fabled of all North Vietnamese military men and a close friend of Ho Chi Minh, dropped in to take a look.

Despite all this, Day thought McCain was dying. He figured the North Vietnamese had dumped the admiral's son in the cell so they could deny culpability, possibly hoping the death could be blamed on the two Americans now staring down at him.

McCain was overwhelmed to be in the company of brother pilots, and, Day recalled, McCain talked constantly all that day and far into the night.

McCain's later memoir would corroborate what various POWs said about him. He wanted desperately to emerge from the shadow of his father and grandfather, both admirals. But he had graduated near the bottom of his class at the Naval Academy, and his career lacked distinction. He was a typical fighter jock: loud, profane, heavy drinking, and womanizing. No matter what he did, he always played to the bleachers.

Despite all this, and despite their eleven-year age difference, Day and McCain became close friends. Both had serious injuries and both believed they would die in prison. Both were fighter pilots who, before they were shot down, had bailed out of jet aircraft. Both were political junkies who talked endless hours about presidential politics.

Day and McCain could not have been more different from their cell mate. Overly was a SAC pilot, a guy who flew multi-engine bombers. The professional and cultural difference between fighter pilots and SAC pilots is vast, like that between a truck driver and a Formula 1 racer. Overly was muted and had little interest in telling flying stories or even talking politics. And he was offended at how McCain spoke endlessly of the women he had bedded, of how he flew Navy jets to South America to visit a girlfriend, and of the girlfriends he had all over the world. Pussy, pussy, pussy — to Overly, that was all McCain talked about. You would think he had scattered his seed like a berserk parakeet. And he was married!

And yet, all three were brothers, and on a fundamental level, the differences did not matter. Overly nursed both men. Because McCain's injuries were so severe, he required special attention. Overly fed McCain, washed him, gave him water, helped him to the bo, and held McCain's penis while he urinated and then shook it for him. McCain had severe diarrhea. Overly wiped McCain's ass and cleansed fecal matter from his legs. McCain would have died without Overly's compassionate and solicitous care.

This is important for many reasons, some of which would not be revealed for several years, some not for decades. But the immediate irony is obvious: the two men who would come to be known by fellow POWs as "tough resisters" — the greatest compliment one POW can give to another — owed their lives to a man who told the guards whatever they wanted to know.

DAY, Overly, and McCain spent their first Christmas in jail together. It was absolutely miserable. Over the camp public-address system they heard POWs singing Christmas carols. The three men could not hold back their tears.

The New Year came without celebration, and the next holiday on the calendar was Tet.

During the thousand years or so of Chinese domination, Tet — the Chinese lunar New Year — had become a national holiday in Vietnam. In 1968, Tet began on January 31. American and Communist forces had earlier agreed to a truce over the holidays, but Communist forces broke the agreement and launched massive attacks throughout South Vietnam. The attacks were poorly planned and badly executed and, with the exception of prolonged fighting in the old city of Hue, were repulsed in a few days. The Tet Offensive was a bitter and costly defeat for the North. Nevertheless, the media — because they knew little of tactics, strategy, or the operational arts, and because many were antiwar — concluded that the North Vietnamese had won a great victory.

The North Vietnamese knew differently; they had been virtually destroyed as a fighting force. After Tet, the North Vietnamese realized, as one of them later said, that the war would not be won on the battlefield but on the streets of American cities. Baby boomers, the most antiauthoritarian generation of Americans ever produced, were coming of age. Five thousand women had gone to Washington a week before to sing war-protest songs as the U.S. Congress opened. Young Americans wrapped themselves in the cloak of self-righteousness and indulged in their favorite pastime of avoiding the draft and protesting the war. At Harvard, Alan Dershowitz was teaching a course on how to legally avoid military service. Musical groups such as Peter, Paul, and Mary were making their reputations singing about the evils of the war. On March 31, President Lyndon Johnson announced he would not seek reelection. He had so mishandled the prosecution of the Vietnam War that he knew he could not be reelected. Robert Kennedy, Eugene McCarthy, and Hubert Humphrey were running against Richard Nixon, and the war was really the only campaign issue. The North Vietnamese realized that all this social unrest, combined with the upcoming presidential election, could be of immense value to their cause. They also realized that, even though the American media were generally ignoring the plight of the POWs, these men had immense propaganda value. Releasing McCain would be a great coup, showing the world that the North Vietnamese were fair and generous.

The North Vietnamese came to McCain and offered to send him home.

McCain, as a number of POWs have written, not only refused in a voice loud enough to be heard by other POWs but called every guard a "cocksucker" or a "fucking son of a bitch" or a "slant-eyed bastard" and said he wanted to be treated like all the other prisoners. He was. He was severely beaten.

Years later when McCain was asked about the incident, he said his actions were prompted by a desire to "boost the spirits" of other POWs. It is a curious and revealing comment. Most tough resisters based their actions on the Code of Conduct, which says prisoners should not accept a parole or special favors. McCain was courageous. But once again he was playing to the bleachers.

Day began each morning by trying to rehabilitate his twisted hands. He placed one finger at a time on the window ledge and pulled down until the finger straightened or the pain became too great. Then another finger. Then another. But there was no progress. He could not move his fingers and he could not lift his arms above shoulder height. He feared that if he lived, he would be crippled for life.

One morning in February, Overly returned from a meeting with prison officials and told Day and McCain he was about to be released; he was going home.

Day looked at him suspiciously. "What did that cost you?"

"Nothing," Overly said.

Day and McCain looked at each other. Overly's hematoma had healed and he had no rope marks or swollen knees — nothing to show he had been tortured. He was thin but relatively fit: the perfect prisoner for the North Vietnamese to release.

"Norris, you are gonna catch a lot of shit over this," Day told him.

"There is no way I would ever take an early release," McCain said.

Almost four decades later, Overly would contest this version of events. He would say he had been tortured but revealed nothing. He would say that he had not violated the Code of Conduct, that he was forced to leave, "expelled" from Hoa Lo.

Overly said he would take a letter to Doris and to McCain's wife, Carol. Day could not write, so he dictated to McCain, "I know, Doris, that you had faith that I lived. This letter confirms your good faith. Pray as I do that we are together soon." Day asked her to send pictures of the children. After much effort, he managed to sign the note in his usual way — "George E. Day" — so Doris would know it truly was from him.

Overly and two other officers were the first pilots released in what those who stayed behind would always call the "Fink Release Program." Later, nine others (eight officers and one enlisted man) would be released early. But 99-plus percent of the POWs would not be repatriated until Operation Homecoming in early 1973. The chasm between the early releases and those who came home in 1973 would never be bridged.

SHORTLY before Christmas 1967, Doris had received a package from the Mistys that contained Bud's personal effects and civilian clothes, along with another pair of flying boots.

She had heard nothing since the initial notification that he had been shot down. She did not know if he was evading, if he had been captured, or if he was dead.

The U.S. government was following what POW wives and the wives of those missing in action called the "Keep-Quiet Policy." President Lyndon Johnson wanted no public awareness that growing numbers of America's fighting men were being shot down and jailed in Hanoi. Air Force officers instructed Doris not to tell anyone her husband had been shot down and was missing. She could say only that her husband was "in Vietnam." Again and again she was told, "Don't talk to the press." "Don't tell anyone your husband has been shot down." "Don't rock the boat." "We are doing all we can."

She might have denied to the world that anything was wrong, but the arrival of Bud's personal belongings somehow made it all so final. As if to put an oppressive stamp on that fact, everything in the package was covered with a heavy dank mildew.

She hung the clothes outside for days to let the Arizona sun burn away the mildew and then washed them and put them away. She told herself that Bud was coming home. And when he came home, he would ask about his boots. A pilot, like a cowboy, is attached to his boots. Every time he puts them on, he remembers the airplanes and the missions he flew while wearing them. Doris knew that when Bud came back, he would want to fly again. The children cleaned and polished the boots and put them in the closet with the neatly pressed uniforms. Seeing the uniforms reminded her of how Bud used to throw his clothes on the floor when he walked in the door. She missed picking up his clothes.

Each night when Doris and the children said their prayers, she prayed for Bud. She put Bud's picture near the bed of each child. She wanted them to remember his face, to remember everything about him. She told them that she did not know when, but their father would be coming home. They should never doubt that fact. But one of the boys was so anxious about his father that he began wetting the bed.

In January 1968, Doris was at the beauty shop when the beautician said, "What is going on with you? You are losing all your hair." Doris knew it was from stress. She bought a wig. Her hair was falling out in clumps and she could not talk to anyone about why this was happening.

On Friday, February 16, 1968, at 11:30 a.m., the phone rang. Doris picked it up and knew by the faint warbled hum that this was a long-distance call. She waited. A voice asked, "Is this Phoenix 278–4082?"

"Yes."

"You are receiving a MARS call from Udorn, Thailand." ("MARS" is a military communications system.)

Her hand flew to her throat. "Okay."

Then another voice asked, "Is this Phoenix 278–4082?"

"Yes, it is."

"Is this Doris Day?"

"Yes, it is." She was growing impatient. What was this about? It had to be news of Bud.

"This is Major Norris Overly and I've just been released from prison in Hanoi. I've been your husband's cell mate since last September. Bud is alive and well and in good spirits."

Doris threw back her head and laughed with joy. "Oh, I knew it," she said. "I love you."

Air Force officials in Thailand would not let Overly talk more than a moment. He told Doris he would call again.

Doris called an officer at Randolph Field, the man who, ever since Bud had been shot down, was her liaison with the Air Force, and told him about the conversation. "Can I tell?" she asked. The officer was disturbed that Overly had called and said, "It's not official yet."

"It is for me. I'm telling my family."

She called her sister in Sioux City. "Bud is alive. He's a POW in Hanoi. He's alive."

Her sister, a devout Lutheran, was not surprised. After all, she had the entire congregation at St. John Lutheran Church praying for Bud.

By now Doris was laughing and crying at the same time. She ran to her next-door neighbor's house and, without knocking, threw open the door and shouted, "My husband is alive! My husband is alive!"

A few days later Overly called again, this time from Hawaii. He said he was putting a letter from Bud in the mail. He told her the letter had been written by Bud's roommate, a naval officer named John McCain, but Bud had signed it. Overly was afraid that if he brought the letter back to the mainland, the Air Force might confiscate it. He said that as soon as he visited his own family, he was coming to see her and to talk with the children. He had promised Bud he would do that.

After Doris hung up, she wondered why this fellow McCain — someone she had never heard of — had written the letter. She pushed the thought from her mind. She would wait.

Within a few days her hair stopped falling out and began growing back. She threw away the wig. And there was no more bedwetting by one of the boys.

On April 22, Overly arrived and said the Air Force had ordered him not to tell her anything about Bud. He paused and stared. She nodded, said, "Okay," and waited.

"I'll tell you about me," Overly said. "Here's what happened to me." And he told her how he had been shot down and captured and placed in a holding area near Vinh, where he was "thrown in with another man."

Again he paused and stared. Doris understood.

"When I first saw him, I thought he was an old man."

Doris broke the charade. She slapped the table. "Norris, my husband is not an old man."

Overly looked at her gently. He held his hand about halfway down his chest and said, "His beard was white and down to here. He is stooped. His right arm was broken in three places and he can't lift it above his shoulder. He walks around with his right arm extended at a forty-five-degree angle with the palm up. He has no use of either hand. Doris, he is an old man."

Doris was not having this. Again she slapped the table. "My husband is not an old man."

Overly talked for hours and told her things about her husband that amazed her. Bud was a very private man. He did not talk of such things to anyone. Yet this stranger seemed to know all about her and the children. He even knew the special way she made salad and why she did not make gravy.

Doris knew that if Bud had told all this to Overly, the two men must have been very close. Then Overly asked, "What aircraft did Bud fly?"

It was an innocuous question, the sort of question everyone asked. But instantly the Sorensen genes kicked in: the World War II resistance in Norway, the oft told stories of how her family had dealt with German intelligence officers. If Bud had not told Overly that he flew an F-100, there could be only one reason: he did not trust this man.

Neither would she.

"A jet," she said with a shrug.

Norris took Steve to visit with him and his family in San Antonio. During the two-week visit, he taught Steve how to water-ski and introduced him to horseback riding, and the two had long man-to-man talks. Overly told Doris that she should buy Steve a horse, that it would help him adapt to his father's being away and would give him something he did not have to share with his brother and two sisters.

Doris bought Steve a horse. Steve thought long and hard about a name. Then he remembered that song his dad was always humming. He named the horse "Misty."

* * *

By March, Day had healed enough that he could nurse McCain, feed him, keep him reasonably clean from the effects of savage diarrhea, and — most of all — encourage him. They were both in such terrible physical shape that a mere cold or a minor infection could have killed either of them. Because neither expected to live, each revealed things to the other that he had never revealed to another soul. They forged a friendship closer and more enduring than that of many brothers. They swore a blood oath. If McCain died, Bud would tell John's parents that his last thoughts were of them and that he died without losing his honor. If Bud died, McCain would seek out Doris and tell her how much Bud loved her and that he had been a highly respected prisoner under terrible conditions.

When the two men were taken from their cell to empty the bo, they were a comical pair, both dirty, both shit streaked, both wearing casts. Day could not use his hands but had some use of his left arm. He had a pronounced limp. McCain could not use his arms but did have some use of his hands. He still could not walk. The two men supported each other, arms wrapped around each other, McCain's legs dragging as they lurched and stumbled, each effort the product of this human Rube Goldberg conglomeration of fighter pilots.

Jack Van Loan was in a cell across the courtyard. He watched from a crack in the door and saw Day trudging along, head down, bent arm pumping, and could tell from the expression on his face that this was one determined man. Word had gotten out among the POWs of his escape and early torture and of his defiance.

"His leadership was omnipresent," Van Loan said. And the POWs knew who McCain was and how he had turned down an early release. When Van Loan saw them lurching toward the showers, he showed his respect in typical fighter pilot fashion.

"Hire the handicapped!" he shouted. "They're funny as hell."

The laughter of other POWs could be heard from inside their cells. Day and McCain laughed with them.

Several POWs also recognized Day's name as belonging to the man who survived both a fire on takeoff in a T-33 and a no-chute bailout from an F-84. Other POWs knew of Day's gunnery scores and the papers he had written about delivering nuclear weapons. They learned the details of his escape to South Vietnam, his being shot when he tried to run, his torture down at Vinh. When one new POW first heard Day's history, he said with reverence, "Now there's a man who has pissed on every tree in the forest."

When Day lurched across the courtyard, other POWs saw ankles that were red from rusty shackles, knees swollen and bleeding from kneeling on concrete floors, and hands virtually useless, and they knew they were looking at someone who had undergone many a torture session. And they knew from his eyes that he had not been broken.

When a newly arrived shoot-down, a Misty named Bob Craner, was placed in an adjacent cell, he told Bud he had been promoted to lieutenant colonel and recommended for four Silver Stars. McCain laughed and said, "Why don't you tell the Bug? Maybe he will give you a fucking parade."

In March the cast was taken off Day's right arm. His arm was bowed at the elbow and would not straighten. McCain pulled and tugged and tried to realign the bones, but it was impossible. He pressed the bones together as tightly as he could and bound the arm with rags. Day continued to worry about his hands, both still curled into claws. For hours every day, McCain acted as a physical therapist for Day, massaging his arms and hands. But Day's fingers always recurled. The nerves in both arms seemed deadened. Then one morning Day managed to wiggle a finger for the first time.

McCain burst into tears.

By now the guards had decided that McCain, against all odds, was going to live and that he could survive alone. He and Day were transferred to different prisons. When McCain and Day separated, both men were near tears. They embraced like brothers, each fearing he would never again see the other, and each dreading what lay ahead.

THE POWs were segregated by rank, the most senior officers kept in a remote portion of Hoa Lo and isolated from other prisoners. The thinking of the guards was that this would deprive the POWs of leadership. Other methods were used too. Some senior officers, such as James Stockdale and Robbie Risner, were tortured so severely that for months on end they could not be leaders. But what the guards did not understand was that in such instances the leadership passed down to a few senior Air Force majors such as Bud Day and Larry Guarino.

Day and Guarino knew that if they were identified as commanders, they would receive special torture. Nevertheless, both accepted the burden of command and both paid the price. Both were almost killed by the Bug. And both became legends among the POWs.

These men could not be more different. Day was a small-town boy from the heartland while Guarino was a street-smart wisecracking Italian from Newark, New Jersey. He was the eleventh American shoot-down of the war and had been in jail since 1965. Via tap code and whispering, Guarino sent out stirring messages almost daily telling POWs to resist until they were about to be permanently crippled or killed.

Though the two men were in frequent communication, solitary confinement meant it would be several years before they actually met. In coming years, Day and Guarino would be the senior ranking officers (SROs) of their cell block or their building or their camp. Their life stories became interwoven as POWs and would remain so after they were released.

AFTER Day and McCain were separated, their actions reflected their natural bent. McCain limped through the courtyard to the bath, waving his casts and shouting, "Ho Chi Minh sucks dead Japanese dicks."

A few months later, McCain was housed in the same building as Guarino. They were separated by two cells but could press cups against the wall and talk for hours every day. Guarino repeatedly counseled the young officer to be more circumspect. A few guards spoke enough English to understand. If they heard McCain, he would be tortured. "Fuck the goddamn gooks," McCain replied. "They are all pricks."

Guarino says that McCain was quite mercurial. One day he shouted into his cup that he wanted some advice.

"What do you want to know?" Guarino replied.

"It's about women."

Guarino rolled his eyes. "Go ahead."

"Sometimes when I am with a woman, I ejaculate too soon."

Guarino could not believe what he was hearing. The brash young McCain wanted sexual advice from a man who had not seen a woman since he was shot down almost three years earlier.

Nevertheless, he responded, "Next time you are about to have sex, think about something else."

"Do you mean I should not have an erection?"

Guarino laughed. "No, you're gonna need one of those."

Years later, he recalled McCain's bravado. "He wanted to grow up and be Bud Day," Guarino said.

SOMEDAY, God willing, all the POWs would go home. Until that day, Bud decided, the POWs who were tortured and continued to resist must not be lumped in with those who went home early. There should be some way to recognize those who adhered to the Code of Conduct. More and more the slogan "Return with Honor" was on Day's mind. That slogan perfectly described what he thought should be the goal of every POW. Later, these ideas would coalesce, and one of the most elite units of the American military would be formed. Until then, though, survival was the order of the day.

LATE every Friday afternoon, Day tapped out a message sent down the line to all POWs under his command: "HH" — happy hour, the traditional Air Force Friday afternoon drinking and hell-raising session. Of course there was nothing to drink and nothing to celebrate. But by recognizing the tradition, the officers maintained a link to the outside world.

Every Sunday morning, Day tapped out "CC" — church call. All the other SROs did the same thing. Most POWs then stood in their individual cells and faced east, the direction of America, placed their hands over their hearts, and said aloud the Pledge of Allegiance. Then they recited the Lord's Prayer, after which they prayed for their fellow POWs who were being tortured; they prayed for the sick and injured POWs and for their families and for America. Day, as did most of the POWs, ended every message with "GBU."

The homeland might have been in turmoil, but here in a forgotten hellhole, a small group of men were keeping alive the America they knew and loved.

In his book *1968: The Year That Rocked the World*, Mark Kurlansky says that four events merged to form a tumultuous year: the civil rights movement, an alienated generation that rejected all authority, war hatred around the world, and the coming of age of television. The last turned out to be particularly important to the American military in general and to the POWs specifically.

The POWs were mostly of a generation that knew of World War II journalists such as Edward R. Murrow and Ernie Pyle. Murrow had reported often on the resourcefulness and courage of the British while Pyle wrote of the indomitable nature of the GI. In World War II, the reporting, books, and movies had generally supported America's war effort. During the Korean War, there were divisions in the press, but usually the reporting was straightforward.

But in Vietnam a fault line developed between the military and the media — with dramatic results.

Virtually every reporter in Vietnam had gotten it wrong about the Tet Offensive — the major dailies, the three networks, the news magazines, radio — they all got it wrong. And the incestuous amplification of their wrongness gave new strength to the anti-war movement and had an enormous impact on American politics. The Tet Offensive was the first time in history that the news media overturned a victory by American troops. Only a few days later, Walter Cronkite, the venerable anchor of *CBS News*, declared that America had lost the war. He qualified his remarks by saying they were personal comments. Nevertheless, he was what was called the "voice of God," and his words had enormous impact. President Johnson said that if he had lost Walter Cronkite, he had lost Middle America. It was not long afterward that Johnson announced he would not run for reelection.

Bud Day and John McCain had talked often about the press. McCain told him how, after he survived the famous fire aboard the aircraft carrier *Forrestal*, a young CBS reporter named Morley Safer had interviewed him. "That guy was antiwar," McCain said.

It was particularly irksome to military people that brash young television reporters not only were argumentative and cynical but were painting themselves as experts on tactics and strategy when, in fact, few of them knew the difference between a company and a battalion. This low opinion of the press was shared by one of America's most prominent authors. John Steinbeck had gone to Vietnam in December 1966, representing *Newsday*. He went into battle with the 1st Cavalry and with Marine assault units. He flew in a Bird Dog over the DMZ. He came under fire several times. In his columns, he said that the media was interested only in "the immediate and the dramatic" and that the real war in Vietnam was not being communicated to people back home. He said that much of what was produced by young reporters was "pure horse manure."

His columns astonished people back home. Why, when so many people opposed the war, was Steinbeck so "hawkish"? Steinbeck, who had received both a Pulitzer Prize and the Nobel Prize for Literature, was attacked by the American press as an old man who had lost his way.

The POWs did not trust the media in general but were especially wary of television and particularly CBS (even more particularly, Walter Cronkite, Morley Safer, and Dan Rather). To the POWs, Walter Cronkite became "Walter Crankcase." And they called the camp public-address system "CBS." The guards asked the prisoners what this meant and were pleased to learn that CBS was a prominent American television network. They never knew that to the POWs, "CBS" meant "camp bullshit system." And the POWs knew that no other daily newspaper in America gave as much space to the antiwar movement as did the *New York Times*.

By late 1968, Doris thought the Keep-Quiet Policy had gone on long enough. She had to do something so people would know about the plight of the POWs. But what? She had heard about a group called the National League of Families of American Prisoners and Missing in Southeast Asia. The group was organized by Sybil Stockdale, wife of Jim Stockdale, and the membership was comprised of families of MIAs and POWs. The sole purpose of the group was to press for the return of all missing Americans in Southeast Asia. Maybe joining them was the first step.

"If the shoe was on the other foot, if I was the one in jail, what would Bud do?" she asked herself. The answer was simple: he would move heaven and earth to rescue her. But how could she change the Air Force? How could she have an impact on American thought? She was from Sioux City, Iowa, and had no experience in these matters. She had not been to college. She prayed and asked what she could do that would not harm Bud or the other POWs.

Her opportunity came just before Bud's second Christmas in jail. Air Force officials at Luke AFB did not want the wives of MIAs or POWs to know how many other similar wives were nearby or who they were. Visits of POW/MIA wives to Luke were scheduled so the wives would never meet. But in December the Air Force received a copy of an East German documentary called *Pilots in Pyjamas* that included footage of a number of the POWs. The Air Force wanted the wives and families to see the documentary and identify as many POWs as possible. The film could stay at Luke only one day before it was sent to California for other POW wives to view. So all the local POW/MIA wives were brought to Luke.

Doris looked around at the women, all sitting silently. This was her opportunity. She was Bud Day's wife; she was The Viking. She took pen and paper from her purse, stood up, turned to the woman next to her, and said, "Hello, I'm Doris Day and I'm a POW wife." She wrote down the woman's name and phone number and said, "I'll call you later." Then she moved on and did the same thing with other wives.

When she returned home, she went down her list and invited the women to her house. It was the first time the MIA and POW wives from the Phoenix area met as a group. She was so excited about the gathering that she burned the chicken she had prepared for dinner.

But it did not matter. Doris told the women the purpose of the meeting was to form an organization of local POW/MIA families and make it part of the National League of Families. Doris was elected president of the group and began making speeches about Bud and the POWs. It was very difficult in the beginning. She could get no more than a few minutes into her story when she noticed people in the audience were crying. Then she would begin crying. She talked to almost every Republican club in Arizona. No Democrat clubs invited her to speak. She met newspaper and television reporters and columnists. She met elected officials up to and including the governor. Later, she was elected the Arizona coordinator for the National League of Families.

One of the most important people she met, one who was to become a lifelong friend, was a wealthy Texan named Ross Perot. In the beginning she had no money, no photographs, nothing to help people understand the plight of the POWs. Perot had formed a POW awareness group called "United We Stand" that gave her bumper stickers and invaluable advice in a dozen areas, and put her in touch with people who could help. With the backing that might make a difference, Doris was going to let America know about the POWs.

And she was going to get the North Vietnamese to acknowledge that Bud Day was a prisoner.

11

Another Summer of Love

D<small>URING</small> the late 1960s, some young Americans wore love beads while others wore the uniform of their country.

Some sang "Where Have All the Flowers Gone" while others sang "God Bless America."

Some young men fled to Canada. Others volunteered to go to Vietnam.

Some stood in the streets of America and clenched their fists in the air. Others huddled in dank cells in North Vietnam and held their hands over their hearts.

Some made speeches and protested about all that was wrong with America. Others maintained their sanity by remembering all that was right with America.

In addition to the physical torture and the primitive living conditions faced by the POWs, they experienced considerable psychological pain. The North Vietnamese withheld letters and packages from home, a move particularly dispiriting to men whose thoughts often soared toward home and who spent hours wondering how their wives and children were faring.

Through the new shoot-downs and through the ever-present "CBS," POWs knew what was going on back home. Congressmen and senators speaking out against the war? Young men burning draft cards? It was terribly demoralizing. If they were forced to listen to one more antiwar speech or one more group singing "Give Peace a Chance," they would pull out their hair. And why were Senator Ted Kennedy, Jane Fonda, former attorney general Ramsey Clark, and others denouncing America's involvement in Vietnam as "immoral"? The war might be immoral to college students and to some politicians and even to much of America, but the POWs were American men at arms and it was their duty to follow the orders and uphold the policies of their lawfully elected civilian leaders.

POWs thought they had been doing their duty. The catchphrase "immoral war" struck at the sacred heart of the POW: the concept of honor.

The POWs believed they had assumed an unlimited liability, up to and including the loss of life in service to their country. Their lives were dedicated to protecting America, and they were willing to make the supreme sacrifice for the *privilege* of so doing. They pressed on with their duty as they saw that duty. While the world might think of them as prisoners *of* war, they thought of themselves as prisoners *at* war; they were simply fighting on a different front.

Particularly painful to the prisoners was the *Bob and Ed Show*, a chatty anti-American prison broadcast by Navy commander Robert Schweitzer and Marine lieutenant colonel Edison Miller, two collaborators who were given special treatment and who were kept isolated from other POWs. In North Vietnamese prison camps, there were 458 American officers and 10 enlisted men (plus some 65 men who died in captivity). A fraction of 1 percent of this number became outcasts. Eight enlisted prisoners were so derisive about the Code of Conduct, so anti-American, so antiwar, and so flagrant in their disobedience of orders that a plot was developed to kill one of them. The SRO squelched the plan.

The POWs did not know it, but back home evidence of the first intimations of a change in government policy toward the prisoners could be seen. Richard Nixon had won the presidency, and in May 1969, Secretary of Defense Melvin Laird met with

Communist negotiators in Paris and waved pictures of emaciated POWs and complained about their condition. It was the first sign that Nixon would be more aggressive than was Lyndon Johnson on the POW issue.

Nixon was familiar with the National League of Families. He also knew about Doris Day because she sent him letters supporting his POW efforts — and he wrote her letters in return. Nixon also knew that Ross Perot was putting his virtually limitless resources into bringing the plight of the POWs to the attention of America. The passion of the wives and the money of Ross Perot were coming together in a great upsurge of emotion from grassroots levels all across America, and Nixon planned to ride that wave.

For Bud Day, the summer of 1969 was a summer of hell.

It began on May 10 when John Dramesi and Ed Atterberry escaped. Even though the Code of Conduct calls for captured American military personnel to make every effort to escape, and even though there were escape committees in every camp, SROs almost universally refused to sanction escape attempts. Aside from the obvious — tall and fair Caucasians did not exactly blend into Hanoi or the North Vietnamese countryside — escapees could not go north, west, or south; geography limited escape routes to getting to the Red River and floating 110 miles to the sea and then hoping to be seen by American aircraft. Chances of finding a Vietnamese to assist in an escape were zero. National pride was high, and in addition, the North Vietnamese government placed a bounty equaling $1,500 on any escaped prisoner. Finally, SROs knew that when escapees were caught — as would inevitably be the case — a terrible retribution would be rendered against all POWs.

There was never a successful escape from a North Vietnamese prison camp. And the unsanctioned effort by Dramesi and Atterberry on a rainy Saturday night before Mother's Day was no exception. The two men got three miles away and were back in jail before noon.

During intense torture sessions, guards usually forced towels down the mouths of POWs to muffle their cries. But this time the guards did not use towels; they wanted other POWs to hear. The screams of Dramesi and Atterberry were heard two blocks away, and Atterberry was killed during his torture session.

The heart of a fighter pilot is too big for his chest. It must be big to accommodate his fighting spirit, his patriotism, his sense of duty, and his willingness to sacrifice. But it is not big enough to contain his anguish when he hears the cries of brother pilots who are being tortured and he can do nothing.

PEACE talks between America and North Vietnam had begun in Paris back in January 1969. And as a first step in winding down the war, America began withdrawing its troops from Vietnam on July 8. The North Vietnamese said they would discuss the "criminals" — the POWs — only after America withdrew its troops. But students of military history knew that the Vietnamese had made the same offer to the French in 1954. After the French withdrew their troops, fewer than one-third of the known French prisoners were repatriated; the others died in captivity from starvation, disease, and torture. If America unilaterally pulled out of the war without making repatriation of the POWs part of the agreement, American POWs might suffer the same fate. Guards often told Day, "You will be the first man shot when the war is over." They meant it. In the more immediate term, Day knew there would be more retribution for the Dramesi/Atterberry escape. He told the men under his command to prepare themselves: murderous reprisals were coming and communications soon would be shut down. "Assume the worst," he tapped out. "They know a lot. Tell them anything obvious. But reveal no classified material."

The POWs recall the summer of 1969 as the time of the most vicious, systematic, and sustained torture of their long imprisonment. A new camp commander appeared and sealed the light and airholes in each cell. The temperature was well over 100 degrees, and POWs sweltered in a darkness that only increased their apprehension. Day and night the shrill and sustained screams of

American pilots echoed through the prisons of North Vietnam. The very jangling of a guard's keys made strong men tremble. They prayed the guard was coming for someone else, and they were racked with both guilt if another man was taken to torture and dread because next time the guard would come for them.

The harshest reprisals were visited upon senior officers who the guards thought were the brains behind the escape attempt but who in reality, for security reasons, had not been told in advance. (In fact, only Dramesi's immediate SRO knew of the escape plans.) Until the summer of 1969, putting a prisoner in the ropes was considered the most painful and debilitating of all forms of torture. But this time the torture was different. A four-foot-long rubber strip cut from a tire was used to beat the Americans. They called it the "fan belt."

Day felt a special apprehension. He was the SRO of a building called the Barn, and he realized he soon would be facing the greatest trial of his life. Midwesterners know two things for certain. The first is how to reduce complex issues down to the basics. So, in the quiet before the guards came for him, Day made a solemn vow, a simple vow of three parts:

I will not do or say or write anything that will embarrass Doris and the children.

I will not do or say or write anything that will embarrass the Air Force.

I will not do or say or write anything that will embarrass my country.

Day knew that, God willing, someday all this would be over, and if he was still alive, he would go home. On that day he was determined to hold his head high.

Return with Honor.

That would be his creed.

He would die before he dishonored his family, the Air Force, or his country.

If he could not return with honor, he would not return at all.

The second thing Midwesterners know about is fortitude. In his *Maxims of War*, Napoleon says, "The first qualification of a soldier is fortitude under fatigue and privation." Most people think courage should be the first qualification. But without the fortitude to survive the terrible times that sometimes are the lot of the soldier, he may not be able to reach the place where courage is required. From his father, Bud Day had learned all there was to know about fortitude.

Early on Wednesday morning, July 16, Day heard the jangle of the guard's keys. The door opened and it was his time.

Like every POW, he thought this might be a mistake, that there would be some sort of intervention, that his captors would change their minds. But as the guard marched him out of the room, Day looked over his shoulder and saw a second guard pick up the small towel that every POW had in his cell.

Being marched off in the predawn darkness toward torture does things to a man's mind. Cold fear knotted Day's stomach and his knees trembled.

Inside the small blood-splattered quiz room, a guard stood against one wall holding a fan belt. On the opposite wall another guard also held a fan belt.

A guard motioned and said, "Drop pants."

Hell cuffs were ratcheted deep into his wrists. Almost immediately his hands began to swell. Irons were clamped around his ankles.

July temperatures in Hanoi, even at dawn, are around 80 degrees. Nevertheless, as Day's pajamas fell to his ankles, he shivered. He was naked before his enemies. And he knew enough about pain to know that eventually he could be made to talk. "If you torture me, I will lie," he told the guards. "And later I will take it all back. I will withdraw whatever I say."

One guard ripped the small towel in half and forced it into Day's mouth.

"Down!" a guard shouted.

Day slumped to his knees and then to his stomach and realized no questions had been asked. This was not about information. This was about punishment.

Dear God, give me strength. Give me strength. Let me endure. Please, God. Don't let me talk. Please.

A guard across the room stood erect, tightened his grip on the fan belt, and grunted as he pushed off from the wall. He raised the belt high above his head and used the momentum of his dash across the room to smash the belt across Day's buttocks.

The towel did not muffle the noise. Day's scream sliced through the dawn, and POWs knew another American had been called to torture.

While the scream still hung in the air, the second guard launched from the wall and brought his fan belt down on Day's buttocks.

One scream merged into another as the guards bounced from wall to wall. From some distant remote place, Day realized the sound of the fan belt on his skin was crisp and sharp. Hour after hour the beating continued, the lashes falling from Day's buttocks to his thighs and then up over his lower back, and after a while the sound of the belt hitting his flesh changed to a soft *splatting* sound and then to a wet plopping noise.

God, give me strength. Don't let me talk. Please, God.

Occasionally, when the guards needed a break, the interrogator asked, "Are you ready to confess your black crimes?"

Each time Day shook his head and the beating continued.

He was frequently reminded that he was a Yankee air pirate with a bad attitude.

Sometime in late morning the beating stopped so Day could eat, so he could have strength to endure the afternoon session. He slowly sipped the thin pumpkin soup and a cup of water.

The men who had beaten Day were tired, and two new guards came in and gripped the fan belts and the session resumed. Late in the afternoon, when these guards were too tired to continue,

Day was dragged to his cell and given another bowl of pumpkin soup.

All he wanted was rest and sleep and to renew his strength for what would come with the new day. But he had not finished his soup when he was ordered to his knees, and the leg irons and hell cuffs were reapplied. When the guards finished screwing down the cuffs into Day's swollen wrists, blood was flowing freely. He was kept on his knees all night. Every time his head nodded in exhaustion, he was prodded with a bayonet.

On the morning of the second day, the torture resumed. Sometime that morning the three hundredth lash from the fan belt fell on Day's buttocks. He lost count after that, too groggy from lack of sleep and too weak to keep track. Guards asked him about the hierarchy of the Pentagon and the CIA, two subjects that obsessed the North Vietnamese and two topics that invariably came up during a torture session. Day had never served in the Pentagon and knew little about the CIA.

The beatings continued.

Dear God, give me strength.

He spent that night on his knees. Because he was so tired and weak, the bayonet pokes were more frequent.

By the third day the shackles had cut so deeply into his ankles that his Achilles tendons were visible. The shiny white of his patella could be seen on both knees.

On the morning of the fourth day, after Day spent another sleepless night on his knees, the guard shouted, "Are you ready to confess your black crimes?"

"I hope your mother dies in a whorehouse," Day replied.

The beating continued.

Now the guards stood at Day's feet when they beat him. The fan belts sliced into his scrotum.

Please. Strength.

That evening he was tottering back and forth on his knees and being prodded so often with a bayonet that the guard ordered him to sit on a stool. Within seconds he fell asleep and slumped to the floor. During the subsequent beating, the guard broke two of Day's front teeth, cutting his own knuckles in the process. This made the guard quite angry, and he slapped Day so hard that he ruptured the prisoner's eardrum.

When Day was dragged off to the quiz room on the morning of the sixth day, his buttocks and thighs were swollen and puffed out about three inches. Atop the hamburger-like flesh, from the middle of his thighs up to the small of his back, a scab was trying to form. Day's lower legs were twice their normal size, and his toes were like overstuffed sausages. A watery fluid oozed from his testicles.

The leg irons and hell cuffs were forced on him.

He dropped his pants and slumped to the floor on the wet place where his blood was trying to congeal atop that of other POWs.

Prayers were not enough. He was forced deep into himself, to the very core of his being. In that dark hour he found the rock to which he would cling, the words that symbolized his deepest beliefs and his deepest desire. If he died, these words would be his last thought.

Return with Honor.

That day he did what every POW did under sustained torture. He broke. He knew he had been crippled for life. He knew he was at the point of death. So he talked. But when he talked, he offered only lies. When the interrogator wanted to know about various escape committees and their functions, Day said there was a transportation committee whose job was to line up trucks to haul POWs out of Hanoi after the next escape. He gave them the names of every committee that every military organization for two hundred years had formed, information so trivial and so frivolous that he was amazed the guards accepted it.

"Who are the committee members?"

"I am the only member of each committee."

The fan belts ripped the scab from his back and flayed his testicles. He said everyone in his building was on every committee, an equal impossibility.

Return with Honor.

That night he was ordered back on the stool. His buttocks were so raw he could not sit on them, so he sat at an angle on his hips. When he fell asleep he was beaten and put on his knees.

Sometime during that long night, he began projectile vomiting a mixture of blood and bile. Uncontrollable bloody diarrhea racked his body. A blood vessel in his stomach had been ruptured from the beating. He slumped in a pool of blood and vomit and piss and shit.

The guards were disgusted.

Return with Honor.

The guard put him on his knees. When he collapsed, the guard beat him until he awakened.

It was not his battered body that he thought about that night. He knew that if he lived, one day the pain would end. But the suffering that came with violating the Code of Conduct would last forever. Never mind that everything he told his guards was fiction or useless information. Never mind that every POW sooner or later talked to the enemy. All Bud Day could think of was that he had gone beyond name, rank, serial number, and date of birth: the Big Four. He was ashamed of himself, and his suffering knew no limits.

The next morning the guard looked at the stinking scarecrow before him and asked, "How do you think of your treatment by the humane and lenient Vietnamese people?"

"My treatment is brutal, uncivilized, inhumane, and far below the standards of the Geneva convention."

"Drop pants."

The guards knew Day was at the point of death, and the beatings lessened in severity. Still, July became August and the beatings continued. The guards wanted Day to write a statement saying the war was immoral. But Day did not have the luxury of free speech that civilians had; he was a serving military officer in the hands of the enemy, and he was bound by the Code of Conduct. He did what he did with full knowledge of the consequences.

"I can't do that."

As the beating began, he shut his eyes, his mind traveled to a different place, and he held on to his rock:

Return with Honor.

By now the guard and Day had fallen into a verbal shorthand.

"Write or not?"

"No write. Never."

"You write."

"No."

"Drop pants."

The beatings continued on a daily basis, but now he received maybe a dozen lashes. Years later he would remember and say, "Happiness is a short quiz."

Sometime near mid-September the beatings ended and Day was dragged off to solitary. The door was barely closed before he crawled to the wall and began tapping that he had been in daily quiz for months and was in bad shape physically and mentally. "Do not send any camp news," he said. "I don't want to know anything that might get someone else tortured."

Larry Guarino tapped back that Day had made his country proud, that he had performed as a U.S. military officer should perform by continuing to be strong. He ended by saying that twenty-six POWs had been beaten to the edge of death. But a few days later, Air Force major Leo Thorsness tapped a message saying that none of the men in the Barn had been tortured because of anything Day said during the quiz.

Day wept.

In June 1969, Doris enrolled at a local junior college and took a course titled On Being a Better Parent.

Many times that summer she awakened in the middle of the night — midday in Hanoi — with the sense that something was terribly wrong. She took Bud's picture down from the dresser and talked to him. She stared into his determined eyes, and it was almost as if he were talking back to her, thinking of her at the same time she was thinking so longingly of him. Many times the thought came to her that he could be sick and dying, that he might not come home.

Doris spent her days cartwheeling from grief to hope. The greatest pain of all was not knowing whether Bud was dead or alive, whether she was a wife or a widow. In this limbo she had only raw courage for sustenance.

Her burden was greater because of the four children. They were uneasy. Once, they had seen her cry and were visibly frightened. At some level they must have been haunted by the fear of again being without a father. She had to remain always upbeat.

But there were times when she went to the bathroom, locked the door, and sobbed.

Doris became coordinator of family services at Luke AFB, the top civilian volunteer on the big base. She continued to visit every local newspaper, radio station, and TV station to talk about POWs. She knew as many reporters and columnists and editors as anyone in Phoenix. She became friends with the mayor and with Arizona congressmen. Anytime she called, the governor came to the phone. She made speeches to any group that would listen. (She recorded every speech so that, when he returned, Bud would know exactly what she had said.) She wrote letters to the North Vietnamese government. Meanwhile, Ross Perot and his people met with many of the POW wives, and together they became an increasingly powerful consortium.

On August 26, 1969, the second anniversary of Bud's shoot-down, Doris felt particularly low. She knew that things were just not right with Bud. She sewed much of the day. When she was sad and lonely, she always scrubbed the house. That evening she sent the children to bed early and stayed up scrubbing the walls until 2 a.m.

She was worried about how she was handling the family real estate investments back in Sioux City. She had someone who was supposed to be doing maintenance. But she had gotten word that the city was about to condemn one of her rental buildings, a structure containing four apartments. Bit by bit, her world seemed to be falling apart.

THE middle years for the POWs ended on September 3, 1969, with the tolling of bells in Hanoi. The guards were mopey and morose; some shed tears. Word got out to the POWs: Ho Chi Minh is dead.

Ho's death marked the end of their systematic and institutionalized torture. The Americans were still occasionally beaten but usually for taunting the guards or flagrantly disobeying camp rules. Day was thus the last American POW to undergo a prolonged period of torture. Afterward, he remained in solitary, in leg irons, and under intense pressure to write a letter saying the war was immoral — the only person in camp still under maximum pressure. Every guard, every cook, every functionary, was committed to making his life one of continuing misery. But even Day sensed things were getting better. He was allowed to wash his pajamas and told to take a shower, his first in months. His back and legs were so sensitive that the harsh lye soap seared his skin. Walking was so painful that he wondered if his knees were permanently damaged.

Another event that had an impact on North Vietnamese thinking about the POWs was that in July, Secretary of State William Rogers had said Hanoi was "lacking humanity" in treatment of POWs. And in August, forty-two U.S. senators issued a statement condemning North Vietnam for its "cruel" treatment of American POWs. The North Vietnamese responded in the usual fashion, that the Americans were not POWs; they were criminals. North Vietnam did not have to identify its criminals nor did it have to release the sick and wounded nor did it have to allow Red Cross inspections. But by now, this response was sounding hollow, and the North Vietnamese knew that.

Still another event that brought on better treatment for the POWs was a press conference held by three more early releases.

Ironically, the press conference occurred on the day that Ho Chi Minh died.

One of the returnees was Seaman Douglas Hegdahl, a nineteen-year-old ammunition handler aboard a Navy ship who, without permission, went topside one night to watch a bombardment and fell overboard. He was picked up by fishermen and turned over to North Vietnamese militia. To the guards, he was a simple, uneducated enlisted man hardly worth their attention. But Hegdahl had a phenomenal memory and knew the names of almost four hundred POWs. Because of this, and because the POWs wanted their identities known to the world, Hegdahl was ordered by superior officers to accept an early release. The two officers with him were under no such orders and were then and are today considered by those they left behind as part of the Fink Release Program.

During the press conference, Hegdahl recounted in stark detail the abuses being suffered by POWs. His account reverberated across America and added to the growing backlash against the North Vietnamese.

Soon afterward, three more POWs were released: Fred Thompson, Joe Carpenter, and Jim Low. Before he was released, Thompson made a tape that was played over "CBS" in which he urged the POWs to follow camp regulations. Guards told the POWs that Thompson had a "good attitude." Day was mortified that all three releases were Air Force officers.

The American media, for the first time, were beginning to take a serious look at the POWs. It started with a cover story in the October issue of *Air Force* magazine. The story was titled "The Forgotten Americans of the Vietnam War" and was reprinted as the lead article in the November issue of *Reader's Digest*. References to the article continued for months. During that stretch, the POWs enjoyed a period of relative calm.

On October 2, Day was given a package from Doris. The package included pictures of the four children. Day reverently sorted through the box and realized all his prayers had been answered.

His family was alive and well. He had written nothing and signed nothing that would have disgraced him. Not one word of criticism against America had escaped his lips.

Rules about the content and weight of packages sent to Hanoi were rigid. Doris found that when she weighed the package, it was several ounces lighter than the maximum. She wanted to send as many items as possible, but what weighed only a few ounces? She settled on a pink nail file. After Day received the package, word went out across the prison camp: Bud Day uses a pink nail file. Other POWs frequently asked if he remembered to push back his cuticles.

Two weeks later, Day was taken out of irons. His spirits raised, his objections became more intense. One day in early December he was loudly protesting his treatment and demanding more privileges for his men. When he was told to be quiet, he said, "You can all go to hell."

About that time another guard came to his room and pushed an American inside. Navy pilot Jack Fellowes of Tucson, Arizona, looked at Day in amazement. The twisted arms, the swollen and bloody knees with the bones shining through, the rust-covered wrists and ankles, told the story — that and the hamburger-like backs of his legs. And the man's eyes. My God, Fellowes thought, they looked like black holes, but they glistened with an unquenchable fire. The frail man wobbled when he tried to stand. His right arm was bowed and his hands were curled.

Whoever he was, this man was a tough resister.

Bud Day's face broke into a big smile. He stuck out his hand. "Hello, pal. I'm Bud Day."

Fellowes's eyes widened. American POWs were scattered in a dozen camps around Hanoi and even up on the Chinese border. But they were shuffled from camp to camp, and most of them had heard the story of Bud Day. It was said that he was one tough son of a bitch, that when he looked at one of his captors, you could strike matches on his eyes. It was said that the very sight of a

North Vietnamese guard made the hair on the back of his neck stand up in anger. And here he was, just after enduring six weeks of the worst that teams of North Vietnamese torturers could dish out, and he was telling them to go to hell.

By late 1969, Norris Overly, the man who had saved the lives of Bud Day and John McCain, was a sought-after speaker. He addressed universities, civic groups, congressional committees, military Dining Ins, state legislatures, the Air Force Academy, and CIA employees. From coast to coast, Overly got standing ovations. He was a former POW and everyone wanted to touch the hem of his garment. He even had a private chat with the Air Force chief of staff.

Overly had made lieutenant colonel during his brief time as a POW and made full colonel not long after he returned. Every promotion since captain had been below the zone. Kidney stones kept him off flying status, but basically any desk job in the Air Force was his for the asking. He picked the Air Force Personnel Center, then under the command of Major General Robert Dixon, the same man Bud Day had invited out on the ramp to fight back in Korea.

Dixon decided which colonels would become generals and boasted that he had destroyed the careers of more colonels than any man in Air Force history. He was a loud, angry man whose nickname was "The Alligator." He terrified his subordinates, but the Air Force would continue promoting him all the way to four-star rank.

Overly thrived in Dixon's office, and Dixon was delighted to have in his command the glamorous former POW, so much so that he helped Overly receive a prestigious assignment to the National War College.

On November 15, 1969, some 250,000 people marched on Washington, the largest antiwar protest in American history.

In December 1969, Ross Perot chartered two jets from Braniff Airlines. One he jammed with everything from Bibles to Christmas dinners and then announced he was taking the goods to the American POWs. The second jet was filled with POW wives and flown to Paris for an appeal to the Vietnamese diplomatic mission there. The North Vietnamese would not allow Perot's food and medicine-laden aircraft to land in Hanoi, but the media coverage as he bounced around Southeast Asia focused world attention on the plight of the POWs, caused considerable embarrassment to the North Vietnamese, and made the Nixon administration wonder if Perot was a loose cannon. The POWs had no such reservations. When the guards told them of "Ross Pirate," they knew he was their friend — indeed, more than that. For the remainder of their lives, the POWs would consider Ross Perot their hero. Day hoped that one day he could meet the combative Texan.

12

The Years of the Locust

AFTER several weeks of recovery, Day, though still wobbly, resumed his job as SRO. His first order was vintage Day: he told the men under his command to cease bowing to the guards.

The next morning the Bug came to preside over the head count and Day refused to bow. It was an act of extraordinary defiance. No matter that the rules were somewhat relaxed in the aftermath of Ho's death, such defiance could not go unpunished.

Again, the Bug ordered Day to bow.

"Back off or I will order my men not to stand up when your guards enter the rooms," Day said.

Fellowes rolled his eyes in amazement. Day could barely stand, and he was defying the Bug.

"I'm tired of bowing to these little pricks," Day told Fellowes.

When Day was not tortured, the POWs knew change was in the air.

Even so, discipline and good order had to be maintained. The Bug's countermove was brilliant. A guard came to the cell and told Day and Fellowes that each could write a letter to his wife. These were the first letters they had been allowed to write. Once finished, they were to bring the letters to the Bug, who would proofread them for proper content before mailing them.

Day and Fellowes walked into the Bug's office carrying their letters. The Bug insisted they bow. Day did not miss a beat. He bent forward so low that his head almost touched his knees, a sign not of respect but of contempt.

The Bug screamed and waved his arms, and his right eye began an erratic journey. He knew that if Day bowed correctly, those under his command would follow.

The Bug smiled and tapped the letters on his desk. Unless Day and Fellowes bowed in a proper, respectful fashion, there would be no letters home to their wives.

"Pound sand," Day said.

The Bug did not understand the colloquialism. But he did understand the tone. He had a guard march Day and Fellowes back to their cell. It would be another year before they were allowed to write home.

PERHAPS nothing reveals Day's constant and unending defiance as much as a single game of checkers.

As the mood of the prison relaxed, one of the guards began playing checkers with the POWs. Each day he would take his board and his checkers and go into individual cells to play. An unofficial agreement among the POWs was to let the guard win. The thinking was that this made the guard feel good and might in some small way lessen the indignities they had to endure.

Day's reputation was such that the guard never asked him to play.

As time went by, the guard defeated every POW in the building, not once but numerous times. This must have given him great confidence because one morning he walked up to Day in the courtyard and said he wanted to play checkers.

Day stared at him a long moment. "Okay."

As the guard walked away to get his checkerboard, Fellowes turned to Day and asked, "What are you going to do?"

"I'm going to whip his ass."

The guard was jovial and expansive as he set up the checkerboard. Fellowes remembers that Day was very intense and studied every move.

He trounced the guard so quickly and so thoroughly that the man was humiliated. The guard stormed out of the room and never again played checkers with a POW.

Fellowes looked at Day with raised eyebrows.

"I didn't want the son of a bitch in my room anyway."

IN January 1970, Ross Perot offered the North Vietnamese $100 million to free the POWs. The North Vietnamese refused and went on "CBS" ridiculing "Ross Pirate." The affection and respect the POWs had for Perot continued to grow.

IT was a few months later that Norris Overly went to Paris to talk with North Vietnam diplomats about the plight of POWs. Overly says the idea for the trip originated in the Pentagon.

He flew to Paris, reported in at the American embassy, then rode the metro out to the distant suburb where the North Vietnamese diplomatic mission was housed and knocked on the door.

"I told them they were making a mistake sending home healthy guys like me. 'Why not release the sick and wounded?' I asked them. 'Why don't you release John McCain?' "

He spent about three fruitless hours talking with a diplomat. When he returned to the States, he reported in as a student at the National War College, a necessary assignment before a colonel can be promoted to general.

OCTOBER rolled around and Day marked his third year in Hanoi. He was one of six men in Heartbreak Hotel, a cell block within the Hilton, and was SRO by default, as Navy commander Ken Cameron had been beaten senseless and was unable to command. Air Force captain Earl Cobeil had been driven insane by torture. Navy lieutenant J. J. Connell was a hard resister who had endured great torture. Day frequently had asked for medical help for the three men, for Red Cross packages they were entitled to receive, for writing materials. The standard answer was "In some moments," which meant never. In mid-October the guards took away Cameron, Cobeil, and Connell, and they were never seen again. Later the North Vietnamese said they had died in a hospital. But Day knew the guards had killed the three Americans.

Now only he and Fellowes and Ben Pollard were in Heartbreak. Their names and the fact that they were prisoners had never been made public by North Vietnam. If the guards had already killed three men, who was to say that the remaining three wouldn't also disappear?

That thought did not slow Day's resistance. He found that by unhooking the wires from the speakers in his cell and rubbing them together, he could short out the entire camp radio system — he could take "CBS" off the air. Thereafter, whenever he did not like what was on the radio — which was often — he shorted out the system and that was that.

EARLY Sunday morning on November 21, 1970, the POWs were awakened by the sound of distant explosions. U.S. Special Forces had made a daring raid into Son Tay, a POW camp about twenty miles southwest of Hanoi, and had killed numerous guards. But the main purpose of the raid — rescue of POWs held there — did not happen because the prisoners had been moved to another camp some four months earlier.

Many in America ridiculed the military and said the raid was a dismal failure. But a bellicose Mendel Rivers, the South Carolina congressman who was then head of the House Armed Services Committee, said the raid showed that American forces could go into Hanoi if they chose. The North Vietnamese must have believed him, because a few days later, all of the American POWs in North Vietnam were moved into Hoa Lo, and many of them were placed in large rooms. For the first time in all their years of captivity, the POWs were together. Men who had tapped messages to each other but had never met now saw each other face-to-face.

New shoot-downs told some of the old heads that no one had seen their parachutes and that they were considered dead. The family of a POW named Porter Halyburton had even held a funeral for him and placed a marker on his grave. Yet here he was, alive.

The POWs appeared to have been jammed helter-skelter into six of the big rooms at the Hilton. But one chamber was different: the guards gave considerable thought to which POWs they placed in Room 7, a twenty-five by seventy–foot room in the back courtyard. That room was for the hard cases.

Today Americans tend to lump all the POWs into one group. That is wrong. The sharpest division is between the twelve men who came home early (excluding Hegdahl) and those who remained until the spring of 1973. If ever you meet a man who was a POW, the first question to ask is "Were you an early release?" If he says yes, you may wish to walk away. If he says no, ask him what room he was in at the Hilton in late 1972. If he says he was in Room 7, you may wish to shake his hand because you are talking to a hard-assed resister, a defiant and unbending air pirate with a bad attitude, a true American hero. Bud Day was there. So were James Stockdale, Robbie Risner, and John McCain. Day and McCain had not seen each other since the spring of 1968. McCain told Day the guards had broken his arm during a quiz. "Damn, John. You must have pissed them off," Day said, thrilled to see his friend alive and still feisty.

In a few more months, Room 7 would become the most famous room in Hoa Lo.

On June 26, 1970, the North Vietnamese for the first time released a list of names of Americans who were captive — 335 of them. Bud Day's name was not included.

Doris was filled with dread. There had been more early releases, and several of those men had called her to say they either had seen

Bud or had heard of him. But if the North Vietnamese would not publicly acknowledge the name of a man — even if he was known to be a POW — that man could disappear and there would be no accounting.

General Chappie James, the Air Force officer in charge of dealing with the POW/MIA wives, came to Luke. Doris had been picked as Military Wife of the Year at Luke and had been a finalist for Air Force Wife of the Year. She was no retiring flower and she was not going to be dissuaded by double-talking Air Force generals. She had hard, specific questions for James. But he was evasive. "We don't want to draw attention to the POWs," he said.

By now, Doris and other wives were writing letters by the hundreds to Hanoi. They were generating more and more newspaper and television coverage of the POWs. With Ross Perot backing them and with the Nixon administration showing an ever-increasing interest in the POWs, the wives sensed a change was coming. But they also knew that with each passing day the chance of loss was even greater.

In late summer of 1970, the Mistys were disbanded. The air war, like the ground war, was winding down. Almost one-fourth of the Mistys had been shot down, some of them several times. And the Mistys had worn out so many F-100Fs that there were simply not enough left in the inventory to carry on.

Former Mistys back in the States decided to mark the occasion with a reunion at Luke AFB. They had a lot to celebrate, as the Mistys had become one of the most storied outfits in Vietnam.

So much had happened since Misty 1 had been shot down. Someone had designed a shoulder flash for them, the word MISTY stitched in white letters against a dark blue background with a red border.

The Mistys had a highly unusual refueling technique, used by no other pilots in Vietnam. Ordinarily a fighter pilot approached a fuel-laden tanker in a very cautious manner. He slowed down, pulled up off the tanker's wing until the speed of the two aircraft was equal, then gently slid in behind the tanker to receive the refueling boom. The departure was equally cautious: a slow and easy drift out to the side until he cleared the tanker, and then a gentle turn.

Not the Mistys. They radioed the tanker, "My nose is cold" — cannons are switched off — "requesting a Misty approach." They zoomed in behind the enormous lumbering tanker, homing in like a beagle sniffing a Saint Bernard, hooked up, topped off, then asked for a "Misty departure," which meant they backed off slightly on the throttle, rolled that puppy inverted, and dove for the deck.

Shit hot!

As part of his indoctrination, every new Misty had been told the story of the outfit's first commanding officer, every new Misty given the mandate to carry on with the same aggressive nature. And at every gathering, every going-home party, the Mistys raised their glasses and offered a toast: "To Misty One and his safe return."

Bill Douglass was a key figure in the Misty reunion at Luke. On his first tour in Vietnam he was a Bird Dog pilot who was shot down and wounded. On his second tour he was a Misty. Then he came back on a third tour as a Thud driver so he could drop bombs on the people who held Bud Day in jail.

When Douglass organized the gathering, he decreed that since Misty 1 was a POW, this had to be a practice reunion. The real thing would be held when the boss returned.

Douglass called Doris and told her that Bud's outfit was meeting at Luke and she was invited. She laughed when she heard that they were called "Misty." Bud loved that song so much.

This was the first time that any of the Mistys had met Doris, and in the beginning the party moved slowly and was very awkward. What do you say to a woman whose husband is in jail? By now the Mistys knew something of the torture the POWs were experiencing. A Misty named Jack Doub had access to highly classified intelligence reports that said Day was being singled out for special torture and might no longer be alive.

But Doris made every Misty relax. Every pilot sat and talked with her, and she made them feel as if they had known each other for years. They talked of Bud as if he might walk in the door any minute.

The party began to loosen up. There was talk of how during a refueling, Charlie Neel stood up in the pit to urinate into a bottle. He looked up at the tanker and saw a camerawoman from a television network shooting tape of the refueling. Exactly what he said over the radio has become garbled with time, but it was something about pleasing the viewing audience back home.

There was talk of Dick Rutan, who, when he had the first predawn flight of the day, would switch on his clearance lights and turn them up brightly so the North Vietnamese gunners would fire at him. And Ed Risinger, who, as a captain and on his own initiative, commandeered three aircraft and led the later-famous "Risinger Raid" into North Vietnam to bomb a SAM site. And the party really loosened up when Ron Fogleman, who later would become a four-star and the chief of staff, swung on a chandelier and sent it crashing to the floor.

At some point in the evening, the Mistys grew serious and presented Doris with a large silver snifter, on which was engraved:

HOLD FOR RETURN OF
LT. COL. GEORGE DAY
MISTY ONE
1ST PRACTICE REUNION 18 JULY 1970

"We'll fill it with champagne when Bud comes home," Douglass said. "He can drink it down at the first reunion." He began talking of what a great leader Bud was and how he set such a high standard for Mistys to follow. Douglass became so emotional he could not continue.

But The Viking could.

She stood up, and her voice carried to every corner of the room. Every Misty stopped what he was doing and gave Doris his full attention. "Bud is very proud of all of you," she said. "He wrote me and said he was flying with the finest men he had ever known."

She talked for about ten minutes and ended by saying, "I pray this is our last practice reunion." She raised her glass and asked the Mistys to join her in a toast. "To my tiger. May he never lose his fight."

All around her, men who had flown down the barrels of AAA guns were weeping.

In December 1970, Senator Ted Kennedy went to Hanoi and brought back an updated list of POWs that, for the first time, included Bud Day's name. After more than three years, the North Vietnamese had finally acknowledged his presence.

A few weeks later, Doris received a package of four letters from Bud. One was dated in September, another in late October, and two more on November 23.

By early 1971 the POWs were experiencing more leniency on the part of the guards and entered into a period of relative calm. In that calm, Day's ideas about forging the POWs into a separate and distinct military unit became more firmly rooted. He tapped out a message to Colonel John Flynn, the senior American prisoner, that the POWs should organize themselves into the 4th Allied POW Wing. The 4th because the Vietnam War was, after World War I, World War II, and Korea, the fourth American war of the century. He told Flynn there was only one appropriate motto: *Return with Honor.* And just because a man had been a POW did not automatically mean he was eligible for membership. Those who came home in the Fink Release Program would not be eligible. Nor would the small group of officers and enlisted personnel who had collaborated.

Flynn endorsed the idea and tapped out a message to that effect.

The POWs began conducting classes about ten hours each day. Day taught business and construction law, contracts, and how to invest in real estate. Other officers taught everything from playing golf (the bamboo "shit stick" used to push fecal matter down a trough served as the club) to architecture to physics to philosophy to math to a half dozen languages. Day became relatively proficient in French and German. The POWs talked of what they wanted to do when they returned to America. One of the favorite ideas was to fly a fighter under the Golden Gate Bridge.

As the guards became more lenient, the POWs became more boisterous. Jim Stockdale sensed how quickly and how viciously the guards could react and tapped out a message telling the POWs to "learn to live with prosperity." But these were, all things considered, good times.

And the fighter pilots who, during the brutal years, had obeyed orders without question now were beginning to be fractious and contentious. They argued endlessly about the meaning and intent of the Code of Conduct, especially the phrase that if captured, "I am required to give only" the Big Four. What did "required" really mean? What did "only" really mean?

It was here that Bud Day's great strength as a leader emerged. And again, it was the sensibilities of a Midwesterner that seized the day. He brooked none of the onanistic arguments from the men under his command. It was all very simple, very straightforward, very unequivocal. And the "SRO is the only guy around here with a vote that counts." POWs in other rooms disagreed with their SROs on virtually everything. But not in Room 7.

As the men grew more rambunctious, the guards grew sullen. The showdown came on Sunday, February 7, 1971, when the POWs in Room 7 decided to hold an organized church service, the first ever in Hoa Lo. The Bug was advised in advance and ordered the POWs not to meet. But plans continued. Robbie Risner, who knew church liturgy as well as any minister, led the service.

The concept of church was unknown to the Bug. It was okay for the POWs to stand around in small groups and talk. But the

Bug equated one man standing in front of a group with the Communist political indoctrination session. To the Bug, Risner was talking his fellow POWs into rebellion.

Risner began by leading the men of Room 7 in the Pledge of Allegiance. The Bug came to the window and ordered him to sit down. Risner ignored him. The POWs sang "Rock of Ages" and "The Old Rugged Cross," and Risner began preaching.

Suddenly the door banged open, and the Bug, accompanied by armed guards, bayonets at the ready, entered, seized Risner, and marched him off to quiz.

After the relaxed attitude of the past few months, this turn of events was shocking. The POWs watched almost in disbelief.

In that frozen moment, Bud Day jumped atop one of the concrete beds, waved his arms in the air, and began singing.

Oh, say can you see
By the dawn's early light

The POWs turned to look at him and a few joined in.

What so prooooooudly we hailed

Now everyone in the room joined in. And with great volume.

At the twilight's last gleaming

Larry Guarino interrupted and began chanting, "This is number seven, number seven, number seven. This is number seven. Where the hell is six?"

The men of Room 6 chimed in.

Gave prooooofff through the night that our flag was still there

Then Room 5 kicked in, followed by Rooms 4, 3, 2, and 1.

(A structure in the courtyard, where the collaborators were housed, did not participate.)

Oh say, does that star spangled banner yet wave
O'er the laaannnd of the free and the hoooomme of the brave

Robbie Risner heard the singing, and his back straightened and his head was high. Later he said he had "felt nine feet tall" when he heard Bud Day leading the POWs in singing the National Anthem.

The song had barely ended before Day began another one. Bud Day is not a singer. But he had the volume and the passion, and everyone knew the words.

My country 'tis of thee, sweet land of liberty

This time the other rooms joined in immediately. And when the chorus came, hundreds of American voices soared up and over the walls of Hoa Lo and through the streets of Hanoi. From every corner of that old and fearsome place of horror and death, a place that had echoed with screams of anguish for more than a half century, voices for the first time were raised in pride and exultation. And it was a song that allowed the POWs to release all that their guards had tried for years to suppress, a song that gave words to their fight, a song that lifted them beyond the walls and back to all that was dear to them.

Goooooooddddd bless America, my hoooooommmmeeee sweet hoooooommeeee

And outside in the streets of Hanoi, passersby, who often averted their eyes when they passed Hoa Lo, stopped in bewilderment. Those were American voices. And they could be heard for blocks.

Hoa Lo was rocking.

Goooooooooddddd bless America, my hoooooommmmmeee sweet hoooooooommmee

On that Sunday morning, the POWs sang every song they could recall. The Air Force Hymn, the Navy Hymn, the Army Hymn, and the Marine Corps Hymn. Then they sang "California, Here I Come" and "Yellow Rose of Texas" and "Georgia on My Mind" and "Sioux City Sue."

The Bug came back, this time with dozens of soldiers. The chin straps on their helmets were snuggled down tightly and bayonets were at the ready. They ran into the room and backed every POW up against the wall with a bayonet tip in his belly. What the guards later referred to as the "Church Riot" was quelled. The guards thought they had prevailed.

But from that moment, the big rooms were known as Camp Unity. And for the rest of their lives, men would be proud they had been in Room 7.

THE day after the "riot," Orson Swindle, a big Marine pilot, tapped a message saying, "You have to stand in line to get in trouble with that crowd." In a short time, Day would meet Swindle, who, along with McCain, would become one of his closest and most lasting friends. Swindle, like many of the POWs, was from a small town — Camilla, Georgia — and had small-town values. He was raised by a grandmother whose constant admonition was "Do the right thing." He was a roguish fellow who, other POWs acknowledge, was the unsurpassed master at giving guards a "fuck you" look.

The Bug considered Bud Day the instigator of the riot; after all, it was he who jumped atop the bed and led the other prisoners in song. The Bug called Day to quiz and lambasted him as a black criminal with a bad attitude, a Yankee air pirate who had killed many women and children and who had never been sincere, never respected the humane and lenient treatment afforded by the people of Vietnam. And then, curiously, he gave Day a letter from Doris. It was his first letter in three years.

Day was now forty-six years old. He was becoming deaf and his eyes were beginning to dim, in large part from being beaten in the face and temples so many times. Day could not read the letter and told the Bug he needed glasses.

"You are an old man," the Bug gloated. "You are going blind. Your wife may take a new husband because you are so crippled."

"Yeah," replied Day, "and she probably has gone to work in the Pentagon for the CIA."

Later, the Bug went through all the rooms at Hoa Lo and picked out the malcontents, the incorrigibles, and the troublemakers. On March 17, the guards loaded thirty-six of these men on a truck. Among them was Bud Day, SRO. McCain and Swindle and Fellowes were also on board. The men were taken to Skid Row, a camp about ten miles southwest of Hanoi.

As they were hauled away, someone said, "Well, there go the Hells Angels."

The North Vietnamese POW camps were all different levels of squalor and misery. Skid Row was among the worst. It was a long building with eighteen cells on either side. Each cell measured six feet by four feet and was a fetid mud hole. The building had no electric lights and no bathing facilities. There was no ventilation.

Bud Day was put on his knees for a day and a night and then pushed into his cell. He celebrated his fourth anniversary as a POW in solitary.

In that bleak place, he remembered the English professor at Morningside who had made him memorize poetry. Then, he had thought it was a waste of time. Now he rejoiced that he remembered and could recite aloud a verse from one of the poems forced upon him:

> *Stone walls do not a prison make,*
> *Nor iron bars a cage;*
> *Minds innocent and quiet take*
> *That for an hermitage;*
> *If I have freedom in my love*
> *And in my soul am free,*
> *Angels alone, that soar above,*
> *Enjoy such liberty.*

THAT Friday afternoon he tapped "HH."

Sunday morning he tapped out a strong "CC." And the Hells Angels stood up, faced east toward America, recited the Pledge of Allegiance, and prayed in their individual ways.

Monsoon rains began early in 1971 and were particularly heavy. The Red River rose and threatened to inundate Skid Row. On June 17, Day and his posse were moved back to Hoa Lo.

POWs peeped through cracks in the doors or slits in the windows and watched the Hells Angels return. They were gaunt and hollow-eyed and limping and covered with filth, but they swaggered. They were the toughest sons of bitches in the Red River Valley, and Bud Day was their leader.

Day and the other malcontents were thrown into Room 2 at Heartbreak Hotel, the most brutal part of Hoa Lo. They were in the cell adjacent to Larry Guarino. One day word went out that Guarino was about to be taken out for exercise. Day peeped through the slit under the door, expecting to see the giant of a man who for years had been sending out such stirring messages of resistance. Guarino was a scrawny little guy who weighed no more than a hundred pounds. Guarino's scarred wrists and ankles and his swollen knees told his story, and his eyes revealed his fighting spirit. Day wept when he saw him.

Most of Day's posse would remain together until they were repatriated. Day was SRO, and as his communications officers he chose McCain and Swindle, two of the most facile "flaggers." McCain would stand on Swindle's shoulders and flag messages through the window to other POWs. (Swindle was the better communicator, but McCain pulled rank on him and stood on his shoulders.)

Day and McCain and Swindle talked politics endlessly. It was here that Day realized he no longer was a Democrat; he had become a Republican, and he thought Richard Nixon and Ronald Reagan were great leaders. The three men particularly liked the tough stance that both Nixon and the California governor had taken against war protesters and demonstrators.

EXCEPT for caring for her four children, Doris Day's sole focus in life was working on POW/MIA issues. She was a child of the heartland, unsophisticated and inexperienced in many matters. But she never doubted that she could change the government of America and the government of North Vietnam. Her husband was in jail and she wanted him home, and she would do whatever it took.

In the spring of 1971, the National League of Families chartered a jet to fly to Geneva for a Red Cross rally, the purpose of which was to appeal to North Vietnam to release the sick and injured POWs.

Doris wanted to go. The four children would understand. She was seeking information about their dad.

Before she left, she attended a dinner to receive an award for her advocacy. Air Force general Chappie James was there and tried to discourage her from taking the trip to Switzerland. "If you were my wife, I wouldn't want you to go," he said.

"Well, Chappie, that's the big difference," she snapped. "You are not Bud Day. He would understand."

James said dealing with representatives of a foreign country was the job of the State Department.

"We don't have diplomatic relations with North Vietnam," Doris replied.

Once the Department of Defense and the State Department realized the wives could not be dissuaded, they relented enough to brief the wives before they departed.

Doris hired a nanny to stay at the house. The woman came the day before Doris left. That night Doris showed her the food she had prepared for the nine days she would be gone. Clothes for those nine days were lined up for each child.

On May 21, she flew to Dallas and then to Dulles, and from there to Geneva. She was among 174 POW/MIA family members.

In Geneva, the family members split into different groups. Doris's party elected to go to Sweden to visit the North Vietnamese embassy in Stockholm. Since she spoke Norwegian, she could understand a bit of Swedish.

Once in Stockholm, she was so nervous that she had diarrhea and was vomiting. But she got control of herself, called the Embassy of the Democratic Republic of Vietnam, and asked for an appointment. When she was told to come to the embassy, she said, "Not just me. My friends also. We have traveled a long way."

The four women and one POW father showed up at the embassy and were escorted to a large room with a big coffee table and lace curtains on the open windows. A large picture of Ho

Chi Minh was on the wall, and a vase filled with red tulips sat in the middle of the coffee table. As they waited, they remembered one part of the State Department briefing: expect the room to be bugged.

The women looked around the room. "I think the bug is behind Uncle Ho," Doris said.

"No, it is in the tulips," said another.

"No, I think it will be in the cuff links of whoever we see," said a third.

After about twenty minutes the consul entered and greeted each wife by name. Doris found to her astonishment that the consul spoke beautiful English. She would not need to speak Norwegian or to have a translator.

The consul sat at the big table and shot his cuffs. He was wearing very large cuff links. The wives tried hard not to laugh.

The slender Vietnamese man took the initiative by opening a folder filled with pictures of babies killed in Vietnam. "This is why your husband is in prison," he said to Doris. "He kills women and children, and bombs churches."

"No, my husband is a good and decent man." She pointed at the pictures. "Those people in the pictures look as if they are in South Vietnam."

Another wife agreed. "Those pictures were taken in South Vietnam."

The consul did not like these aggressive American women and launched into a litany of crimes alleged to have been perpetrated by their husbands.

"But what about the Geneva convention?" asked Doris.

"These men are criminals. The Geneva convention does not apply to criminals."

"I have not heard from my husband," Doris said. She was determined to keep the initiative, to talk about the wives' agenda and not the consul's.

"Mrs. Day, how can you say that? You received a letter in the last group sent out."

She was shocked. How did a consul in Stockholm know she had received a letter in Phoenix?

"He is not receiving packages."

"How do you know that?"

The consul opened another folder and took from it picture after picture of civil rights disturbances, of antiwar marches. He had newspaper clippings from each wife's state of residence. He asked Doris about prison riots in Arizona.

She was stunned. The idea that the North Vietnamese subscribed to a clipping service covering such stories rattled her. But there was more.

"Mrs. Day, we don't want your son coming to our country to fight in a few years."

Doris was speechless. The consul knew that Steve was almost of draft age.

When she left she knew that the consul, and the government he represented, did not care if her husband was in jail another year or another ten years.

This was an even bigger battle than she had realized. Doris knew she would have to become even more active in politics. George McGovern was running against Nixon and supported a unilateral withdrawal of American troops from Vietnam, a move that would have left the POWs to the mercy of the North Vietnamese. Nixon was her man.

On July 2, 1971, the *Phoenix Gazette* quoted Doris as praising the Nixon administration, and speaking on behalf of POW/MIA wives, she said Nixon "has our total and unqualified support." She said the wives, unlike much of America and for obvious reasons, opposed an immediate and unilateral withdrawal from Vietnam. She received a letter of thanks from Nixon, the first of a half dozen he would send her.

That was important to Doris. But even more important was the fact that the Lutherans at St. John Lutheran Church back in Sioux City continued to pray for her husband. And they did.

13

The Freedom Bird

As was the case in 1968, the Vietnam War was the pivotal issue in the 1972 presidential campaign, and the two candidates — Richard Nixon and George McGovern — could not have been more opposite in their views. The hawkish Nixon wanted a military victory and to bring the POWs home. The dovish McGovern wanted America to pull out of Vietnam immediately and to settle the POW issue later.

The antiwar movement was at the height of its power, and McGovern was its darling. Nevertheless, the movement did not have a face; there was no single leader.

That changed on April 22, 1971, in Room 4221 of the New Senate Office Building. At 11:05 a.m., Senator J. W. Fulbright, chairman of the Committee on Foreign Relations, called his committee to order and asked a twenty-seven-year-old Vietnam veteran to speak. The decorated veteran was a reserve naval officer and a leader of a group called Vietnam Veterans Against the War. Handsome and eloquent, he delivered a showstopping speech, flawless in presentation and devastating in content.

He began by saying that his presence was symbolic, that he represented a group of a thousand that, in turn, represented a much larger group of Vietnam veterans, and were it possible for all of them to attend, they would give the same testimony he was about to give.

Then he talked of "war crimes" being committed in Southeast Asia, not isolated instances but "crimes committed on a day-to-day basis with the full awareness of officers at all levels of command." He said American troops raped Vietnamese civilians; cut off their ears, heads, and limbs; applied electric shock to genitals; blew up bodies; and randomly shot at civilians. He said American troops shot cattle and dogs for fun and razed villages "in fashion reminiscent of Genghis Khan." He said that in the Vietnam veteran, America "has created a monster," that these men were given the chance "to die for the biggest nothing in history."

He asked for an immediate withdrawal from Vietnam and said veterans "are ashamed of and hated what we were called on to do in Southeast Asia." He estimated that 60 to 80 percent of U.S. servicemen in Vietnam "stay stoned twenty-four hours a day."

The impassioned young man grew more intense. He was educated and polished, and the ribbons on his fatigues gave great weight to his words. Senator Fulbright and the packed chamber listened closely. Television cameras representing the major networks and reporters from the major dailies were there when he said Vietnam was a racial war in that black soldiers "provided the highest percentage of casualties" and that free-fire zones — places where U.S. soldiers shot at anything that moved — showed "America placed a cheapness on the lives of Orientals." He said weapons were used in Vietnam that "I do not believe this country would dream of using" in Europe or any non–third world country. In response to one question, he said America "murdered" two hundred thousand Vietnamese annually.

One line the reserve officer uttered was particularly powerful. It crystallized the feeling of the antiwar movement, was the ideal sound bite, and decades later would still be repeated: "How do you ask a man to be the last man to die for a mistake?"

Several times he returned to his theme of an immediate withdrawal from Vietnam, saying it was the "will of the people."

What the extensive media coverage of that morning's testimony overlooked was that rarely, if ever, in American history had a military officer so turned military customs and regulations and laws on their heads. America was withdrawing its troops, but 284,000 remained in South Vietnam. The testimony before the Fulbright committee indicted those troops, their commanders, and their civilian leaders in Washington and placed the POWs in great jeopardy by declaring them to be war criminals.

The officer added that America should pay "extensive reparations" to North Vietnam and that President Nixon's talk of withdrawing from Vietnam with honor was "whitewashing ourselves." He said he had been to Paris to talk with North Vietnamese delegations to the peace talks. This would mean a junior officer in the Navy was attempting to negotiate foreign policy with the enemy. He supported the North Vietnamese proposal of having America set a date for withdrawal of all troops so that men should not continue "to die for nothing."

A few days later, in early May, the guards at one building in Hoa Lo called a group of POWs into the courtyard. A sheet was draped over a clothesline, and the guards showed a 16 mm film clip of the officer's testimony.

A number of POWs would later say that, from that point forward, when they were called to quiz, the guards always mentioned the young man's testimony. After all, that testimony substantiated the North Vietnamese oft-stated position that the POWs were murderers.

Day was at Skid Row when the film clip was shown. When he returned, he was told of the officer's testimony.

"Who is he? What's his name?" Day asked.

"John Kerry."

Day shrugged. "A no-name dingbat."

In April 1972, Norris Overly became deputy commander for operations at Mather AFB in California. He still was making speeches about the POWs, how badly they were treated, how isolated they were, and how he had been freed to offset the bad image North Vietnam had regarding POWs. In May, the *Copperhead*, a newspaper published by the Air National Guard in Phoenix, quoted Overly as saying the North Vietnamese policy of releasing a few POWs had not gotten them anywhere at the peace talks in Paris, so they had stopped releasing prisoners.

The Air Force looked upon Overly and the other early releases as heroes. And America clasped the early releases to her bosom. (One was given a new car by the people of his hometown. When North Vietnamese guards showed POWs the picture of the man and his car, a POW asked why there was no yellow stripe down the top.) In June, Overly became a wing commander at Mather. Becoming a "Wing King" is one of the best jobs a colonel can have in the Air Force. And commanding a wing opens the way to becoming a general.

A month after Overly became a wing commander, one of the most celebrated and controversial events of the Vietnam War took place in Hanoi. Numerous politicians, including Senator Ted Kennedy and former attorney general Ramsey Clark, had visited Hanoi. Celebrity activists such as Jesuit priest Daniel Berrigan, Reverend William Sloane Coffin, and convicted "Chicago Seven" conspirator Tom Hayden were also among those who visited. But in July it was a glamorous and outspoken movie star who was hosted by the Communist leadership.

Jane Fonda.

While near Hanoi, Fonda put on the helmet of a Vietnamese soldier and sang antiwar songs. She sat in the gunner's seat of a AAA battery to "encourage" North Vietnamese soldiers fighting against "American imperialist air raiders." She made numerous broadcasts over Radio Hanoi — broadcasts the POWs were forced to listen to over "CBS" as she denounced Richard Nixon as a "true killer" and lamented his "crimes" against the Vietnamese and said he was "lying" when he said the war was winding down. Over "CBS" the guards played a tape of Fonda and a group of women outside an army base in New Jersey singing a song called "Fuck the Army."

Fonda came to Hoa Lo and met with seven POWs. One of them, Navy lieutenant commander David Hoffman, was tortured until he agreed to appear. (McCain says he was "knocked around" in an unsuccessful effort to make him meet with Fonda.) Among the POWs who showed up voluntarily were Lieutenant Colonel Edison Miller of the Marines and Commander Walter Eugene Wilber of the Navy.

The legal definition of "treason" includes a phrase about providing "aid and comfort to the enemy." Bud Day and, for that matter, almost all of the POWs say that Fonda had done just that and should have been tried for treason.

They would never forgive her.

Not long after Fonda left Hanoi, a new shoot-down entered Hoa Lo. P. K. Robinson, who had been a Misty, brought Day up to speed on the unit's accomplishments and how the Air Force and Marines were using F-4 Phantoms as Fast FACs. He said that until they disbanded, the Mistys had continued to use the tactics Day had developed, tactics that had never been compromised. Day nodded and blinked back the tears.

Back home, the presidential election was heating up. McGovern said that, if elected, he would go to Hanoi to ask for the release of the POWs. At Hoa Lo, his speech was played over "CBS" and enraged the POWs. They wanted to come out of jail standing tall and proud. They did not want a president of the United States begging for their release. Day was so angry he jumped atop a bed and told the POWs under his command, "If that son of a bitch wins and comes to Hanoi, I will personally kick his ass, then I will step over his prostrate body and lead all of you to Australia."

The POWs cheered.

But the exodus to Down Under was not necessary. Nixon won in what turned out to be one of the most lopsided presidential elections in history — a clear refutation of the antiwar rhetoric. When Nixon subsequently began bombing North Vietnam, Doris sent a telegram to the White House saying, "Dear Mr. President, you just put a smile on my husband's face." She signed it "Wife of POW George E. Day." She almost immediately received a thank-you note from Nixon.

By late 1972, only 27,000 U.S. troops remained in South Vietnam, not enough to apply military pressure on North Vietnam to end the war. Only airpower remained.

YEARS later a POW would be interviewed by the Historical Office in the Office of the Secretary of Defense. He told the historians that POW policy was that only the SRO in a room or a building or a camp could speak officially to the guards and that Day was the only SRO who sometimes had to delegate this duty because "when they started bullshitting him," he knew it was possible he might "punch the guy in the fucking face." Once, Orson Swindle, a big, badass Marine, looked at Day, stooped over with that rolling gait, his skinny bowed arm pumping in determination, his eyes shining in defiance, and asked him, "Bud, why are you so goddamned tough? How do you do it?"

Day smiled. "Ors, if I'm not, I know that when I get home, Doris will kick my ass."

Day was as rigid with fellow POWs as he was with the guards.

A few weeks after Day and his posse returned from Skid Row, the guards added several POWs to the room. One was a full colonel named Jim Bean. The guards knew that with a colonel in the room, Day no longer would be SRO. What the guards did not know was that because of his conciliatory ways toward his captors, Bean had been relieved of command authority by the senior American POWs.

That day the guards were harassing the POWs in the courtyard. Bud ordered the men under his command to go back in their cells. Bean refused. Late that night, Day pulled Bean aside for a private chat. He kept his voice down. But the room was small and

Swindle and Fellowes and others heard when Day said, "Colonel, you are not in command. And if you try to exercise command, I will throw you and everything you own out in the yard."

The men in Room 2 lay there in the darkness, eyes wide. They were not surprised when the colonel meekly accepted Day's leadership.

THEN there was Hubert Flesher, a captain who was very much full of himself. It was Day's practice to give the men under his command a job. If they had a job, he could later write ERs about their performance. With these ERs they could more easily merge into the Air Force once they were repatriated. Day doesn't remember what Flesher's job was, only that the captain refused to perform his duties. "This job is to keep you in the system," Day explained. "This will get you promoted when you go home." Flesher still refused. Finally, Day went to him and said, "You are on your own. When it gets to be ER time, I'm not looking out for you."

ON February 13, Doris picked up the telephone and a voice said, "This is Melvin Laird. I'm having a press conference in Phoenix and wondered if you would you like to meet me there."

She paused. This can't be *the* Melvin Laird, the secretary of defense.

But it was. He was coming to Phoenix and he wanted to meet the woman who had become such a leader among the POW wives, the woman who had written numerous letters to the president. Nixon knew who she was. And that was why Laird was calling.

"Will you join me for lunch?" he repeated.

"Yes."

Dorie and Melvin Laird had a private lunch, and she told him about the obstacles still faced by POW wives. She sat in the front row at Laird's press conference when he talked of the administration's commitment to bringing the POWs home.

Then she went home, and for yet another day in a long string of days, Doris was strong for her children.

So much time was passing. The children were growing up and sometimes expressed concern that they could not remember what Dad looked like. She pulled out the old home movies of Bud playing in the yard with the children, made popcorn, and delighted as the children laughed, pointed at their dad on the screen, and said, "I remember when we did that." Every night she had a family meeting and told the children more about their father. She wanted his memory to stay fresh in their minds. She told them that before they said their prayers they should look at his picture beside their bed. Remember his face. Remember what he looks like. He is coming home.

The calendars she kept showed day-by-day expenditures, every dime she had spent while Bud was away. Since Bud went to Vietnam, she had been on a strict budget. Most of Bud's salary was being put in the bank. Her diaries recorded everything that happened to her and the children — day by day, month by month, and year by year accounting. She could pick a date, go to a calendar, and see what she and the children had done that day. She kept all of their report cards and all the little toys and pictures and trinkets of childhood. One day Bud would be home, and she wanted him to know everything that had happened, to see everything the children had done, to be aware of everything.

In October she publicly endorsed Richard Nixon in his reelection campaign and said she was "disgusted" with McGovern's attempt to use the POWs in his "contemptible" Vietnam policy; she said McGovern would leave the POWs to the mercy of the North Vietnamese.

In November 1972 she wrote in her diary how very tired she was of being a POW wife and that she longed "to go back to being a mop squeezer."

As Christmas 1972 approached, Swindle organized a group of POWs into what was called the "Hanoi Players" to perform their interpretation of Dickens's *A Christmas Carol*. Swindle played

Christmas Past, Christmas Present, and Christmas Future. Jack Fellowes was Tiny Tim.

McCain was Scrooge.

It was not the usual solemn performance of this Christmas classic. Tiny Tim had diarrhea and was wearing a diaper. Props were few. The script was ad-libbed and was both crude and profane.

Scrooge wore a cotton lamb-chop beard, pranced about, and contorted his face, and had there been scenery, it would have been said he chewed on it. McCain's performance was over the top, his cocky, party-animal side in full splendor.

In a scene where Christmas Future told Scrooge that his time was coming, that he would pay for being such an unpleasant fellow, McCain and Swindle were standing over the room's five-gallon latrine bucket, which was being used to depict a tombstone. The dialogue was interrupted several times when Fellowes needed to use the bucket.

It was the first Christmas in five years that Bud Day had something to laugh about.

ON the night of December 18, the POWs in Hoa Lo were awakened by the shriek of falling bombs. Day knew the sound well. Wave after wave of B-52s dropped stick after stick of bombs. The AAA and SAM defenses around Hanoi fired in salvos, but the bombs kept falling. As the guards cowered in fear, POWs stood and cheered and shouted and laughed.

Some bombs fell so close that the blast pressure could be felt inside Hoa Lo. With dawn came smaller attack aircraft, the A-6s, F-105s, and F-111s. Hanoi was hammered all day long. That night the B-52s returned.

For the first time in the long war, North Vietnam was learning what unleashed American airpower was all about. To the POWs it was the greatest fireworks display they had ever seen.

But not all American aircraft made it home, and almost immediately the captured crews were promptly paraded before reporters.

In the past, crewmen met the press only after being beaten and told what to say. Now it was clear the POWs were simply being held as hostages in the peace negotiations. The propaganda ruse was off. Now it was simply a test of will between Nixon and North Vietnam.

Night after night the POWs were circled with bombs, many so close to Hoa Lo that guards realized the B-52 navigators were using the prison as an offset point for bombers. But Hoa Lo was the safest place for miles around. Seen from the air, Hanoi was burning. But in the middle of the city was a dark circle of safety. Suddenly, government bureaucrats and everyday citizens were knocking at the gates of Hoa Lo. Everyone in Hanoi wanted to be inside, close to the trapped Americans.

The emotional bond between the military and the POWs was never more apparent than during those days. Some Navy aircraft had both the pilot's name and the name of a POW written under the cockpit. Occasionally, Air Force attack aircraft would come off a bombing run, drop down Misty-low, come screaming across Hoa Lo, and light the burner. Inside, POWs were jarred out of their beds, but they came out cheering. Their brothers had not forgotten them.

This was Nixon's famed "Christmas Bombing," or as it was officially known, Operation Linebacker II. It continued, with a short break for Christmas, for eleven days. And on the last few days, not a single SAM was fired at American aircraft. Not a single AAA battery was firing. On December 29, some 150 aircraft attacked North Vietnam, and none were lost.

The massive bombing campaign was the last card Nixon had left to play. Congress was threatening to cut off money financing the war. America wanted an end to the fighting. At the same time, the POWs were the last card the North Vietnamese had to play; only Hanoi knew how many Americans were there. It was a poker game with some of the highest stakes in history.

BACK home the antiwar and anti-Nixon mood was still strong. Doris received numerous phone calls from the media asking what she thought about the Christmas Bombing.

"I think it is great," she said.

"But aren't you afraid your husband might be killed?"

Doris was exasperated. These people knew so little of the military. And their politics were quite clear. But she controlled herself and said, "The men dropping the bombs are Bud's brothers. They know what they are doing. I suppose an accident could happen, but even if it did, I support the president one hundred percent."

At this point there always was a brief silence before the reporter said, "Are you sure that's how you feel?"

"Absolutely."

ON December 30, the White House stopped bombing because the North Vietnamese wanted to resume the peace talks. Soon afterward the Paris Peace Accords resumed and moved along quickly. The POW release was a big part of the talks.

The high-stakes poker game was over and Nixon had won.

The newest POWs, those shot down during the Christmas Bombing, were altogether different from those who had been there five years or so. They entered a relative country-club atmosphere and thought they were tough guys when they barked at the guards. But they were humble when they saw the men they had heard so much about during the past few years: Bud Day, Robbie Risner, Jim Stockdale, Larry Guarino, John McCain, Jerry Denton. No one was sure these guys were even alive. And there they were, old and bent and not giving an inch.

Now the American prisoners began receiving three meals a day, more blankets, more clothes. Had the POWs known that back home much of America was castigating Nixon for the bombing, it would not have mattered. They did not care. Because the POWs knew then and will tell you so today that "Nixon bombed us out of jail."

Then a prisoner who spoke Vietnamese heard guards saying that the war was over and that the "prisoners" and "detainees" — as the guards now called them — soon would be released. Within hours, every POW knew. Senior American officers remembered the propaganda films of French prisoners reacting with jubilation when they were told of their release after years as prisoners of the Vietnamese, and they wanted no such record. The word was passed down: show no emotion.

A few days later, POWs were assembled for the official announcement. Risner called them to attention. And these men who had grown old in prison, these men who had endured unspeakable pain, these men whose friends had died around them, slapped the heels of their rubber sandals together in a big "splat."

Risner marched the men into the courtyard. This was the first public appearance of the 4th Allied POW Wing, and the members were determined to show the guards a thing or two about the discipline of American men at arms. The cadets at West Point or Annapolis or the Air Force Academy could not have looked sharper than did the POWs when they marched into the courtyard that day. Shoulders back. Eyes forward. Perfect cadence.

The 4th Allied POW Wing was shit hot.

The camp commander stood in front of the solemn group and looked around. A half dozen cameramen were in place to record the joyous reaction to his news. But when he told the Americans they were going home, not a man moved, not a man smiled, not a man showed the slightest tic of emotion.

The camp commander frowned. He took a few steps forward and asked Risner, "Don't you understand? You are going home."

"Yes, we understand."

The POWs would leave in three groups. And they would leave as they had always wanted: in order of shoot-down, with an exception made for the sick and injured. Split up by date of shoot-down, Day and McCain and Swindle went to separate buildings.

The camp commander was still frustrated about not getting taped footage of emotional Americans. He ordered a group of POWs to collect brooms, mops, and buckets and to clean the camp. The POWs looked to Day for guidance. He waited as the commander did a slow burn, then he sauntered forth and said, "In some moments."

Day left on March 14, part of the third group to depart. The gates of Hoa Lo clanged shut behind them. The group rode by bus out to Gia Lam Airport and stepped onto the tarmac and stood in formation, still unblinking, still unsmiling, still showing not one shred of emotion.

People in America would see the film and wonder why the POWs seemed so subdued.

For more years than they wanted to remember, the POWs had held the moral high ground. They were not criminals; they were American fighting men, prisoners at war, and they had won. They knew this. And the North Vietnamese knew it too.

On that March morning, as the POWs awaited the arrival of the transport aircraft that would take them home, the spirits of a hundred battlefields stirred once again. The brothers of the POWs, the men who died at Valley Forge and Gettysburg, the warriors buried under the countless crosses at Normandy and in graves all across the Pacific, the valiant souls who died in Korea and the 58,000 who died in Vietnam, nodded in approval and settled back into the dust of the ages. Now they could truly rest in peace. Because these pampered fighter pilots, these cantankerous prima donnas, had set a new and higher standard of conduct for the American fighting man. And as the continuum of American warriors moved forward, the younger generation and those that followed would know what was expected.

Who would have believed it?

Who would have believed it?

From the time he entered Hoa Lo, Bud Day had always hoped he would go home someday. Now someday was here.

He watched the shiny C-141 Starlifter land that morning. She was cleaned and polished and gleamed in the morning sun, and on the fuselage was written UNITED STATES OF AMERICA. An American flag was painted on the tail.

When he saw that flag, Day had to bite his lips to hold back the tears.

The government he served had not forgotten him.

The big silver Freedom Bird was there to take him home.

The Americans remained solemn as they were handed off one by one to American escort officers. They walked up the ramp in the rear of the C-141 and were greeted by nurses who hugged and kissed them. The men smelled the nurses' perfume and they were homesick as never before. Some of the POWs were afraid the aircraft might be called back to the terminal. Some had great fear of being shot down by the North Vietnamese Air Force. They could not accept that they were free. They strapped into their seats, and when the aircraft taxied onto the active runway, the four powerful engines rose to a crescendo that echoed across the tarmac, the aircraft lifted off, and there was a hesitant cheer. A few minutes later the pilot announced over the PA system, "Gentlemen, we are feet wet. We have cleared North Vietnamese airspace. Next stop, Clark Field in the Philippines." Now the men laughed and cheered and pumped their fists in the air and slapped each other on the back.

After five years and seven months and thirteen days, Bud Day was going home.

And he was returning with honor.

14

Three's In . . . With Unfinished Business

WHEN Bud Day and the POWs walked into the hospital at Clark AFB, the doctors and nurses and all the staff stood and applauded. Day had some emergency dental work done to repair the front teeth broken by a guard. Doctors found he was riddled with hookworms, whipworms, and something called "gatamoeba coli." He was deaf in his right ear from countless blows to his head. His right arm was bowed. And doctors bit their lips when they saw his buttocks and the backs of his legs, still red and inflamed almost three years after his summer of hell.

He underwent a debriefing by an intelligence officer and was fitted for a new uniform. He looked at the jacket, replete with the silver eagles of a full colonel, the wings of a command pilot, and the medals he earned while in jail. He was overcome by emotion as he buttoned the jacket and looked in the mirror. This was what it was all about, this uniform. It was to maintain the honor of this uniform that he had stood fast in the POW years.

He took another look in the mirror. He was quite thin. But he was still a squared-away officer.

The most important thing that happened at Clark was that he was allowed to call Doris. She had sent pictures to Clark showing what she and the children looked like. Bud held the pictures as he called, and as he tells it, when he heard her voice he "almost melted into the telephone."

"Welcome home," she said. "The kids are okay. How are you?"

"I'm fine. Everything is healed."

Already a number of returning POWs were finding that their wives had divorced them or that a divorce would be waiting as soon as they arrived at home. Others would find their marriages falling apart within a few years. But Bud and Doris remained untouched by these swirling marital currents. They were best friends, and their marriage had strengthened in the past six years.

At Clark, Day also made a disturbing discovery about what his years in confinement had done. A pilot friend visited him in the hospital, every pocket of his flight suit bulging with miniatures of scotch, bourbon, and vodka. Day had been a scotch drinker, but at Clark he found he had to force it down. Something had happened to his taste buds while he was in jail. He tried the bourbon and vodka with the same results.

Then the POWs took off for March AFB in California. Aboard the C-141 on the flight to California was a liaison officer who went to Day and said, "You are senior and will be first off the aircraft. You will be expected to make a brief speech."

The ramp at March was filled with hundreds of spectators, many of whom waved flags and banners. America put aside its internal dissent and embraced the POWs. There was something healing about their return, and the nation welcomed them as no other military people serving in Vietnam had been welcomed.

Brigadier General Robin Olds, former wing commander of a highly aggressive group of Vietnam-era fighter pilots known as the "Wolfpack" and a man who was a living legend in the Air Force, greeted Day when he came down the steps. The two men exchanged crisp salutes, then embraced. Bud Day was back on U.S. soil, back with his own.

Doris was watching from the crowd and remembered what Norris Overly told her about Bud's arms. She saw the salute and said, "Oh, he's not crippled."

Day walked to the microphone and began his remarks by saying he was thankful for the support of all those present and particularly to President Nixon, who "bombed us out of jail." He continued talking, not knowing that Doris was mumbling, "That's enough, Bud. That's enough." A few sentences later, Day heard the staccato clicking of high heels running across the tarmac. He would know that sound anywhere. It was The Viking, running toward him, arms outstretched, a glorious smile on her face. And behind her were the four children. His speech halted as he moved toward her and then stopped, arms waiting, as Doris flew to him.

Steve now was a strapping blond-haired boy who picked up his father and twirled him around.

The Day family headed to the VIP rooms at March; Bud and Doris had a room, and across the hall were separate quarters for the children. Doris sang "Misty" to Bud, and they turned off the lights. Day was so used to sleeping on concrete that he could not sleep in the bed. During the night he lay down on the floor. Doris looked down at him and said, "Bud, you've got to learn to sleep on a bed."

"Yeah, you're right."

The most important item on the agenda was medical assistance for Bud. He went to see Dave Martyn, a former Air Force doctor he had known at Niagara Falls who was now in a civilian practice at nearby Newport Beach. At Martyn's office, Day explained what had happened and how John McCain had tried to straighten his right arm. "I'm not sure McCain was a good orthopedic guy," Day joked.

"Let's start with X-rays," the doctor suggested.

Later the doctor said that an operation to break and reset the arm would be relatively easy. But the nerve controlling his biceps was stretched or severed. Another nerve, which controls hand muscles, was only a thread. Breaking and resetting the bones could straighten Day's arm but probably would destroy the nerve, rendering his right arm immobile. It was not worth the risk. For the rest of his life, Day would be a poster boy for the efficacy of the Bug.

Day began what would become months of physical therapy — a process he called "legalized torture" — that caused his arm to spasm during the night. The spasms brought on a recurring nightmare that the Bug had called him to torture and he was back in the ropes. Day began taking sleeping pills to get through the night. He would take the pills the rest of his life. Sometimes the nightmares were stronger than the pills and he would have to take part of another pill to find a fitful rest.

Back in Phoenix, Doris sat down with Bud and showed him the bankbook. She had saved more than $70,000 and spent only the allotment money he had assigned to her. She showed Bud her diaries, ledgers, and calendars that chronicled every expenditure over the past sixty-seven months. She was apologetic that some $600 could not be accounted for. "Doris, that's close enough," he said.

He looked around the house and was pleased with most of what he saw. A notable exception was the bed in the master bedroom. It was covered with white fur and had pink velour pillows.

"Doris, that has to go," Day said.

When not at home recovering, Day was caught up in a never-ending round of hospital visits, social appearances, and intelligence debriefings. The latter were particularly important for Day, as he was the last man to see Cobeil, Connell, and Cameron alive. He told his debriefer how the three officers had been taken away and probably tortured to death. But most important of all, he told them that the early releases — members of the Fink Release Program — had not been picked at random; that those officers actively competed for the chance to go home early; that they tried to outdo each other in cooperating with the guards and in their criticism of America. The debriefer reeled in shock. Almost every returning POW was telling the same story and had the same explosive anger, the same determination to set things right.

Senior leaders thought that if they did nothing, if the POWs were given some leave, some time to settle down and get back into the mainstream, this anger would dissipate. They were wrong.

* * *

JEREMIAH Denton had been SRO in the first aircraft of POWs to leave Hanoi in 1973. When he arrived at Clark, he made two phone calls: the first to his wife, the second to Ross Perot. On behalf of the POWs, he thanked Perot for all he had done.

"I told him that rather than thanking me, he ought to thank the Son Tay Raiders. No one thanked them," Perot said. The men who had assaulted the POW camp west of Hanoi in November 1970 were ridiculed by the media because they had attacked an empty camp. But they were revered within the military.

The more Perot talked, the more enthusiastic he became about the idea of getting the POWs together with the Raiders. The White House was talking about a big welcome-home party for the POWs in May, but Perot wanted to do something before then. Much to the annoyance of the White House, he began planning a Texas-style welcome-home party.

Hundreds of returning POWs received airline tickets to San Francisco, where Perot had taken over the Fairmont Hotel. For the POWs and the Raiders, everything was free. Perot even put an envelope filled with a generous amount of "bar money" in each room. For good measure, he brought in John Wayne and Red Skelton and Ernest Borgnine to party with the POWs and the Raiders.

When Day arrived, he told Doris the bathroom in his suite was bigger than five or six cells back at the Hilton.

The Raiders, most of whom were in their early twenties, looked on the POWs as avatars of ancient warriors, men who had endured years of torture but had kept the faith. And every time they looked upon a POW, there was respect and awe and the unspoken question: "Could I have endured what this man endured? Could I have held up?"

The POWs, on the other hand, looked on the Raiders as brave and daring young men who had risked their lives to save them, men whose raid scared the hell out of Hanoi and was responsible for the POWs' being removed from solitary and put in the big rooms.

After a few drinks these barriers were broken down, and the brotherhood of men at arms emerged as the POWs and the Son Tay Raiders began having one hell of a celebration. At some point in the evening, John Wayne took to the podium and growled, "Awright, pilgrims. Send your women to their rooms. We are going to have a party." He commandeered a large boat, and the POWs and the Raiders got rip-roaring drunk. They rode under the Golden Gate Bridge and sang patriotic songs and howled at the moon. They saw Alcatraz and decided it was nowhere near as scary as its sibling in Hanoi.

The next day there was a parade through Haight-Asbury, where manhole covers were slid aside and hundreds of balloons popped out. There was confetti and ticker tape and a glorious welcome by the people of San Francisco. It was one of the biggest parades in the city's history.

Meanwhile, stories about the torture of POWs were published in several national publications. Jane Fonda was quoted as saying the POWs were "hypocrites and liars."

On May 24, President Nixon welcomed the POWs to the White House. It was then and remains today the largest seated dinner ever thrown at the White House: 1,280 people seated in a tent on the South Lawn. Bob Hope was master of ceremonies. Jimmy Stewart and John Wayne and Sammy Davis Jr. and Irving Berlin were there. The chief of staff of every branch of the service was there, along with a few active-duty members of each service.

This gathering had the full attention of television networks and major newspapers. But the media — as did much of America — lumped all the POWs (early releases and those repatriated in early 1973) together.

With Day, the reckoning began when he arrived at the Phoenix airport for his departure and saw one of the early releases. "Why are you here?" Day asked.

The man smiled and said he was going to the party at the White House.

"This gathering is for honorable men. You are not welcome."

The same thing happened at the airport in Washington when Doris recognized an officer and said, "Thank you for your service while you were in Hanoi." She was amazed when Bud pulled her away and angrily said to the man, "I can't believe you have the audacity to come here in the company of honorable men."

Before the dinner at the White House, there was a reception — appropriately enough — at the Washington Hilton. Although there were a number of POWs senior to Day, he was the acknowledged leader and, as such, not only introduced Nixon and thanked him "for bombing us out of jail" but presented the president with a handsome plaque that he commissioned and paid for — a plaque from the POWs inscribed to RICHARD THE LION HEARTED.

After the reception, the POWs boarded buses for the ride to the White House. Day was in the front seat. Leo Thorsness was near the back and witnessed what happened next.

Howie Rutledge, during his POW years, had been a tough resister, a light that could not be extinguished. When he saw Edison Miller, the Marine officer who had been half of the *Bob and Ed Show*, he exploded with anger. He seized Miller by the lapels of his mess dress uniform and tried to stuff him through the window. The bus driver and the military minder up front were astonished. It was their great honor to accompany to the White House the most revered group of officers in America. And one was trying to stuff another through the window? What was going on?

After a few minutes, someone pulled Rutledge off Miller and then pulled Miller from the window.

At the White House, Jack Van Loan looked up from his table and saw a face he dimly recognized but could not place. He stood up, stuck out his hand, and said, "I'm Jack Van Loan."

"Hi, Jack. I'm Gene Wilber." Wilber, a collaborator, sat down across the table.

Van Loan stared in disbelief. "You son of a bitch!" he shouted as he lunged across the table. His wife seized his jacket and tugged hard, whispering, "Not here. Not here."

Van Loan straightened his medal-bedecked uniform, sat down, turned to the sergeant in the next seat, and said, "I'm giving you a direct order. You are not to speak to the officer across the table. If he asks you anything, you are not to answer. Do you understand me?"

The sergeant, one of the active-duty personnel attending the party, nodded, his eyes big with astonishment.

The White House party was a glorious time for the POWs, a chance for them all to be together again, to say their proper good-byes before they left for new duty stations.

Larry Guarino found himself sitting next to John Wayne. Being the irrepressible man that he is, the still hollow-eyed Guarino — now up to maybe 120 pounds — turned to Wayne and said, "You know, Duke, I thought of you when I was in jail."

"You did?" growled Wayne, a smile tugging at his lips. Only his best friends called him "Duke." He was flattered to be called that by this famous POW.

"Yeah. When the guards came to take me to quiz, I asked myself, 'What would the Duke do?' I tried to model myself after what I thought you would do."

"Yeah? What happened?"

Guarino smiled, put a hand on Wayne's shoulder, and said, "You know, Duke. They beat the living shit out of me."

Wayne stared a moment. Then he laughed. But tears were running down his cheeks.

Nixon by then was in the throes of Watergate, and his presidency was in trouble. But in this room he was a hero. They gave him a standing and prolonged ovation.

ON May 28, only a few days after they returned from Washington, Colonel and Mrs. George E. Day were remarried. It was their twenty-fourth wedding anniversary. Doris wanted to wait another year until their twenty-fifth, but Bud was not sure he would live another year, and life was too precious and too fleeting to post-pone the important things. So in front of an Air Force chaplain, with no guests, they renewed their wedding vows and then had a quiet dinner with the chaplain and the chaplain's wife.

BECAUSE Doris had lived in Phoenix for six years and because of her long involvement with the Republican Party, Day was hon-ored at a Republican dinner and given a gold watch. But that was only a hint of what was to come. It seemed that America could not do enough for the former POWs. They were given parades, cars, and free vacations anywhere in the world; were honored at count-less dinners; received hundreds of requests to make speeches; and were idolized as few military groups ever have been idolized. Within all branches of the U.S. military, the near canonization of the former POWs was in full blossom. These men were venerated to a degree that civilians simply cannot understand.

In previous wars, POWs were identified by the conflict during which they served. For instance, "He was a POW in World War II" or "He was a POW in Korea." But for these men, no qualifier was needed. For the rest of their lives, they would be identified by "He was a POW," and it would be understood.

The POWs were the rallying point around which America could begin to come back together. The POWs were America's heroes.

And these heroes were obsessed with the early releases.

The POWs had fully expected to find these men, if not in stockades, at least drummed out of the military. Day was aston-ished to learn that Norris Overly was a wing commander and on the list to become a brigadier general. The military considered the other early releases heroes and had promoted them and given them assignments that almost guaranteed future promotions.

"What stupid idiot promoted these bozos?" Day publicly wondered.

Because he was Bud Day and his story was becoming widely known, his comment was widely circulated, especially since the "stupid idiot" happened to be General Robert Dixon, now the four-star commander of the Tactical Air Command.

Perhaps the most revealing story about Dixon is that he was so abrasive and so abusive with his power, such an unpleasant fellow, that when he played golf, he played alone.

An outsider who does not understand military culture might expect Day to cut Overly a little slack — that forgiveness was in order. But that would not happen. For Day, a fundamental principle was at stake: American military men must know that if they violate the Code of Conduct, there will be consequences. Now it was payback time. And not just for those who had come home early but for those who, during their internment, were — to use Day's phrase — "poor performers."

Day, as did Larry Guarino, Jeremiah Denton, Robbie Risner, Jim Stockdale, John Flynn, and a few other senior officers, began writing ERs on the men who were their subordinates in Hanoi. When the military saw the ERs, they were astonished. The early releases had been taken at their word when they said they were sent home as a goodwill gesture on the part of the North Vietnamese. These men were stars of the military, and some had been given highly visible jobs or, like Overly, fast-tracked for senior leadership. Now the military was discovering, as Larry Guarino said, "Not all of our pilots were valiant." It was hard for military leadership to understand that although almost every POW who had stayed behind had been broken at one time or another, they had neither divulged classified information nor were disloyal.

Robbie Risner is a good example. He was promoted to brigadier general while he was in jail, and then the Air Force heard that he had been broken and had signed certain statements. The Air Force withdrew his promotion. The other POWs said they were the only ones who knew whether or not a man had served honorably and that Robbie Risner was one of the Air Force's greatest heroes. The Air Force reinstated the promotion, which probably made Risner the only Air Force colonel twice promoted to general.

If the POWs rallied around Robbie Risner, they were bitter in their denunciation of those in the Fink Release Program.

Fred Thompson, the early release who taped a message to the other POWs that they should obey camp regulations, the man whom the guards described as "having a good attitude," now was — of all places — up at Fairchild AFB at the survival school, teaching young pilots how to handle interrogations if they ever were captured by the enemy.

Following the Hanoi ER, he was relieved of duty.

Jim Bean, the colonel whom Day had relieved of command, was sent to a military school, where he was scorned by other POWs. He soon retired.

Hubert Flesher, who had refused to carry out the tasks Day assigned to him, was "Freedom 01," the first POW to be requalified in a fighter at Randolph AFB. He was on the promotion list for lieutenant colonel and was being assigned to the National War College. After Day's ER, the promotion came through but the assignment to the War College was canceled. Flesher knew his career was over and in a fit of pique called the *Sacramento Bee* and complained about the mean-spirited Colonel George Day who had ruined his career. The reporter called Day, who remembers that he said, "It's all true. He is a loser and a meathead."

When Pentagon officials saw Day's ER on Overly, they were alarmed. This officer was a protégé of General Dixon. They showed the ER to other senior POWs and said, "What do you think of this?" They backed up Day. Overly's promotion to brigadier general was canceled, and he was relieved of duty as wing commander. Following a tour as the vice wing commander at Lowry AFB in Denver, he served a bit longer in a staff job before retiring.

General Dixon was the man who, a few years earlier as chief of the Air Force Personnel Center, had promoted the early returnees. Now he was embarrassed that those men were being ostracized by the POWs.

Another dynamic — unknown to the general public — was taking place about this same time. Larry Guarino, who was a camp SRO for most of his years in Hanoi, wrote Day's ER and said, "I believe the Air Force should push him for the highest position of responsibility." He said Day "is a man of exceptional integrity, unbounded vigor, and unquestionable patriotism, with a potential of becoming a national figure of considerable advantage to his country."

This is the ER that should have guaranteed Day's promotion to general officer. And that was what Day wanted. Retirement was put on hold.

Guarino also wrote up two Air Force officers for the Medal of Honor (MOH), America's highest award for valor. The award for Lance Sijan was posthumous. He was a young Air Force Academy graduate who was shot down in November 1967 and, despite a concussion and a compound leg fracture, evaded capture for forty-six days. In the short time he was at Hoa Lo before he died, every minute was spent planning an escape. His story was an inspiration to all POWs.

The second recommendation was for Colonel George E. Day.

Guarino kept quiet the fact that he had written the recommendations.

Senior military officers from all branches of the military must consider each recommendation for the Medal of Honor. They go to a secure room in the bowels of the Pentagon, a place known as "The Tank," where they consider the merits of each proposal. With Sijan and Day, the process would take several years and — with Day — become involved in presidential politics. But both would be approved.

Inevitably, the Medal of Honor delegation was complicated by interservice rivalries. At one point, Guarino was approached by several Navy admirals who said, "We think the Navy should get a Medal of Honor. The Air Force is getting two; we want one."

Guarino waited.

"We think Jim Stockdale should get the medal," one admiral told him. "And we want you to write him up for it."

"May I ask why Jim Stockdale?"

"Because he was senior," snapped one of the admirals.

"Yes, sir," Guarino said.

Years later Guarino would laugh about this and say that at the time he thought, *Funny, I didn't know seniority was a basis for receiving the Medal of Honor.*

(This does not mean, and Guarino did not mean to imply, that Stockdale was not a tough resister and an inspirational leader who was deeply loved and respected by the POWs. But the citation for his Medal of Honor talks mostly of how he inflicted injuries on himself to avoid speaking to peace delegations. It reads, as some POWs — not Guarino or Day — say in private, "like a recommendation for a Bronze Star.")

Then a Marine Corps general came to Guarino and said, "You recommended the Medal of Honor for two Air Force officers and a Navy officer. We think the Marine Corps should have a recipient."

"Sir, do you have anyone in mind?" Guarino asked.

The general waved his hand dismissively. "No, you were there. You knew the Marine Corps personnel. You pick an officer and write a recommendation. We'll take care of it from there."

Guarino by now was annoyed at how this process was turning out to be so political. But he also was a career officer, and he did what he was told. He wrote up a recommendation for a Marine Corps officer who had died of typhoid fever in a remote camp up on the Chinese border. The Marines had envisioned a tough resister, maybe a man who was tortured and died for his defiance. They did not want to award the medal to a man who had died of typhoid fever. The issue was dropped.

On the civilian side, Day came home to a country altogether different from the one he had left six years earlier.

He did not like the jeans his daughters wore; they reminded him of the Depression, when jeans were all that people in Riverside could afford, and they somehow reminded him of the conformity of his Communist captors. Doris mediated the solution: the girls could wear jeans to school but not at home.

One Sunday, Colonel and Mrs. Day attended the St. Thomas Evangelical Lutheran Church at 5237 West Thomas Road in Phoenix, where everyone in the congregation knew who he was. So did the minister, a young and militant antiwar activist. At one point in his remarks, the preacher injected an antiwar sentiment into his sermon, then paused for dramatic effect. In that pause, Day, in a voice heard throughout the congregation, said, "That's a lie."

After the service was over, the minister stood in the door to shake the hands of those who had been present. He avoided Day. Afterward, the Days found another Lutheran church, one where the minister was more concerned with things spiritual than with things temporal.

To take his mind off such things, Day decided to resume his golf game. But he could not hold a driver. His arms and hands had so little strength that, with every swing, he lost control of the club and it went flying down the green. Golf now was a part of his past. He would never again pick up a golf club.

Now that the boss was home, now that Misty 1 was back in uniform, the Mistys could have a real reunion. They came to Luke AFB in the summer of 1973.

Bill Douglass and Ray Bevivino arrived early. Day met them at the airport and was walking with them to his car when he saw a man urinating on a van at the front door of Sky Harbor Airport.

Douglass and Bevivino were amazed when Day cursed, grabbed the man by his lapels, and threw him against a van and began lecturing him about peeing in public where women and children might see him. The man not only was considerably bigger than Day but was strong and young. Nevertheless, the power of Day's personality was such that the man did not resist. Day summoned the police and filed a public-indecency complaint against the parking-lot urinator, who later was fired from his job as a schoolteacher.

At the reunion, Day was presented with the silver goblet that Doris had been holding for his return. Bill Douglass filled the goblet with champagne and gave it to Day with the admonition, "Drink all of it."

He tried.

It was a raucous, fighter pilot sort of party. The Mistys had heard talk of awards and decorations for Day and were proud of their leader. For much of the night they drank and replayed the old missions.

Day, in turn, was immensely proud of the Mistys. He nodded in approval as he was given all the statistics on what the Mistys had done during their three years of existence. They were amazing men. Later, two Mistys, Tony McPeak and Ron Fogleman, would become four-star generals and chiefs of staff. Don Shepperd would become a two-star who headed up the Air National Guard and later would become a commentator for CNN. Dick Rutan would become the first man ever to fly an airplane around the world without refueling.

Douglass was master of ceremonies and tried to make a speech about Day, but as usual in these instances, he became so emotional he could not speak. Day could. He stood up and talked about his experiences in Hanoi and how it was so important to him that the North Vietnamese had never learned about the Mistys.

During the evening, young fighter pilots at Luke heard the Mistys were having a reunion, and they hung around the door of the Goldwater Room hoping for a look at one of these legends. These young pilots were invincible — superior to all other life-forms. But they grew humble upon hearing that Mistys were in the building — as well they should.

By late summer of 1973, Day and Guarino and several other commanders, men who were SROs in Hanoi, were upset that no formal action had been taken against the men in the Fink Release Program. The commanders asked for a meeting with General John Flynn and Admiral James Stockdale, the highest-ranking POWs. At the meeting, Day delivered an ultimatum: "If you don't file court-martial charges, we will."

Stockdale replied by filing court-martial charges against Edison Miller and Walter Eugene Wilber, accusing them of mutiny and attempting to cause insubordination.

Colonel Ted Guy initiated court-martial proceedings against eight enlisted men who, as the so-called Peace Committee, had — he claimed — openly collaborated with the enemy. He charged them with disobeying the lawful orders of a superior officer, acting in conspiracy with the enemy, and aiding the enemy.

In rapid succession, charges were filed against the eleven officers who had accepted early releases. But after Abel Kavanaugh, one of the enlisted men, committed suicide on June 27, all charges against all personnel were ordered dropped. For better or worse, the POWs were all lumped together in the mind of the public, and the White House did not want a series of bitter and highly public courts-martial. Those charged were allowed to quietly leave the service. They returned to their homes in far-flung corners of America, civilians beyond the reach of military justice. Because their experiences remained unknown by the general public, they were revered in their hometowns and in their adopted towns.

The POWs would not go public on an issue their superiors clearly wanted closed. But their anger toward the early releases was unabated. Day came up with a solution. He incorporated a group known as the NAM-POWs and was the first president. One of the bylaws, subtle enough to be overlooked by most, said membership was open to those who had served honorably in the prison camps of North Vietnam. "Served honorably" was the operative phrase. Early releases and members of the Peace Committee — as the controversial enlisted men called themselves — were not eligible for membership.

The NAM-POWs, from the moment of their creation, had more moral authority than any other veterans' group in America.

THE POWs had been out of the cockpit and out of Air Force life for years. Word from the White House was to give them any job, any assignment that they wanted. And on the surface, that is what happened. But in fact, the military struggled to find a place for the former POWs.

Getting back on flying status was a top priority for many Air Force pilots. They went to Randolph Field near San Antonio, where they had their "Freedom Flights" in the T-38 supersonic trainer. They thought that once they requalified, they would get jobs in the operational Air Force.

But the bureaucrats who ran the Air Force were not too sure about the POWs. Their only frame of reference was Korea and brainwashing and *The Manchurian Candidate*. The POWs might be ticking time bombs. It would be best to watch them for a while, to place them in jobs where they could do little harm until their measure had been taken. School was a safe place. Many of the POWs were assigned to Command and Staff College or the War College or other military colleges. Some were assigned to civilian universities for advanced degrees.

The Air Force would not give Day a command job in the fighter community. So, very much against his wishes, Day enrolled in the political science PhD program at Arizona State University.

When not studying or in class, he spent hours every day writing ERs, getting his people from prison back into the mainstream of the Air Force. He wrote them up for medals. Air Force jets arrived at Luke once or twice a week to take him to other Air Force bases to make speeches about his POW experiences, about leadership, about adhering to the Code of Conduct. All the while he was steaming. When he returned from Vietnam, he had changed his mind about retiring. He wanted to get requalified in a fighter and become the director of operations at Luke. From there it would be easy to become a wing commander, an almost obligatory step before he could be considered for promotion to general officer. He wanted to be promoted to general, but he had no intention of taking a staff job.

Day was deeply unhappy. He still was one of the most educated men in the Air Force and, at this point, did not need a PhD. He asked Robbie Risner about the jet-requalification program and what he thought of the T-38. Risner replied, "Every kid ought to have one." He suggested that Day requalify in the F-4 Phantom. "It's like an F-100 with two engines," he said.

For months it seemed the Air Force ignored Day's wishes. Then in the spring of 1974 he was ordered to go to Luke to be requalified. He would do so in the F-4 and in a twenty-five-hour course for senior officers.

But there were a few problems. He had a history of head trauma, loss of consciousness, and gastrointestinal hemorrhage; a deformed right arm; and injury of peripheral nerves. It is an understatement to say his overall physical condition was not at the level expected for fighter pilots.

Nevertheless, he was given a check ride. His right hand was so weak that he could not adjust some of the critical cockpit switches. Unseen by his check pilot in the rear seat, he reached across with his left hand to make the adjustments. And he had to use both hands to pull high-G maneuvers.

But by now the story of Bud Day had made its way throughout the Air Force. If Bud Day could take off and land a jet aircraft, the Air Force would put him back in the cockpit. He requalified in less than twenty hours. It took thirteen waivers, but Bud Day was back on flying status.

Then, in September 1974, Day received orders to report to Eglin AFB in the Florida panhandle, where he would be vice commander of the 33rd Tactical Fighter Wing. He had a job that easily led to his becoming a wing commander. From there, he would be on track for promotion to general.

But General Dixon was lying in wait.

15

Over the Side

ALL Day remembered from his time in the Florida panhandle was Panama City and the stench of the paper mills and a dozen tacky little beach towns. But when he tapped into the Air Force network, he was told that he had landed a great job. "This is a shit-hot deal," he remembers being told. "It's a TAC base. You are not responsible for the chapel and the BX [base exchange]. All you have is the airstrip, a few fire engines, and your own people. There are only two squadrons in the wing and you could get promoted."

So it was with considerable hope and with great expectations that Colonel Day and his family moved to Eglin AFB in the fall of 1974. But that hope and those expectations soon would be squashed by petty Air Force politics. Eglin would be Day's last assignment, and it would be a bitter one.

Day, like many of the POWs, came back from Hanoi as a full-throttle kind of guy. There was so much catching up to do. And, again like many of the POWs, whatever pretense or posturing or just plain old *bullshit* there might have been about him had been stripped away in Hanoi. The POWs had nothing to prove to anyone. Ask a POW a question and — if he wants to answer it — you get a straight, stripped-down, no-frills answer. Order a POW to perform a task and it will be done to the best of his ability. There was a purity about them that made them — and these are odd words to describe such men — *innocent*, even *naive*. Most of those who remained in the military were lieutenant colonels or colonels, ranks in which politics and political awareness are important. But POWs were concerned with doing the *right* thing rather than the *political* thing. To them, there was no gray area; the world was black and white.

That was Bud Day.

He believed that God had saved his life many times so he could perform a certain task — to be an inspiring leader during the POW years by following when he was junior, leading when he was senior, and always setting the example. Now that job was done. And at his core was peace and serenity. He thought the remainder of his military career would be relatively uneventful. All he wanted was to be promoted, to have the chance to go back to Sioux City in the autumn of every year to go pheasant hunting and maybe pick up a few Bing Bars, and then to retire and practice law. Eglin was the stepping-stone to the rest of his life.

He had barely arrived at Eglin when he was ordered to Louisiana to investigate the crash of an F-4. The commander of the 9th Air Force, a three-star who reported to General Dixon, sent down word that he thought the wing commander in Louisiana was at fault, that his lack of leadership was the reason a pilot crashed. The three-star was named James Hartinger, a diminutive fellow who referred to himself in the third person as "The Ger." Day investigated, determined the accident was not the fault of the wing commander, and so stated in his report.

When Day was Misty 1, he had warriors working for him. Birds of a feather, if you will. The other side of that coin is obvious: bureaucrats also flock together. And in the Air Force there are far more bureaucrats than there are warriors. The people working for General Dixon either were like him or were fired or transferred out of TAC. The three-star had Day's report rewritten and fired the wing commander.

* * *

OFF base, Day was finding he had moved to a strange part of America. The First Congressional District of Florida then ran roughly from Pensacola to Panama City. It long has had the highest concentration of ex-military people of any congressional district in America — about 110,000. They are drawn here by warm weather, shopping privileges at the BX and commissary, and free medical care at the military bases. The small towns around Eglin — Shalimar, Fort Walton Beach, Valparaiso, Niceville — are inextricably tied to the military. Much of Okaloosa County is taken up by Eglin AFB. There is Eglin Parkway and Freedom Boulevard and Commando Boulevard and Doolittle Street and other streets that remind visitors they are in a patriotic and conservative community. Naval Air Station Pensacola, the primary flight-training base for Navy and Marine Corps pilots, is forty miles west. Hurlburt Field, center of Air Force Special Operations, is nearby. So are Duke Field and — to the east about forty miles — Tyndall AFB.

All this Day found good. He was among his own. But in other ways that was not true. Most military people travel widely during their careers; they are transferred about every three years, often to overseas postings, and in many ways are very sophisticated.

But one of the names for the panhandle is "LA" — as in "Lower Alabama" — and the beaches here and to the east often are referred to as the Redneck Riviera. It was pickup-truck country, predominantly protestant and then yellow-dog Democrat to the core. Day had never seen or heard of the sort of politics he found in the First District. Democrats held every elective city, county, state, and national job. Bob Sikes, congressman from the First District, was the political boss of the panhandle. He had more seniority in the district than anyone but God and was almost as omnipotent. Sikes called himself the "He Coon," because the male racoon knew where the food was and how to get the water. Sikes brought in more pork than a meatpacking house, and it seemed that coon tails, signifying the driver's allegiance to Sikes, waved from the antennae of every pickup truck in the First District.

When Day and Doris took Steve to register to vote, they told the registrar they wanted to register as Republicans. The reaction they got was about the same as if they had said they wanted to register as *Catholics.*

"Ain't no use in you all registering as no Republicans because there ain't no Republicans to vote for," the elderly registrar said.

Day was appalled. Because of Nixon and because of the long conversations he and McCain had in jail about politics, he was a committed and devoted Republican. He thought there should be Republican candidates running in every race in the district.

Day was then and remains so today a man of elaborate and courtly manners. But he does have his hot buttons. And the registrar had punched one.

"When I need advice on how to register to vote, I'll ask for it," he said. "Until then, hand me the paper and I'll register as a Republican."

When he left the registrar's office, he had that same head-up, arm-pumping, determined, and hard-eyed look of defiance that Jack Van Loan had noticed in the yard at the Hanoi Hilton. Turning to Doris, Day said, "We're going to have to do something about this."

DAY's life at Eglin existed on two parallel but distinctly different tracks. On one level, he was one of the most famous officers in the Air Force. Speaking invitations poured in from around the world, and he and Doris made several trips to Europe. As more and more people learned about his escape and his hard-nosed resistance, the legend of Bud Day grew. He received numerous combat medals, and word had gotten out that he had been recommended for the Medal of Honor.

But at the same time, Day was having to deal with two enervating facts. First were the bitter realities of an Air Force in the post-Vietnam era.

The F-15 — the follow-on aircraft to the F-4 — would not be operational for a few more years, and numerous upgrades were necessary to bring the ancient F-4 back up to combat-ready status. The two squadrons of F-4s in the wing of which Day was vice commander were weary airplanes. They had stress cracks in the wings, a problem that necessitated major modifications. The heavy G-loads of combat flying had caused leaks in the fuel tanks. The aircraft had to be rewired.

Dixon had decreed that all TAC squadrons have 65 percent of their aircraft combat ready, an impossible target. Indeed, for most of the mid- and late 1970s, only about 20 percent of Air Force tactical squadrons were combat ready. Wing commanders who wanted to keep their jobs reported to Dixon that their wing was 65 percent combat ready, whatever the reality.

Day's boss was no different, sending up report after report saying the wing was at 65 percent readiness, and Day knew it was a lie.

Day's experience was a microcosm of what was happening throughout the Air Force at the time. The Air Force has the meanest and most petty bureaucracy of all the services. This is in part because the Air Force defines its mission by the type of aircraft it flies; it is in the hardware-acquisition business rather than the war-fighting business. Even today there are roughly 74,000 officers in the Air Force, about 13,000 of whom are pilots. Most of those pilots fly noncombat aircraft; about 2,000 are combat pilots. Thus, a case can be made that the Air Force is not really a fighting force. It is a bureaucracy, the main purpose of which is to buy ever more expensive aircraft.

Day's second problem was that General Dixon disliked him intensely for the "stupid idiot" comment. While most of the Air Force revered the former POWs, word had come back to Day that Dixon did not. He sent a letter to all Air Force colonels in TAC who had been POWs and told them that they should not expect to be promoted simply because they had been POWs, that they had to prove themselves, that they had to be reassimilated into the Air Force, and that their superiors must agree they were suitable for command in a tactical unit. This sounds fair enough. But the tone of the letter was such that many recipients considered it harsh, even mean-spirited, especially after Dixon was widely quoted as having said, "None of those neurotic POWs will ever become wing commanders in TAC."

About this time, a pistol went missing from a sealed crate in the Eglin weapons-storage area, a serious breach in security. Day's boss was fired and Day thought that his time had come, that he would be promoted to wing commander. But instead of giving Day the job, Dixon summoned a colonel from Thailand to take over, a move that not only humiliated Day but sent a signal that he would not be promoted.

Bud Day realized his Air Force clock had run down.

SHORTLY before Christmas, the Ford administration sent Day and now commander John McCain to Saigon to meet the president of South Vietnam and to receive the National Order of Vietnam, that country's equivalent of the Medal of Honor.

While in Saigon, the two officers visited U.S. ambassador Graham Martin, who told them that the war was going well in South Vietnam, that this was a country that had repulsed its enemies for a thousand years.

"It was insane drivel," Day said. "It was like being lectured to by the drunkest guy in the bar at four a.m."

Four months later, in April 1975, South Vietnam fell to Communist forces in the North.

WITH the end of the war and concurrent budget cutbacks, flying hours for Air Force fighter pilots were radically cut. Squadron officers were limited to five hours per month — not enough to maintain proficiency in a high-performance jet aircraft. Day flew only occasionally so the younger pilots would have more flying time, but when he did, young pilots competed to fly with him. His greatest joy in those days was going out onto the bombing range with young pilots.

It was a tradition that before going to the range, every pilot bet a quarter on every bomb dropped. The young pilots had great hand-eye coordination, great motor skills, and almost instantaneous reaction time. They figured they could easily best Colonel Bud Day; after all, in 1975 he was fifty years old, wore glasses, limped, and was beginning to aquire a slight stoop. To the young pilots, he was an old man.

But that old man waxed their asses.

It was uncanny how his bullets, bombs, and rockets went where they were supposed to go. And when it came to night-bombing or night-gunnery practices, no one in the wing was in his league.

But then, no one in the wing had been a Misty.

The young pilots would have been even more chagrined had they known the full extent of Day's injuries and the practical effects of those injuries. He still had to cross his left hand over his body to operate some of the switches. He had to use two hands to honk the F-4 around in high-G maneuvers. An impartial check pilot would have grounded him. But there he was.

When McCain was transferred to Jacksonville, Florida — about three hundred miles away — as commander of an air group, he and Day and their wives saw one another frequently.

One afternoon McCain flew to Eglin and met Day in the officers' club. Day had been flying and was still in his flight suit. The men sat at the bar, two of the most famous and most widely recognized of all POWs, drinking and talking about the old days and about politics. A young captain swaggered up. He was not from one of the operational fighter squadrons in Day's wing but rather from the test squadron (a group that tested new weapons or new technology). He was tall and trim, a recruiting-poster sort of fighter pilot. The captain greeted Commander McCain, then turned to Day and said, "Colonel, may I ask why you have those leather clips on your flight suit?"

Day looked down at the leather tag attached to the end of every zipper clip. He was aware that younger pilots thought the clips useless and cut them off.

"Because it's government property and part of the uniform."

"It's not necessary, sir."

"I think it is."

The captain reached out and flicked one of the clips.

"Only the old guys wear these."

"Captain, I think you'd better go back to your table and sit down."

Day was tolerant of junior officers even when those officers were fueled more by booze than by recognition of military courtesies. But McCain recognized the change of tone in Day's voice. He saw Day's eyes turn glacial, and he knew what was coming.

"I think your flight suit would look better without them," the captain said. He reached out and seized one of the clips, intending to rip it off the flight suit. But before he could do so, Day leaped off the bar stool. With his weak right hand and his withered right arm, he knocked the young captain on his ass.

Officers from all around the big room looked around to see Colonel Day, fist still clenched, and the astonished captain looking up and rubbing his jaw. There was a moment of absolute silence. Then the officers broke out in applause.

McCain howled with laughter.

The captain stood up and returned to his group. Day went back to his bar stool and resumed his conversation with McCain.

Word swept across Eglin and throughout the Air Force: "Bud Day punched out a captain in the officers' club."

"Yeah, *that* Bud Day."

A few weeks later the pilots from the 58th Fighter Squadron gave Day a set of boxing gloves emblazoned with the squadron insignia — a gorilla.

Colonels do not publicly punch out captains. Had any other colonel in the Air Force done this, or if the young captain had pressed charges, Day might have been court-martialed.

* * *

IN early 1975 Day received an unofficial call from a former Misty who was working in the chief of staff's office: "Sir, you have been recommended for the Medal of Honor." He was told to expect an official call and to prepare for a trip to Washington, where President Ford would award the medal.

Doris bought new clothes for herself and the children. And they waited for the summons.

Then Day received notice he was to receive the Air Force Cross (AFC). He assumed the Medal of Honor had been downgraded, a not-uncommon practice. In any case, the AFC is the highest medal awarded by the Air Force. The three-star who flew to Eglin to pin on the medal said it was the first he had ever awarded. The citation that accompanied the medal indicated that it was awarded for failing to give jailers any information during the sustained torture in the summer of 1969.

A few weeks after receiving the AFC, Day was notified that he would also receive the Medal of Honor. The friend in the chief of staff's office privately told him that when he came to Washington, the chief was giving him a surprise: a spot promotion — one outside normal promotion channels — to brigadier general.

Uncomfortably close to all this was a request from the Ford White House asking Day to work in President Ford's election campaign. Ford had taken over as president when Nixon resigned and now sought election to the office. But Bud Day was a Reagan supporter. After Day incorporated the NAM-POWs, he invited Reagan to be the featured speaker at the 1974 and 1975 reunions of the POWs. He turned Ford down. It would be another year — on March 6, 1976 — before Ford awarded the medal, waiting until Betty Ford was campaigning in Florida and could point to Day's Medal of Honor as an example of how her husband supported the military.

And Day was not promoted to general. He was told that a spot promotion for an Air Force officer would have meant a spot promotion for a Navy officer also, and since Stockdale (also awarded the Medal of Honor) was a relatively new admiral, it was too soon to give him another star. Day looked at the citation that went with the MOH and saw it was dated a year earlier. He was incensed that Ford had so politicized America's highest award for valor.

(It was a disappointing time for Day. Out in Sioux City, Paul Jackson, one of Day's boyhood friends, had organized a write-in campaign for Day to fill a congressional seat. It came to nought.)

The overwhelming majority of Medal of Honor recipients are ground fighters, Army or Marines, with a few in the Navy and even fewer in the Air Force. For a member of the Air Force to receive the MOH is such a rare event that the recipient is granted a private visit with the chief of staff. When Day arrived at the office of General David Jones, he was ushered straight in and made comfortable, and in the ensuing small talk, the general asked, "How are things going with the POWs?"

"General, is that a rhetorical question or are you really interested?"

Jones blinked. The chief of staff is a demigod surrounded by sycophants who strew roses in his path. Almost never does the chief hear blunt talk.

"I'm really interested."

"Then the answer is 'Not worth a damn.'"

Day told of Sam Johnson, a former POW who, even though he was senior in rank to several of his superiors, was number five in the command structure at a wing at Seymour Johnson AFB. He told how he did not get the wing at Eglin. Day went on about how the Air Force continued to treat the former POWs as second-class officers when, in fact, they had proven their character and their ability in a way that few other officers were ever called upon to do.

Unspoken but hanging in the air was the obverse side of Day's argument: the men in TAC (who had not been POWs) who had been promoted to general officers usually were Dixon's men, officers who had said their wings were 65 percent combat ready.

Within a week after Day's courtesy call, the chief ordered General Dixon to give the tactical fighter wing at Homestead AFB to Sam Johnson. Johnson later retired from the Air Force and became a long-serving congressman from Texas.

After Vietnam, there had been so much turmoil over the Code of Conduct and what it meant and how it should be followed that a special group of officers was convened to study the code and determine if it needed revising. Bud Day was the senior Air Force representative on that review board. In that capacity, he occasionally traveled to the Pentagon. On one of his visits, he was told that General Dixon wanted to see him. Dixon's office as TAC commander was at Langley Field in Virginia, but he borrowed a Pentagon office for his session with Day.

Day entered the meeting with a unique aura. By now he had some seventy medals. In fact, there were no more combat medals to give him; he had them all. He was the only man in Air Force history to receive both the AFC and the MOH, a man so venerated in the Air Force that his picture now hung outside the office of the chief of staff.

Nevertheless, Dixon made him cool his heels for three hours. When Day finally was ushered into the office, Dixon was shaking with anger. He chewed Day out for going over his head and telling Jones about the POWs. Then Dixon launched a diatribe about the former POWs and their demands for promotion. "I'm tired of you guys riding that horse," he fumed.

The comment made Day the angriest he had been since he was in Hanoi. "General, if that's all," Day said. He stood up and left the office.

Some thirty years later when Day told this story, he grew visibly furious. "I had to get out of that office," Day said. "If I had stayed, I would have punched him out. And it would not be good to see headlines about a Medal of Honor recipient punching a general officer."

But Day had more on his mind than battling Dixon. He called an aide to former president Richard Nixon and said, "Would you ask President Nixon if he will reaward my Medal of Honor?"

The aide was a bit nonplussed by the request. Former president Nixon was living in exile in San Clemente, in disgrace after resigning from the presidency. But the aide knew that Nixon was a revered figure to the POWs. And he knew that Bud Day was one of Nixon's most outspoken supporters.

"Colonel, I'm not sure what you mean by reawarding the medal."

Day told the aide about the year's delay in awarding his MOH and how he thought the medal should be above politics, even presidential politics. He reaffirmed his respect for Nixon and told the aide, "I would be honored for President Nixon to be the president who awarded me the Medal of Honor. That would be the one that counts."

Nixon agreed. So Day and Doris flew to California. At San Clemente, Day and Doris had a private chat with the former president. During the conversation, Nixon told Day, "You know, I wish I had started the last bombing campaign sooner. It would have brought all of you home earlier."

Day assured him he had done just fine. Then the little group grew formal, and Nixon removed the Medal of Honor from its box. Day stood at attention, shoulders back, eyes straight ahead. And Nixon spoke for a moment of Day's courage and patriotism and the example he had set for young officers and for all Americans. He hooked the medal around Day's neck, stepped back, shook hands with Day, and smiled.

In 1976 a CBS producer asked McCain and Day if they would return to Vietnam with Cronkite and be the featured part of a documentary — two of America's best-known POWs doing the reconciliation thing. McCain accepted. Day refused. Then one of Cronkite's staffers called Day, tried to schmooze with him, and asked, "Wouldn't you like to go back to Vietnam?"

Day paused. He had no respect for the man he still referred to as "Walter Crankcase," the weak dick who stood up after Tet and said America was losing the war. Then he said, "Yes, I would. Leading a four-shipper of F-100s carrying wall-to-wall nape."

"I'm sorry you feel that way."

"I'm not."

So McCain went to Vietnam with Cronkite and made the documentary.

This was the first instance of what would become, over the next three decades, a pattern of McCain going one way and Day another. They remained the closest of friends. But each was head-strong and each had his own path to tread.

Indeed, Day was out on the range one day, rolling in for a gun pass, when he caught a 20 mm ricochet on the canopy of his F-4. The bullet hit in front of his face on a trajectory that, had the canopy not been bullet resistant, would have taken his head off. The thought occurred to him that if he was being protected in this fashion, maybe his work on earth was not yet done, maybe there was another mission.

But what could it be?

WHEN Day was passed over for the job of wing commander, word quickly passed through the Air Force. Day's admirers began working behind the scenes, and soon he had a phone call offering him a job with the Armed Forces Staff College, where he would be in charge of training field-grade officers for higher jobs. He would be occupying a general's slot; thus it was a job from which he could be promoted to general.

But it was not a job in the operational Air Force. Day had spent his professional Air Force life either in SAC or in TAC and did not want his last assignment to be what he called a "weenie staff job." He turned down the assignment, knowing that by doing so, he would not retire as a general.

With no reason for staying in the Air Force, Day began making plans for retirement, a procedure that career officers refer to as "going over the side." It had been twenty-five years since he joined the Air

Force. With his time in the Marine Corps and the Army Reserves, he had given more than thirty years of his life to his country. He had been stationed at bases in America, England, Japan, and South Vietnam. But his longest duty station was Hanoi.

Day decided not to go back to Sioux City. He had bought property in Shalimar, a town that abuts Eglin, and another piece near Pensacola. He wanted to build a house and settle down and practice law. When he told Doris he was going to put in his retirement papers, she asked him to delay for a year. She had just been elected president of the Officers' Wives Club and wanted to serve out her term.

Day could not say no. "She did a lot of waiting around for me," he said. "I could wait for her for a year."

His last year in the Air Force was a sad postscript to his career. He could not stay in the wing where he had been passed over for the top job, so he went to General Bill Evans, a fighter pilot friend, and said, "General, I need a job in the legal office for my last year in the Air Force."

"Go over there and tell them I sent you," Evans said.

Day never said a word to his bosses in TAC. He simply drove over to the legal office and went to work. When he took a new flight physical, the flight surgeon again reminded Day he should not be flying with his disabilities. This time the doctor added a sobering codicil: "If you continue flying until you retire, you will not be entitled to disability payments."

That made sense. If a man is fit enough to fly, he certainly is not disabled.

Day was grounded.

He was in such wretched physical condition that he was declared 75 percent disabled, a category that meant he would not have to pay income tax. He refused, saying, "I want to pay taxes. I have to contribute." His disability was lowered to 60 percent.

America's greatest living war hero spent his last year in the Air Force doing malpractice work, studying for the Florida bar exam, and shuffling papers.

* * *

ON one side of the Days' property in Shalimar was Choctawhatchee Bay, and on the other side was a bayou. They brought in a dredge and funneled tons of fill dirt onto the property to raise the elevation farther above sea level and then began building a two-story brick house such as they had admired on Country Club Drive back in Sioux City. Two-story brick houses are not the typical waterfront property found in Florida. But that is what Bud and Doris had dreamed of for almost thirty years.

Day took the bar exam in February 1976 and three months later was told he had passed. He bought a building on Beal Parkway in Fort Walton Beach, met a young lawyer named Tim Meade, and set up a two-man law office.

In the fall, Doris asked Bud to again postpone his retirement. She had been elected parliamentarian of the Officers' Wives Club.

"Doris, they can elect another parliamentarian," he said.

He wanted to retire on December 10, 1976, which would have been the thirty-fourth anniversary of the day he joined the Marine Corps. But predictably the Air Force would not grant his request, and he retired in February 1977.

When he did so, Day's friends, including many POWs and a few Mistys, flew in from around the world. Speeches by senior Air Force generals were gracious, as were Day's responses.

It was an elegant send-off, and Day revealed not the slightest hint of the disappointment in his heart.

16

Good-bye Yellow Dogs

In 1978 it had been twenty-nine years since Bud Day had graduated from law school, and except for a little collection work in South Dakota and representing a few wayward airmen in courts-martial, he had never practiced law. Now, at fifty-three, he was setting up a law practice in a town where he knew few civilians.

He went about this in the common-sense fashion one would expect from a man of the Midwest. He knew that simply hanging out a shingle would not make him a litigator. So during much of 1977 and part of 1978, he spent hundreds of hours attending various schools. He went to Washington, DC, and took a course on how to try a medical malpractice suit. He went down to Gainesville and took a course sponsored by the Florida Trial Lawyers Association on how to try cases. Every time he came across an area where he felt unsure, he went back to school. Six hours on introduction of evidence. Six hours on examination of witnesses. In every school, not only was he older than the other students but he was older than the high-powered lawyers who taught the courses.

His law practice was in a one-story plain-Jane sort of building on one of Fort Walton Beach's main north-south roads, a road whose chockablock businesses reveal the city's lack of restraint on zoning matters. He was not one of those lawyers who thought it necessary to let their offices reflect their affluence to impress potential clients. The parking lot out back was then and remains today a refuge for homeless people, public urinators, and an element that operates on the windy side of the law — a place where visitors must keep a sharp eye. (Day grumbles about the urinators. But the Florida variety, unlike those in Arizona, are fleet of foot.)

Day specialized in personal-injury litigation and in representing young pilots who had run afoul of Air Force bureaucracy. He represented a number of former POWs in their efforts to receive disability payments from the military, including Jim Stockdale, John Flynn, Orson Swindle, and a half dozen others.

Day knew well that the military sometimes eats its young. One such instance was the *Marantes* case at Hurlburt Field. David Marantes was a young Hispanic officer, highly accomplished and clearly on a fast track. He was kicked out of the Air Force in such a high-handed manner that not only did he lose his benefits but his honor was impugned. The decision, which emanated from senior officers and had elements of racism, received considerable attention in the *Air Force Times*. Day was ultimately successful in changing the conditions of the officer's discharge and restoring his benefits.

Another case Day handled was quite important, even though he lost. It began when the widow of an Air Force sergeant came to Day. For years her husband had suffered from serious headaches. Military doctors never gave him a thorough examination. Eventually the doctors decided to test the sergeant for a brain tumor and sent him to the military hospital at Lackland AFB. A tumor was discovered, the sergeant was operated on, and then he was left in his bed, unsupervised and with no instructions. He got out of bed, fell and hit his head, then crawled back into bed, where he lay for twelve days with no one checking on him. He vomited, aspirated the vomit, contracted pneumonia, and died. The sergeant's widow asked Day to file a malpractice suit against the government.

Day was outraged by the government's callous indifference toward the sergeant. The facts of the case were clear, and he expected a favorable verdict. But he was steamrolled by government lawyers. He says that he was "outspent and outwitnessed," that he "did not have the ammo or the gas to fight them." The U.S. government, Day realized, is a juggernaut that wins suits because it has virtually unlimited resources to hire witnesses and experts.

When Day returned to Fort Walton Beach, he went to a Jacksonville lawyer who had won a $20 million malpractice case against the government and from him learned the subtleties of how to fight the U.S. government in court. After that, it would be years before he lost a case in federal court.

DAY occasionally wondered about that 20 mm ricochet off his canopy. Was his life saved that day on the range because there was yet another job for him? He was a civilian lawyer on the Florida panhandle, not the most obvious place to be if he still had a big job to perform.

As the years went by, and as the honors and speaking invitations continued to pour in from around the world, as his law practice thrived and his portfolio of investment properties grew, the memory of that day on the range began to fade. During those decades, his life followed two distinct paths. The first was connected to the U.S. military. Day was one of the most highly prized speakers in the U.S. military, particularly for Dining Outs. General officers are considered prize catches for these events, but Bud Day was the avatar of all that Air Force officers hoped to be. His speeches were red, white, and blue.

In fact, for a long time Day could not talk of his experiences without weeping. The embarrassment he felt about his tears caused him to consider giving up public speaking. But with Doris's help, he learned to control himself. "Bud, you've got to get through this," Doris counseled. "It is important for people to know about what you went through. You have to be able to talk about it."

And as tough as it was, he rarely said no. When the Air Force Reserve unit from Sioux City went on temporary duty to Eglin, someone suggested, "Why don't we call Colonel Day and see if he will have a drink with us?" Day was delighted. He came out and answered all the questions about the Mistys, his shoot-down, his escape, and his time in Hanoi. He tended to talk in a flat, dispassionate voice about his escape and in a general way about his time in Hanoi, almost as if he were talking of someone else's experience. But if someone had read his medal citations — and many military people had — they knew his Air Force Cross was awarded for the months of torture he underwent in the summer of 1969. They wanted to know about the torture. (Even now, Day, if pressed, glosses over that time quickly.) He left after an hour or so. When the group from Sioux City asked for the check, they were told that "Colonel Day picked up the bill."

Day particularly enjoyed attending NAM-POW reunions, a three- or four-day affair. One night is casual: POWs wear a flight suit–like garment called a "party suit" on which are sewn numerous patches. A favorite, and one that these men wear proudly, says YANKEE AIR PIRATE.

McCain had little time for the reunions. The only time he ever attended was in the mid-1980s, when he flew in for one day and disappeared without telling anyone he was leaving.

For several years, on every August 26, his shoot-down date, Day had what he called an "Oh, Shit! Party" to celebrate. He invited other POWs and showed videotapes of Operation Homecoming. Afterward, there were always nightmares.

IN addition to making speeches to military groups, Day spoke to dozens of service clubs along the panhandle. In most of those speeches, Day came down hard on Communism. Once, he was speaking to a group and, as is his habit, was slamming his hand against the lectern, talking about the "gooks" who had tortured him and who still ran Vietnam. He grew so impassioned that Bill Campbell, a local newspaper columnist, leaned over to the person next to him and whispered, "I hope no one here has an Asian gardener. If they do, they will go home and kill him."

In much of America, Day's unrepentant warrior mode and his blunt way of speaking might have caused him to be pigeonholed, even marginalized. But in the Florida panhandle, he was preaching to the choir. From the beginning, people stared and pointed him out in restaurants. It was almost impossible in the mid-1970s, and is even more so today, for him to eat in a local restaurant without someone coming up to him and, with great diffidence and in a voice choked with emotion, saying, "Colonel Day, thank you for what you did for our country." Or a simple "Thank you, sir."

The second part of Day's postretirement career was in politics, though not so much in elective office. (In 1978, he was elected state committeeman for the Republican Party in the First District and would hold the job until 1984, when he decided not to run again. He also lost a race for a county commission seat.) Day's real political impact was during the 1980s, when he was a driving force in converting the First Congressional District of Florida into a Republican stronghold.

To fully understand the dynamics of what happened, we must go back to 1964, the dawning of the Republican Party in the South. Barry Goldwater, the Republican senator from Arizona, carried several southern states with his subliminal appeal to racist sentiments and a jingoistic drumbeat on Vietnam. Lyndon Johnson won the election, but the Republican seed had been broadcast across fertile ground. In 1968 came the violent and disastrous Democratic National Convention in Chicago. LBJ pulled out of the race, and Nixon and his "Southern Strategy" carried the South. In 1972, Democrat George McGovern suffered an overwhelming defeat when Nixon again carried the South.

By the early 1970s a new political mood had settled across the South. Moderates held governor's offices throughout the region. Largely as a result of the 1965 Voting Rights Act, blacks were becoming a political force throughout the South, almost entirely in the Democratic Party. Nearly every southern state shifted significantly to the center but remained Democratic. Jimmy Carter embodied this and in 1976 defeated Gerald Ford for the presidency.

But the Carter victory was a small bump in the road. Day had retired from the Air Force, entered the practice of law, and got involved in Republican Party politics at the moment when most southern states were ripe for plucking by Republicans. He was the right man in the right place at the right time.

In 1978, a Republican ran for a county commission seat in Okaloosa County. It was a close election, but he lost. Then the absentee ballots were counted, and the Republican was declared the winner. Almost every absentee ballot came from a military man. And Bud Day, an ardent Republican and a man known to virtually every military man in the district, had campaigned actively for the Republican candidate. From that point forward, Day preached that Democrats could be beaten and that military people — read Republicans — could swing an election.

Once Ronald Reagan secured the Republican nomination in 1980, the South became GOP country. Reagan carried about 68 percent of the vote in Florida's First District. Day was Reagan's national chairman for veterans and traveled around the country with the candidate.

In 1979, California governor Jerry Brown appointed Edison Miller, half of the *Bob and Ed Show* in Hanoi, as a supervisor — county commissioner — in the Third District of Orange County. In 1980, that appointed term was over and Miller had to run for election.

More than two hundred former POWs signed a letter that was sent to some hundred thousand voters in the district. The letter said that Miller "cooperated with the enemy to the detriment of his fellow American prisoners of war" and that he "wrote articles" for the Communists against the interests of his government. The letter claimed that Miller violated his oath as a military officer, that he disobeyed the lawful orders of his superiors, and that he "does not have the dedication to duty, to his country, or to a sense of public service which would qualify him for any public office." The letter ended by calling on voters in the district to reject Miller.

They did. He received only 16 percent of the vote and later filed a defamation suit against the POWs. Bud Day was one of several lawyers who represented the POWs on a pro bono basis. The court granted the POWs' request for a summary judgment that threw Miller's suit out of court. Miller appealed, but his appeal was tossed out.

Day was in and out of the hospital often during the 1980s. He underwent surgery on his left shoulder, his back, and his right shoulder, all in an attempt to overcome the Bug's work. Scar chips remained on his buttocks from the beating with the fan belts, and sitting would always be painful. Cortisone shots for his shoulder, which had been dislocated from being in the ropes, would become familiar to him. He had extensive dental surgery. But no neurosurgeon could erase the memories.

Day was recovering from surgery when, on November 11, 1982, he was the featured military speaker at the dedication of "The Wall," the Vietnam Veterans Memorial in Washington.

In the early 1980s, Pat Holloran ran for superintendent of elections as a Republican and defeated the longtime officeholder, a Democrat and close friend of Sikes.

The yellow dogs were running.

By 1984, city council seats in Fort Walton Beach were shared by Republicans and Democrats. The mayor professed to be an independent, but many suspected she was a closet Republican, especially after she fired the city manager and the police chief.

The Democrats tried to crank up a recall election for the mayor, and one of the fired Democrats sued the three Republicans on the city council. Since firing the Democrat was an official act, those being sued asked the city to pay their legal fees. The city counsel, a Democrat, refused, and a bitter legal battled ensued.

In the city hall dispute, Day represented two of the Republicans. He won every step of the way, but after each victory, a local Democrat judge issued an order vacating the judgment. Finally, Day took the issue to the Florida Court of Appeals in Tallahassee, which ordered the local judge to issue no more orders in the case. In December 1991, the state circuit court ordered the city to pay the legal bill. Day received some $360,000, at that time the largest fee a Florida city had ever been forced to pay a lawyer. One day Wayne Waddell, a POW from Atlanta, came through Fort Walton Beach, nodded approvingly when he saw that both Bud and Dorie were driving Cadillacs, and said, "Damn, Bud. You must be making lots of money."

"Money won't buy you happiness," Day said. "But it will buy you a big car to go looking for it."

WHILE the legal battle with city hall was going on, Day and a few others, most of them retired military officers, had joined together and taken over the small Republican Party in Okaloosa County. Their timing was perfect. People from around the country were migrating to the Sun Belt, many of them to the Florida panhandle. In addition, the population was aging, and many people become more conservative as they grow older. Eglin AFB was expanding, and thus the local population of retired officers — almost all of whom were Republican — was growing.

During the 1988 presidential campaign, Day had initially campaigned energetically for George H. W. Bush. Day understood the realities of presidential politics, but he thought Bush ran a mean and vicious campaign against Michael Dukakis, so Day later withdrew from the campaign. Black and white, right or wrong, good or bad — that's the world of Bud Day. Even though he was a committed Republican and the leadership of the country was at stake, Bush had not behaved honorably and Day wanted no part of it.

After Sikes was accused of using his political influence to benefit his real estate holdings and was forced to retire from Congress, a Republican local television anchor named Joe Scarborough was elected to his seat in 1995. Then, in 2001, to the considerable annoyance of local Republicans, Scarborough returned to television and the First District congressional seat was open. Day was determined that a Republican win the race. One of the candidates was a retired Air Force officer who knew that Bud Day influenced a large number of voters. The retired officer came to Day expecting an endorsement. But Day told the retired officer he was not seasoned enough for Congress and threw his support behind an intense former state legislator named Jeff Miller. Miller won the race.

From that point forward, whenever there was a Republican primary in the panhandle, Day not only got entreaties for his endorsement but received dozens of phone calls and hundreds of e-mails asking whom he planned to support. And by the mid-1990s, from Panama City to Pensacola, there was only one elected Democrat, a county commissioner in Escambia County.

DAY'S closest friends among the POWs remained McCain, whom he always referred to affectionately as "that dumb Irishman," and Orson Swindle, whom he called "Ors." In 1980, McCain was a Navy captain stationed in Jacksonville. When McCain got divorced, Day handled the legal work. McCain remarried a month later and soon retired from the Navy and moved to his new wife's hometown of Phoenix, Arizona. In 1982, he ran for a congressional seat in Arizona's First District. Bud and Doris flew to Phoenix and spent a week campaigning for him. Doris pulled out her detailed notebooks and began calling the newspaper and television reporters and the local and state politicians she had worked with when Bud was in jail. McCain won the election and a few years later won a Senate seat.

In 2005, McCain was interviewed in Phoenix and asked what influence, if any, Doris had on that election. "Everyone knew Dorie," McCain said. "She gave me instant credibility. She was very important in my winning that first race."

In his early years in the Senate, McCain had a reputation as a hothead, a man whose anger was barely under control, a man who, when criticized by constituents, baited and taunted them. Day shook his head and laughed. McCain had not changed from the days when he ran around the courtyard taunting the guards.

* * *

DURING the late 1970s, the 1980s, and well into the 1990s, dozens of POWs wrote of their experiences in Hanoi. Most of those books are formulaic. They begin with the shoot-down and go through the torture and the boredom and the release. Few stand on literary merit. But McCain's book would be significant because he was a U.S. senator when it was published in 1999. Jim Stockdale's book *In Love and War* was published in 1984 and was important for a reason entirely unnoticed by the general public. The most highly classified development of the POW years, and one that even today the POWs will not talk about, is that the CIA devised a way to occasionally have two-way communication with the POWs. Stockdale's book revealed not only that there was such a system but the details of how it worked. Barry Goldwater, a general in the Air Force Reserves and a powerhouse in the Senate on defense matters, was so angry that he wrote Day and said, "I continue to be shocked at the book that was written by Jim Stockdale. I can't imagine him doing it, but the damage has been done." He later confronted Day and asked, "What the hell's the matter with Jim Stockdale babbling about the comm system?" Day couldn't figure it out either.

Day was writing his own book, which would be ready for publication in 1989. But various publishers turned it down, saying it was "too red, white, and blue." Day published it himself in 1990. The title: *Return with Honor.* For years the book was used in terminal-cancer wards of local hospitals to illustrate that no matter how bleak a situation might appear to be, there is always hope.

WHEN 1990 arrived, Bud Day was about to turn sixty-five, the age when many men retire. At home, things had gone well for Bud and Doris. Because he was an MOH recipient, his children were eligible to apply for an appointment to any of the service academies. But Steve became a master mariner, the skipper of large oceangoing vessels that he ferried around the world. George Jr., the quiet and intense boy, entered the Air Force Academy, graduated in 1985, and began an Air Force career.

After high school, Sonja married and had three daughters. Sandra married, had three children — one a Marine — and is now in business school working on her master's degree.

In 1993, Day attended a reunion in Montana. The Dining Out part of the event was presided over by Marine Corps general Walter Boomer, assistant commandant of the Marine Corps. During the ceremony, he summoned Day forward and had him stand at attention. He charged Day with "committing an offense against the mess."

Day was bewildered. The general said Day was not wearing medals to which he was entitled. When Day again expressed bewilderment, the general said he did not see the Marine Corps Good Conduct Medal. He pinned on Day the medal that Day's court-martial had prevented him from receiving when he mustered out of the Marine Corps back in 1945.

Afterward, Day would remove one of the combat medals from the crowded left breast of his uniform and proudly replace it with the Good Conduct Medal.

ALL the medals in the world could not change the fact that Vietnam veterans were the most scorned and rejected men ever to wear the American military uniform. When they came home, they got no parades; they got shouts of "baby killer" and "rapist," and they were spit on and reviled. Rotten fruit and human feces were hurled at them.

Most of them remembered with pride their time in Vietnam. They married and had children. As those children grew up and the Vietnam War became a popular topic to teach in schools, they came home and asked their fathers, "Daddy, did you burn villages when you were in Vietnam?" Or "Daddy, did you ever cut the ears off a Vietnamese?" Or "Were you at My Lai? Did you kill civilians?" Or "Did black American soldiers die in greater numbers than white American soldiers in Vietnam?"

Some three million American troops went through Vietnam, and in any group that size there will be those who operate beyond the pale. My Lai was an aberration, not the norm. Civilians were killed, but it was not an institutionalized policy that came from the highest levels of command. There were soldiers who used drugs, but they were not in the majority. Two-thirds of the men who fought in Vietnam were volunteers, not draftees. And 12.1 percent of American fatalities were black soldiers, a rate roughly corresponding to their number in society. Suicides among Vietnam veterans were no greater than in society as a whole. Joblessness was less than in the general population. Some 91 percent of the veterans were glad they had served their country.

Most Vietnam veterans had seen countless acts of courage. They believed their comrades were the best young men in America. James Webb, a highly decorated Marine officer, a former secretary of the Navy, and a bestselling novelist, would write passionately about the Vietnam warriors, saying they "fought with a tenacity and quality that may never be truly understood." Many Vietnam vets knew the popular perception of the war was a travesty. For this, many of them, but particularly the POWs, blamed John Kerry.

They believed Kerry's 1971 testimony was the template from which almost every Vietnam movie was made.

Except for *The Green Berets* — a John Wayne movie of the World War II type that was savaged by reviewers — no commercial movies about Vietnam appeared until after the mid-1970s, five years or so after Kerry's testimony. And almost every one of those movies — *Coming Home*, *The Deer Hunter*, *Apocalypse Now*, *Platoon* (which won the 1986 Academy Award and was considered the most "realistic" of the Vietnam movies), *Full Metal Jacket*, *The Siege of Firebase Gloria*, *Hamburger Hill*, *Casualties of War*, *Gardens of Stone*, and *Born on the Fourth of July* — included American soldiers as John Kerry had portrayed them in his testimony: crazed, dope-smoking, civilian-killing psychotics who, once they came home, were ticking bombs.

For many Americans, the most compelling statements about the Vietnam War were found in those movies, and many veterans believe that, by extension, Kerry was responsible for America's erroneous beliefs about Vietnam. That this belief may not be widely held outside the military is not the point. To many Vietnam veterans, particularly the POWs — some of whom were knocked around while the guards repeated Kerry's testimony and some of whom believe Kerry's testimony extended the war — Kerry had wronged a generation of honorable men; he had stolen their honor. This was their truth. And they ached for the chance to make things right.

DURING the 1992 presidential election, Day volunteered again to campaign for President Bush. He did not approve of Bush's campaign techniques, but he would work for the president because Bill Clinton was the Democratic candidate.

Years later, on June 12, 2005, Alan Ehrenhalt began a review of *The Survivor: Bill Clinton in the White House* on the front page of the *New York Times Book Review* by saying, "Millions of Americans despise Bill Clinton." He said Clinton haters believe that the former president was "immature, self-absorbed," and indecisive; that he lacked discipline and was reluctant to use military force even when needed.

Ehrenhalt's review did not begin to plumb the depths of revulsion that military people felt in 1992 (and still feel) toward Bill Clinton. From the time he first appeared on the national stage, Clinton's pouting expression, lip biting, and what they considered to be his inveterate womanizing, noninhaling-dope-smoking behavior made him — and this is not too strong a word — *loathed* by military people. Everything about "Slick Willie," they found repugnant.

For Bud Day, Clinton personified not only the self-indulgence and fuzzy thinking of the Democrats but weakness as well. He had no self-discipline, no integrity, no patriotism. He had no principles. He was a man without honor. And he had no military background, which was okay, but — as Robert Patterson described in *Dereliction of Duty*, he was openly contemptuous of the military, which was not okay.

When Clinton won (due in large part to the fact that third-party candidate Ross Perot received 19 percent of the vote), Day believed the republic was in danger.

Making things worse had been an attack Day could not help but take personally. Perot's running mate was Admiral James Stockdale. After a stumbling performance during a nationally televised debate, Stockdale was savaged by the media. Day knew that Stockdale was one of the most brilliant men ever to wear a uniform. To have reporters ridicule him widened even further the gap between the military and the media.

Clinton lifted the economic embargo on Vietnam and appointed Pete Peterson, a former POW, as the first American ambassador to Vietnam. Day thought Vietnam should remain isolated. He could not imagine a former POW being a Democrat, much less taking a job in the Clinton administration. He wrote Peterson a letter in which he all but called the ambassador a traitor. Clearly, Day had the same tightly focused right-or-wrong view of the world that he always had. The single-mindedness that enabled him to be a great leader in Hanoi was still there. It was not always appropriate in the civilian world. In coming years it would sometimes be even less appropriate. He would seem rigid and incapable of forgiveness.

About a year after Clinton was elected, Day drove up to Maxwell AFB in Montgomery, where the Air Force operates several schools for young officers. Part of the curriculum includes bringing in distinguished retired officers to talk to the young officers. Day was one of several MOH recipients on a panel that appeared before newly minted graduates of the Squadron Officer School. Doris was sitting in the audience with the brigadier general who was commander of the school. One of the young graduates asked if each of the old warriors would give his opinion of President Clinton. The other officers gave the proper answer: they were loyal to the commander in chief, no matter who he might be. Then it was Day's turn, and he said, "I wouldn't trust that . . ." He paused, unwilling to use the profanity on the tip of his tongue.

Then the dam broke. "I wouldn't trust that son of a bitch as far as I could throw him."

Doris said the base commander went rigid with shock. And it would not be until the base commander was transferred and a new commander appeared that Day would be invited back to Maxwell.

In the summer of 1995, Day received in the mail his copy of the *Retired Officer Magazine* and read a story saying the U.S. government no longer was allowing military retirees over the age of sixty-five into military hospitals. These old retirees were losing their free medical benefits and were being forced into the Medicare program, which meant they would have to pay for part of their medical coverage. Medical care was very much on Day's mind. His physical condition was such that he had been declared 100 percent disabled. Day figured the article was wrong, another media foul-up.

By now Day believed his major life's work was over. He had been retired almost two decades. The 20 mm ricochet was just a close shave and not a sign that there remained another mission for him. Vietnam was why God had saved him from death so many times.

The travel and invitations to speak continued. His children were living proof of the good job Doris had done during Day's almost six years' absence. His law practice was thriving. The awards and honors were an unceasing river. The health problems caused by the Bug were as under control as they would ever be.

A few days after Day read the article, he drove out to the hospital at Eglin to pick up a supply of medicine.

"Colonel, I'm sorry. But I can't fill that," said the pharmacist.

"Why not?"

"This is an active-duty drug."

"What do you mean?"

"We don't give it to retirees."

"What's the basis for that?"

"It costs too much. These pills are three dollars each."

Day nodded tightly, spun away, and went looking for the highest-ranking hospital official he could find, the deputy hospital commander, and said, "I have a real bitch."

"What is that, Colonel?"

When he explained what happened, the deputy commander nodded and said, "That's a dollar decision. We get allocated so much money, and our job is to take care of the active-duty force."

"I think your job goes quite a bit further than the active-duty force. We were included in that allocation."

"Sir, you're going to have to talk to the hospital commander about that."

By now Day had up a full head of steam. Added to his natural combativeness was a sense of outrage and indignation. When he went into the Marine Corps in 1942, the recruiter told him that if he served twenty years, he would have free lifetime medical benefits. He was told the same thing when he joined the Air Force. In the years since he retired, his medical benefits and his medical care had been free. The people affected by this new ruling — and he was one of them — were World War II– and Korean-era veterans, what TV anchorman Tom Brokaw would call in his book the "greatest generation." More than a million of these men were still alive, and they had been receiving free medical benefits for years. Those benefits were as much a part of military culture as saluting the flag or saying "sir" to superiors.

Day went down the hall, eyes hard and right arm pumping. He found the flight surgeon, a man who had treated him in the past, told him what happened, and said, "This is a lot of bullshit."

The major agreed. "I can't believe the government is sniping away at you old guys."

"Where did this come from?"

"The White House. President Clinton did this."

Day's face hardened.

17

Once More
unto the Breach

DAY was profoundly disturbed as he drove home from Eglin.

If this business of no drugs or hospital privileges for the over-sixty-five retirees was true throughout the military — and it had to be; Eglin could not be the only Air Force base in America doing this — the ramifications were almost impossible to comprehend. He did not know then how many over-sixty-five retirees, spouses, and widows there were, but he guessed — with considerable accuracy, as it later turned out — at least a million, maybe two.

Two crucial distinctions here: First is the difference between "veteran" and "retiree." If a person serves a single tour in the military, he is a veteran. But he must spend at least twenty years in the military to be a retiree. All retirees are veterans, but not every veteran is a retiree. The loss of free medical care applied only to retirees from the World War II and Korean era. Second, military hospitals and Veterans Administration (VA) hospitals are separate entities. A military hospital is on a military base. VA hospitals are scattered around the country and initially could be used by any veteran — not just retirees — who had a service-connected illness. (Today a veteran can go to a VA hospital whether or not his illness is service connected.) The distinction between "veteran" and "retiree" and between "military hospital" and "VA hospital" often was not understood, even by members of Congress or by federal judges.

Maybe two million people's promised free lifetime medical benefits had been taken away by Bill Clinton.

This simply could not be true. Free lifetime medical benefits were one of the single biggest reasons people made a career of the military, part of the trade-off for a career that paid far less than its civilian counterparts. Day's government, the government whose uniform he wore for thirty years, the government whose policies he upheld for five years, seven months, and thirteen days in Hanoi, the government he spent most of his life defending, would not cut loose the old guys from free medical benefits, not when they were at a time in their lives when they most needed those benefits, not when so many of them were living only on retirement pay and Social Security and would be financially devastated by the loss of those benefits.

When Day arrived at home, he dug through his old copies of the *Retired Officer Magazine* and reread the article about free medical benefits being dropped for retirees over sixty-five. He threw the magazine aside. "I was so damn mad I could hardly see," he remembers. Ever since he had retired almost twenty years ago, the government had honored the promise it made to him when he first enlisted in the Marine Corps. Now they had breached the contract; they had broken the promise.

And military recruiters were still promising young enlistees, "You give us twenty years and we will give you free lifetime medical care."

Congressmen, senators, federal judges, and federal employees received largely free care through a program called the Federal Employees Health Benefits Program (FEHBP). There were frequent newspaper stories about government officials entering Walter Reed Army Medical Center near Washington. Their treatment was free.

Day, as he does with everything of importance, wanted to run all this past Doris for her reaction. When he did, she looked at him in disbelief.

The more Day thought about the ramifications of what had happened, the more disturbed he became.

For Clinton to single out military retirees and have them bear the burden of his cost-cutting was unspeakable. He probably figured these men were too old and too few and too incompetent to fight back. Thousands of Korean- and World War II–era retirees died every month. In another ten years there would be only a handful left.

Day got little sleep that night. He had to do something. He could not let this stand.

Early the next morning the phone rang. It was the hospital pharmacist from Eglin. "Colonel, you can come out and get your prescription," he said. "It's all squared away. You are good to go."

The hospital commander called a few minutes later and apologized profusely for the "mix-up" of the previous day. There can be no doubt that when the hospital commander was told what had happened, he put the incident in context: *A famous POW, America's most decorated living officer, an MOH recipient, turned away from the Eglin pharmacy over a prescription. My God, if the papers got wind of this.* Plus, the officer in question was a lawyer who specialized in litigating against the military and had an almost-perfect batting average.

But Day was having none of it. "You guys have to do better," he said. "You are being funded to take care of us. This is a breach of contract. It is pretty chintzy, especially on medicine, to screw us around. This is the cheapest issue. If you have to operate on us and put us in hospital rooms, that's high dollar. But for pissant prescriptions of ninety dollars? That's pretty poor judgment."

"There's not just one of you, Colonel. That ninety gets multiplied. Some prescriptions run hundreds of dollars a month."

"I don't care. They told me if I did twenty years that I would get free medical care, and that's what I expect."

"Sir, we're doing our best."

That night at dinner he casually said to Doris, "I'm thinking of suing the government over the medical-benefits issue."

She stared at him. She knew how difficult it was to sue the U.S. government. "Oh, Bud," she said impatiently.

ABOUT that time, Ted Raymond, a columnist for the local newspaper, wrote a piece about how military retirees had lost their free medical care. Day called him and they talked for more than an hour. Raymond himself was a retiree who had done extensive research before writing his column. He told Day that in 1956 a law had been passed stipulating that free medical care for retirees would be on a "space available" basis. In the beginning, this had no impact on retirees because there was always space available. But then, depending on where they lived and what military facilities were near them, some retirees were turned away. As military spending was reduced and bases began closing, more and more retirees were affected. All of this led to almost every veterans' organization going into the insurance business — selling supplemental health insurance policies.

Raymond remembers that the last thing Day said before he hung up was "I'm going to have to do something about this." Day did not know it, but groups of retirees, upset by the change, were forming in Georgia, North Carolina, South Carolina, Texas, and several other places around the Sun Belt. They did not then know about each other's existence. They were getting media coverage but only in their local newspapers. What they needed was a leader to unite them.

Perhaps only a litigator truly understands just how difficult it is to pursue a cause of action against the U.S. government. The principle of sovereign immunity — the ironclad idea that the government, simply because it is the government, has immunity against lawsuits — is a daunting obstacle. A few exceptions to the principle exist, but lawyers find it difficult in the extreme to meet those exceptions.

Day began spending hours in his law library, looking for a statute he could use to override sovereign immunity, something that could serve as the vehicle to penetrate the barricades that protect the government. The first of those barricades, especially to lawyers who practice beyond the Beltway, is that litigation against the government must be filed in federal court in Washington, DC. This means that all pleadings, hearings, and arguments must be conducted in Washington — an onerous burden to a lawyer in Florida.

In the next few months, Day spent more than a hundred hours researching the law and talking with other lawyers about whether or not he had a cause of action and, if so, how best to press forward. In the end, only one statute applied, a single obscure law under whose umbrella he could stand: the "Little Tucker Act," which, reduced to the relevant basics, says that sovereign immunity can be waived for claims founded upon an express or implied contract with the government and that an action can be brought in a federal district court if the claim does not exceed $10,000. To Day, this latter point was one of the most appealing aspects of Little Tucker. He could file in Pensacola, less than an hour's drive from his office.

Now that he knew how to proceed, he wanted the widest possible base of support. This was going to be an expensive proposition, and he needed help. When the government lawyers looked at his pleadings and realized that this action out of a two-lawyer firm affected maybe two million people, they were going to unleash every resource at their command.

About 397,000 retired officers belonged to what was then called The Retired Officers Association (TROA). (The name has since been changed to Military Officers Association of America [MOAA].) Day expected full support from the group; after all, the core of the association's membership was affected. But when he called TROA, he was astonished. Retired three-star Mike Nelson, the top man at TROA, said that the case could not be won and that his in-house counsel advised him not to get involved.

Day then called the TROA counsel, a former Coast Guard lawyer, who said that Day was relying on the wrong case law, that he could not sue the government and recover damages.

Day did not believe this. "Well, down in Florida, the way we know who won a lawsuit is to look at who walks away with the money."

"You need to read the case law a bit closer," said the TROA lawyer.

Day hung up, thinking he was talking "to a full-of-crap corporate lawyer who did not want to rock the boat."

(Day later realized the reason for TROA's reluctance. The organization purported to be an advocacy group for retired officers. But its biggest source of income was from selling insurance to its members — particularly Medicare supplements, for which the lowest premium was around $300 per year. Assuming only 200,000 members — slightly more than half of TROA's membership — bought the Medicare supplements, a successful lawsuit on Day's part could cost TROA about $60 million annually in lost premiums.)

Day then called the American Legion, whose leaders told Day he had no claim and no standing and should not sue the government. It was the same with the Veterans of Foreign Wars, the Air Force Association, and the Fleet Reserve Association. Each either failed to support the lawsuit or would give it only lip service. All these veterans' groups said the same thing: "A lawsuit has no chance. The best chance for change is for you to turn this over to us and let us influence legislation."

The obstacles against Day were greater than ever.

For weeks he was torn between the almost heretical idea of suing the government to which he had devoted most of his life, and the equally heretical idea of allowing a great wrong against old warriors to go unanswered. As he debated, he continued to research. During his reading he came across a decision out of the Ninth Circuit of the U.S. Court of Appeals that seized his attention. The Ninth Circuit is in California, and its decisions — at least to those who take a conservative approach to the law — sometimes are bizarre. But *Winstar v. the United States* involved several government-backed S and Ls that went broke, and it offered the crucial comment that when the government is involved in a contract dispute, it will be treated like any other party: *sovereign immunity does not apply.* Even better, the *Winstar* case resulted in a multibillion-dollar judgment against the government. The case stood up through the appellate process.

Still, Day was undecided. If a lawyer files suit in federal court and the court decides that he has no cause of action, that his lawsuit is capricious or a misuse of the judicial process, not only will the case be thrown out but the lawyer can be forced to pay the cost of the proceedings.

Finally, there was another issue that nagged at Day. He was seventy years old, and it could take years for this case to find its way through the courts. The effects of the injuries caused by the Bug grew worse each month. He tired quickly. His eyesight was beginning to falter; often he wore socks that clashed with his suits. His hearing was deteriorating. Sometimes when he was trying to remember a name or a fact or a legal citation, it took a minute or so to retrieve the information. A courtroom is no place for a slow-thinking advocate. And while he was a relaxed, skilled, and even humorous informal speaker, appearing in federal court is a very formal matter with rigid rules of deportment and procedure. He privately wondered if he was physically and mentally up to such a daunting campaign. Could he well serve two million veterans on a matter of such crucial importance, on a matter that would lock him in bitter and protracted combat against the U.S. government? To take the case would be a life-changing decision. It would consume almost every waking moment for years to come. But if he didn't step up, who would?

Through the fall and winter of 1995 and through the spring and early summer of 1996, Day went back and forth, trying to decide what to do. The one thought that kept coming back was the simple idea that the government had broken its vow to the over-sixty-five warriors. That was wrong. A promise was a promise. The fundamental principle went back to George Washington, who, in asking the Continental Congress to provide care for veterans, said that the willingness of young people to serve in war was directly proportional to their perception of how veterans of earlier wars were treated.

One Friday night, Day was at home sipping a glass of white Z. His mind was on the retirees, but slowly, almost involuntarily, he became involved in the movie playing on the television set. It was called *The Verdict* and starred James Mason and Paul Newman. Newman played the role of an aging down-at-the-heels lawyer who was opposed in court by a big and prestigious law firm that had virtually unlimited resources. Everyone agreed Newman had a no-win case and should accept a generous offer to settle out of court. Instead he went to court and, against seemingly impossible odds, won.

It was a powerful do-the-right-thing sort of movie. And when it was over, Bud Day had an epiphany.

God had not spared his life a half dozen times to make him strong enough to withstand the travail of North Vietnamese prisons. No, Hanoi was only to toughen him up for the big job, for the real reason he was put on earth. That 20 mm ricochet was a notice that he still had work to do. And the nineteen years since he had retired was the time he needed to gain the skills for this last big job.

At last he knew what God had been saving him for.

He had what he thought was his final mission.

He would sue the Clinton administration on behalf of his comrades.

He would file the suit pro se, that is, he would be the plaintiff.

And he would go into battle the way Mistys always go into battle . . . alone.

THE next morning he got up and told Doris he was going to the office to catch up on some paperwork. All day Saturday and Sunday he spent drawing up the complaint. On Monday, July 16, 1996, he drove forty miles to Pensacola and filed suit against the secretary of defense. It was a shotgun attack with a half dozen allegations. Little Tucker was his big gun, but he also said there had been "an illegal taking" under the Fifth Amendment. He wanted damages for breach of contract.

Bill Kaczor, the longtime Associated Press reporter in Pensacola, heard about the suit. Kaczor had opened the AP bureau in 1984 and over the years found that his superiors in Miami had a very narrow interest in stories coming from the panhandle: hurricanes, shark attacks, and the bombing of abortion clinics — that was about it. This story was no different. Kaczor read the pleadings and said to himself, "It is obvious these guys have a case." He filed his piece and sent it to Miami, where it was put on the "Florida wire." This meant the story ran in the relatively small dailies in the panhandle and in a few papers in Georgia and Alabama.

Day came back to his office in Fort Walton Beach, walked into Doris's corner office, and said, "Well, Mama, I filed that complaint against the government."

For a moment she was speechless. Then she said, "Bud, you are nuts."

He smiled and shrugged. "Well, maybe."

"You are not only nuts, you are absolutely nuts."

He smiled and walked down the hall to his office. He was in the Pack. He had penetrated enemy airspace and the AAA could start anytime.

IT is a safe generalization to say most national media either do not understand military issues or do not think those issues are relevant, interesting, or newsworthy. As a result, what was to become one of the most poignant stories of the decade, a story that — at a fundamental life-affecting level — deeply touched some two million Americans, was overlooked by the media. One or two pieces would later appear in the national media, but the big story, the dramatic story of how America's most decorated warrior went into battle with his government, was overlooked. It was then and remains today largely unknown to the general public, overshadowed by what seemed to reporters to be a much bigger and much more important saga that was beginning to unfold in Washington — a story that, over the next three years, seemed at every turn to flare up and overshadow Bud Day's lawsuit. A young woman named Monica Lewinsky had come to work at the White House as an unpaid intern and had begun a sexual relationship with President Bill Clinton. In early 1996 Lewinsky was transferred to the Pentagon, where she met a career government worker named Linda Tripp. In the summer of 1996, Lewinsky began to tell Tripp of her relationship with Clinton. Shortly thereafter, Tripp began taping the conversations. In October 1997, just three months after Day filed his suit, Tripp met with Michael Isikoff of *Newsweek* and played the tapes for him. In December 1997, Lewinsky would be subpoenaed by lawyers for Paula Jones, a woman who was suing Clinton on sexual harassment charges. That same month, Lewinsky went to the White House for the last time, met privately with Clinton, and later said he encouraged her to be "evasive" when she answered questions from Jones's lawyers.

As the sordid tale of Bill Clinton, Paula Jones, and Monica Lewinsky became the top news story in America, and as everything Bud Day did on behalf of several million retirees was ignored, Bud Day became incensed: this not only was an affirmation to him of how Clinton had disgraced the White House but was an affirmation of how the media was so profoundly out of tune with the world of the military.

SOMETIMES the nightmares were so strong that they overrode the pills, and when dawn came Bud was so tired he would stay in bed a half hour or so longer than usual. So it was on Wednesday morning, two days after the suit was filed and the day after Kaczor's story appeared. At about 8:30 a.m. his secretary called and said, "Colonel Day, the office is full of men wanting to see you, and the answering machine is filled up with messages. I wish you would come on down here. I don't know anything about this lawsuit."

"What men? What do they want?"

"They are upset. They want to know why you didn't put out the word on this lawsuit. They are here to volunteer to help you."

Day arrived at his office to find the parking lot full. Inside, several dozen old men were jammed into the front office and were filling the halls. They were all talking at the top of their voices. They were from as far west as Pensacola and from as far east as Panama City. They came down from Alabama and Georgia, and they came independently of one another. There was no organized campaign where one person phoned or sent an e-mail to another. It was spontaneous. They read the story on Tuesday in their local newspaper, looked up the address of Bud Day's law office, and Wednesday morning got in their cars and started driving. When they arrived, they found the others there.

The men recognized Bud Day when he entered and descended upon him, clapping him on the back and thanking him for filing the lawsuit on their behalf. But most of all, they wanted to know what they could do to help. They were in their late sixties, their seventies and eighties. Among them were men who were mentally quick and sharp, men who knew how to organize people and issues as only military people can.

There were also men with crutches, walkers, and canes. They were palsied, wore hearing aids, were a bit gimpy, and sometimes their senior moments lasted more than a moment. Their history was in their eyes, and their sacrifices in their scars. There had been many overseas deployments that separated them from their families. Countless times they had to uproot their families and move to another base, often to substandard quarters that were always too hot or too cold. Their children grew up not knowing where home was. They had suffered financially because of their service to America. Their youth was a distant memory, and their future held little promise.

But they were still warriors. Their hearts beat as resolutely as when they stormed the beaches on Pacific islands, as when they fought across Europe, and as when they tried to stay warm in the snows of Korea. They were ready to march.

Some of them were financially comfortable. But others lived on retirement pay and Social Security. Paying the Medicare supplement was a big hit in their wallets. For some retired enlisted personnel, the choice was stark: food or medicine. Every man present knew of retirees who were devastated by the actions of the Clinton administration.

Now Bud Day had sounded the call to arms. And Bud Day was a man they would follow. They were ready to do battle one more time, but this time against the government to which they had devoted their most productive years, the government for which they had shed their blood, the government for which they had sacrificed so much. They were about to go to war with Uncle Sam.

And it broke their hearts.

DAY took charge of the meeting and said there was not enough room for everyone in his office. He arbitrarily picked a half dozen men, sent the others home, and told them to stand by.

"This thing is bigger than we are," he said to those who remained. "We need to get organized. We need to qualify the people who are involved. We need phones. We need computers. We need everything."

He gave the north wing of his office building to the retirees. He said he would install additional phone lines and a computer.

Several of the men Day picked to stay for the first meeting would play a crucial role in what followed. One was Robert Geasland, a West Point graduate and retired Air Force colonel with a gift for organizing and writing. He also had access to lists of West Point and Naval Academy graduates going back decades. It was Geasland who said the retirees were a class act group of guys and should be called the "Class Act Group," or "CAG." It was also he who said of Day, "He is, by nature, incapable of allowing injustice to go unchallenged."

Jim Bahl, a retired Air Force officer, would be the bean counter, the man in charge of keeping track of money. Tom Pentecost, a former Marine, would be the computer wizard; he would be in charge of putting names and data into computers and keeping everything current. Within a few months, Pentecost would have a database that included the names of some thirty thousand retirees.

But the two men who would become symbolic of CAG were William O. Schism and Robert Reinlie. It would be difficult to find two men more representative of the "greatest generation," two better poster boys for the life experiences of those affected by the government's broken promise.

Schism enlisted in the Navy in 1943 and served a flying tour in a combat zone. After the war was over, he went to college, then joined the Air Force as an officer. He flew combat missions in Vietnam. In 1995 his free military-hospital care was terminated by the Clinton administration. Now Medicare cost him $525.60 per year, plus that same amount for his wife. The Medicare supplement policy cost him and his wife $3,335.85 per year.

Reinlie had joined the Army Air Forces in 1942 when things were going very badly for America. He flew thirty combat missions over Europe in a B-17. When the war was over, he went into the Air Force Reserves and was recalled to active duty in 1951, when the Korean War began.

Both men had received free medical care until 1995.

On advice of the Florida Bar, Day decided to change his pleadings. He removed himself as the plaintiff and, on December 11, 1996, amended the pleadings to make Schism and Reinlie the plaintiffs.

Every morning when Day arrived at the office, he found a dozen old warhorses pawing the pavement, anxious to go to work. Inside, every telephone answering machine was loaded to capacity. His office e-mail, his personal e-mail, and the CAG e-mail contained hundreds of messages. The daily mail brought dozens of letters from men who wanted to become involved. Most letters contained checks. The phone rang all day long. Word was out beyond the Southeast. Retirees were calling from all over the country.

Day was building up a war chest for the looming battle. But he had faced the government before and knew he could never match the Department of Justice when it came to expert witnesses and resources and people. He told CAG that he would accept only expenses, that he would not bill his comrades for his legal services unless or until they won something. He gave them keys to his office and put them on shifts to enter names on the computer, to return phone calls and e-mails, to answer the mail, and to screen potential CAG members. To qualify, a person had to have joined the military before 1956, served at least twenty years, and been honorably discharged.

On March 6, 1997, Bud Day faced off with a U.S. government lawyer at the federal courthouse in Pensacola. The courtroom was packed with retirees. The government was represented by Martha Hirschfield, a young woman who, Geasland later wrote, "was crawling around in heavy diapers" during the Vietnam War and thus knew nothing about values and practices of the Vietnam era, much less those of World War II. (When military people are criticized, the first thing they want to know is the service record of the person doing the criticizing. Their thinking, and this is almost universal, is that if you haven't been there, if you haven't worn the uniform, if you haven't been shot at, then you don't know what you are talking about, so sit down and be quiet. This argument is specious and irrelevant. Nevertheless, it holds great weight with those who served.)

Judge Roger Vinson asked Hirschfield if there were any precedents, any U.S. statutes that controlled the case; she said no. The judge took the case under advisement.

When Day left the courthouse, several hundred retirees were waiting. They gathered around him, cheering, shaking his hand, and thanking him.

On June 10, 1997, Judge Vinson agreed to let the case go forward, and the proceedings moved into "discovery" — the process by which the plaintiff and the defendant provide whatever evidence they have to each other so that when the case comes to trial, the court can weigh all the evidence and make a decision.

Those who have never entered a courtroom tend to think of legal proceedings as dry and plodding, even boring and of little consequence. Nothing could be further from the truth. All the drama of the human experience, from birth to death, is played out in the courtroom. And if one can hear the underlying harmonies, then one knows the courtroom can be a bloody arena with enormous stakes. It helps to have the law on your side, but that does not always ensure victory. The almost universal presence in the courtroom, or somewhere on the exterior of the courthouse, of a blindfolded woman holding the scales of justice is misleading in the extreme. Justice is not blind, and courtrooms are not about justice. Being an advocate is like being an old Western gunfighter who stands in the middle of the street and takes on all comers. The winner is the fastest and most skillful gun.

On March 14, 1997, Air Force chief of staff Ronald Fogleman presided over the dedication of the new Colonel George E. "Bud" Day Academic Building at the Air Force Survival School at Fairchild AFB near Spokane. The building was named for Day because, after his escape in Vietnam, he traveled farther than any other graduate in the history of the survival school.

The event was significant in a number of respects, the most important of which is the Air Force regulation that says buildings will be numbered, not named. On those rare times when the Air Force does name a building after a person, that person usually is long dead. The Air Force's naming a building after a living officer had few precedents. But General Fogleman said waiving the regulations in this instance was one of the easiest decisions he ever made.

WITHOUT getting bogged down in what became months of legal maneuvering, of motions and countermotions, suffice it to say that

Bud Day did not believe the government was entirely forthcoming in its presentation. Day knew the government had old manuals and recruiting material that would prove his case. But he could not find them. He filed interrogatories, part of the discovery process in which the plaintiff asks the defendant questions about the case. The government responded by saying the discovery motions were burdensome and onerous and would take too much manpower and be prohibitively expensive. On September 17, 1997, Judge Vinson issued an order saying the burden and expense to the government of discovery outweighed the benefits. He said the government did not have to respond to the interrogatories. Day offered the services of CAG members, retired military officers who would be delighted to help out the Justice Department. The offer was refused.

The government position was that no one in the military had the authority to bind the government to a promise of free lifetime medical care. This argument implied that all military recruiters were rogue agents who made promises without the authority of the government. Of course, few organizations are as rule-bound as is the U.S. military. It is a crime for an officer to make a false official statement. Yet the government's position implied that hundreds, perhaps thousands, of recruiting officials had, over the decades, done precisely that.

Day pointed out in one of his motions that the government claimed it was not bound by promises of lifetime medical care to retirees while at the same time military recruiters continued to use "this extremely valuable retirement benefit as a key recruiting tool." Indeed, as Veterans Day approached in November, Bill Kaczor noted in a story that on an Internet Web site, the U.S. Army was continuing to make promises of free medical care while at the same time government attorneys were asserting in court that no such guarantee existed.

(A few months later, U.S. military recruiters stopped telling enlistees, potential reenlistees, and officers of free lifetime medical care.

Recruiting films and brochures and anything containing references to free lifetime medical care were tossed out and replaced with material that did not contain the promise.)

Day's trepidation about fighting the government was proving to be well founded. But in late 1997 he sent an e-mail to all members of CAG saying that "defeat is not an option" and that he was pressing forward with all the forces at his command. As a military man, he knew that multiple thrusts are a proven strategy. He did not want to put the fate of the retirees entirely on the judicial approach. As a backup, he also would go the legislative route.

Mississippi was proving to be a ripe recruiting ground for CAG. Then congressman Ronnie Shows attended a CAG meeting in his Mississippi district. He told Day about his father, who was a disabled World War II veteran, and said, "I will do whatever I can to help you get a bill passed. But I am a freshman congressman. I have no clout. You need someone in the Senate who can help."

While Shows prepared and introduced a House bill to restore benefits, Day talked to Senator Tim Johnson of South Dakota, who agreed to support the legislation in the upper chamber. McCain, for reasons that are unclear, was reluctant to lend his support until Day called him for a heart-to-heart. Neither man will reveal the content of the conversation, but whatever it was finally convinced McCain to support the legislation.

The bill began making its way through Congress.

In February 1998, Day filed a motion in federal court in Pensacola, charging that the government was withholding crucial evidence. Both Day and the government asked for summary judgment in their behalf.

Day came to feel increasingly isolated during the months of court proceedings. The judge called Day "Mr. Day" while he called the government lawyers by their first names and was fraternal, almost jocular, with them. Day showed respect toward the judge but not the obeisance shown by the government lawyer.

And sometimes his indignation toward the government's position was palpable while the government lawyer was cool and almost clinical. Occasionally when Day sat down and crossed his legs, his socks were not in harmony with his suit. The government lawyer dressed like a Washington lawyer.

But Bud was not alone. Bob Geasland drove to Washington and, in a Navy medical library, found Navy Manuals of the Medical Department (MEDMAN) from 1922 and 1945 showing that free medical care for Navy and Marine Corps retirees had the force of law. Geasland also found the crucial "Forrestal Memo."

James Forrestal was secretary of the Navy and then, in 1947, became America's first secretary of defense. As secretary of the Navy, he signed a document that clearly set forth the military policy of using free medical care as a recruiting tool, of telling enlisted men and officers alike, *You give us twenty years and we will give you and your spouse free lifetime medical care, plus a retirement pay that equals 50 percent of your salary when on active duty.*

Now Geasland had documented Army, Navy, and Marine Corps practices. At Maxwell Field, he found the Air Force had piggybacked on Army regulations when it became a separate branch of the military. Indeed, his research showed that as far back as 1811, there had been an organized government effort to provide health care for improvident veterans. Sailors and Marines were assessed ten cents per month to build regional hospitals in Charleston, Boston, Philadelphia, and Pensacola. The heart of the hospital-fund legislation directed the secretary of the Navy to write the regulations concerning which military members would be admitted. Congress was completely out of the loop on hospital usage; all it did was appropriate additional construction funds. In fact, until 1956 and the "space available" law, Congress had never dictated the conditions under which retirees would be admitted to military hospitals.

On September 1, 1998, Judge Vinson entered a decision on civil document Case No. 3:96 CV 349/RV. The order was brief and said that while there was no question that certain representations were made to members of the military regarding health care, the issue was whether those representations were contractually binding. He did not think so and tossed Day's case out of court. To put this in perspective, the civilian analogy would be if the government decided to stop paying Social Security and a federal court upheld the decision.

Day's action was predictable.

He appealed.

18

The Fat Lady Never Sings

On September 22, 1998, Day met in Washington with about 150 retirees for a rally on the West Steps of the Capitol. This "Convention to Educate Congress" about health care was one of dozens of trips Day would make to Washington to talk with members of the House and Senate about the broken promise to America's military retirees.

Most members of Congress treated him with respect and gave him time to tell his story. But a few young staffers treated him with open disdain. He never took it personally, never became angry. And he forgot it before he was ten steps down the hall.

For these trips, he was, as always, paid only expenses. He stayed in cheap hotels across the Potomac in Virginia. He traveled by metro.

It was not unusual for him to be recognized by passengers, almost always military or ex-military people who had heard him speak at one place or another over the years. The conversation was always the same. The passenger would approach deferentially and say, "Excuse me, sir, but are you Colonel Day?"

That fetching boyish smile would break out on Day's face. He would clap the other person on the shoulder and say, "Sure am, pal. How you doing?"

Then the passenger would reach out to shake hands and say, "Great honor, sir. Great honor."

During the years the lawsuit was in the courts, Day would make many trips to Washington. But this trip was special. James Stockdale was there.

By now, Stockdale was beginning the long, slow decline into Alzheimer's disease that would claim his life in less than a decade. People stared as Stockdale and Day stood on the steps of the Capitol to address the retirees. A violent and fast-moving rainstorm suddenly moved in and sent spectators and the retirees scattering for the shelter of nearby buildings. Stockdale and Day remained. Of course they would.

Day opened an umbrella and held it over Stockdale so his prepared statement would not be soaked.

Stockdale began, "With heavy heart I have come to the nation's capital to ask the Congress of the United States to honor America's commitment to its military veterans." As he slowly spoke, Day stood a step above him, protecting him with the umbrella, staring straight ahead, jaw firm and jutting as the rain lashed him.

The sight of the two men, both MOH recipients, both heroes of Hanoi, both military legends, was enough to make the other retirees emerge from the protection of nearby buildings and gather to hear their comments.

Tom Philpott, who writes a syndicated column called Military Update, was there. He wrote that Stockdale spoke of honor and sacrifice and the sanctity of promises kept. Philpott finished his column with "And it was hard not to compare these men and their words with the moral vacuum at the White House, a mile and an age away."

Other than Philpott, who wrote about Bud Day's case extensively, there was almost no media coverage. In late September 1998, the big story was not about America's broken promise to some two million military retirees; the big story was about Bill Clinton's broken promise to his wife.

* * *

In December 1998, Bud Day filed documents indicating he would appeal the decision of the district court judge in Pensacola to the U.S. Court of Appeals for the Federal Circuit in Washington, a court that has nationwide jurisdiction in specialized cases.

It is in the appellate courts — particularly in the U.S. Court of Appeals for the Federal Circuit, which is considered only a half step below the Supreme Court — that legal writing reaches its zenith. Lawyers appearing in these courts know their briefs can become part of the legal canon. They strive for elegant and soaring prose that approaches literature. They favor pinstripe suits. They eschew emotion and manifest the pure essence of the legal thought process.

Not Bud Day. There was nothing delicate or rarefied about his brief, nothing of the épée designed to delicately puncture. He came in swinging a two-handed battle sword that mowed down everything before it. His appeal was a gutbucket document of indignation and outrage, a scathing denunciation of both the government lawyer and the federal judge in Pensacola. He said Hirschfield was either incompetent or a liar in that she made false representations about existing statutes and knew or should have known that she was not being truthful. He told how the plaintiffs had begun discovery but were "cut off early by the trial judge." He said Vinson "improperly limited plaintiffs' discovery and thus improperly shifted the burden to the plaintiff to disprove the defendant's defense with evidence in the defendant's control." In a sentence dripping with sarcasm, he wrote, "District court found that the secretaries of the Army, Navy, and defense, its officers and agents in DOD, and military recruiters did not have authority to bind the government to promises of free lifetime medical care." He used exclamation points as a hammer, saying that the judge "erred in applying both the facts and the law" and that the precedent used by the judge was "too old, too narrow, and too mean to apply in this case!!" He added that "it cannot be the intention of Congress or the Executive Department (defendant) to provide the aged Private Ryans a discriminatory hemlock drink from the cup of life after reaching age sixty-five. If in fact that is the intention, then this government of William Jefferson Clinton is not worth fighting for."

DAY had a lot riding on his court appearance before the three-judge panel. By now, more than ten thousand retirees, each individually qualified as affected by the Clinton cost-cutting measure and therefore eligible to participate in what Day hoped would become a class action suit, had signed up for CAG. (Eventually there would be more than thirty thousand.) Day spent months preparing the appellate brief. Almost two million people were depending on him, and the three-judge panel, if it upheld the decision of the district court, could dash their hopes. Such an outcome would mean Bud Day had to abort his final mission. And that was unacceptable.

WHEN John McCain ran for president in 2000, Orson Swindle worked in the campaign's national headquarters. One of his main jobs was coordinating the support of veterans around the country. Florida was a crucial state because about 1.7 million veterans live there — a powerful political force. Bud Day worked tirelessly for McCain.

George Bush showed that he had his father's political skills when he characterized McCain as a man who had undergone so much torture in Hanoi that he could not stand up under the pressure of the presidency. Day was furious. Yet when McCain withdrew from the race, Day switched his support to Bush, a man who spoke often of the need to honor the nation's veterans and to protect retiree benefits. And besides, Albert Gore was Bill Clinton's Mini Me.

ON March 6, 2000, the night before he was to present his case to the three-judge federal panel, Day went to the hotel restaurant for a bowl of soup. He was exhausted and had a bad cold. At the restaurant he was seized with a terrible coughing spell. Later, as he went over his presentation, his throat was so sore he could not finish. He lost his voice. In despair, he swallowed his sleeping pills and a host of other medicines and went to bed.

Day had just turned seventy-five, an age when few lawyers continue to practice. Four long years had passed since this matter began. He had gone through another surgery on his shoulder. He was becoming more forgetful, less able to summon facts immediately. And even though he had given hundreds, perhaps thousands, of speeches in the last quarter of a century, he still stiffened up somewhat in the formal setting of a courtroom. His mouth became dry and his hands trembled. His hearing was at the point where he often used a blank stare and a raised eyebrow to have people repeat whatever they said. Soon he would get a hearing aid.

The next morning Day was elated. His voice had returned. He dressed in a starched white shirt, solemn gray suit, and sober tie. His shoes were polished until they gleamed.

Doris checked his socks. Bud had a pair of Christmas socks, bright red with green Christmas trees on them, that he liked to wear no matter the season. But today Doris made sure he wore black socks.

Doris sent Bud on his way. She was running late and would be along soon.

The U.S. Court of Appeals for the Federal Circuit is located on Madison Place, a small street between Pennsylvania Avenue and H Street that is closed to vehicular traffic. Day walked in and saw that his case was number two on the docket.

Rarely does an advocate have a day in the courtroom such as Bud Day had before the three-judge panel. It was, to use his phrase, "a slam dunk." Every question the court asked him was sympathetic and understanding, and he responded quickly with relevant case law. His memory was sharp and his tongue was persuasive. The secretary of the Navy had offered free lifetime medical care to sailors and Marines in the 1918 issue of the MEDMAN. Those promises, funded by Congress, were carried out over more than seventy-seven years.

The government lawyer was E. Roy Hawkens. Sitting beside him was a JAG officer. Day could not believe that a man in uniform would oppose his case. The officer's mere presence made it appear that the military was fighting the retirees.

The foundation of the government argument was that the promises of free medical care might have been made, but there was no statute authorizing the promise and therefore the promises were without authority and were not enforceable. It was the familiar "rogue agent defense" — the agents had no authority to make the promises, and therefore the promises were not legal.

Judge Pauline Newman said, "You're not telling us that these promises were not made; you're just saying they don't have to be kept?"

"Regretfully, that is the case," Hawkens said.

The judge pointed out that the government's promise was never conditional; the promise was made for life.

"The current Congress is not bound by the generosity of benevolence of a previous Congress," said Hawkens.

Judge H. Robert Mayer asked if there were not someone in the chain of command who had authority to bind the government to the promise that had been made.

Hawkens said the promise was a "well-meaning misunderstanding resulting in an unauthorized representation" that could not be enforced to the extent of drawing on the treasury.

When Day left the courtroom late that morning, he knew he had won. There was only one way the court could rule.

IN October 2000, the "Keep the Promise Bill" introduced by Representative Ronnie Shows passed through Congress. In its final form, the bill became known as "TRICARE for Life." It was a staggering win for Bud Day in that the law gave the retirees far more than he had asked.

Not only did the law allow military retirees to use military — and civilian — hospitals for their care and medicine but it provided a low-cost mail-in pharmacy program that meant retirees did not have to drive fifty or a hundred miles to buy drugs at a military hospital. And Congress expanded the coverage to include retirees under sixty-five. The law did not cover ears, eyes, and dental. (The "ears" part is important because many retired pilots have significant hearing loss from being around aircraft engines for so many years.) And retirees still had to pay for Part B of Medicare, the supplement that covers doctor fees. But TRICARE for Life meant that Bud Day had returned to the retirees about 95 percent of what the Clinton administration had taken away. And for the remainder of his life, no matter where he went, elderly retirees would come to him with tears in their eyes and thank him.

Before the federal panel ruled, there was the end of the bitterly contested presidential campaign. Day was proud of how the veterans and retirees in the First District turned out. Indeed, voters across the panhandle voted so heavily for Bush that CBS — and the other networks — did a lot of backpedaling and adjusting and explaining and correcting before reporting that Bush had carried the state.

Later, on January 19, 2001, at a preinaugural "Salute to America's Veterans," Bush would say, "In order to make sure that morale is high with those who wear the uniform today, we must keep our commitment to those who wore the uniform in the past. . . . We will make sure promises made to our veterans will be promises kept."

Even though Day won a major battle in Congress, he had not won the war. He wanted to absolve retirees of having to pay Part B of Medicare. And he wanted them reimbursed — up to $10,000 each — for their medical expenses since 1995.

On February 8, 2001, Day received news that the three-judge federal panel had reversed the district court. The judges sent the case back to Pensacola and ordered the district judge to decide how much to pay the retirees to make them whole. In a scathing decision, the three-judge panel said the district court judge erred in applying both the facts and the law, that Vinson had "misread case law" probably because he was taking "one-liners out of headnotes without a full review of the facts, or misapprehension of the case."

Because of what would happen later, it must be noted that the then chief judge on the three-judge panel was H. Robert Mayer, a graduate of West Point and a highly decorated former Army Ranger who wore a Combat Infantryman Badge. He had been appointed by Ronald Reagan. Judge S. Jay Plager, appointed by George H. W. Bush, had been a Navy commander who served in the Korean War. Both of these men had been among the many promised free medical care if they spent twenty years in uniform. Judge Pauline Newman, appointed by Reagan, also ruled in favor of the retirees.

The idea that a federal judge might order the government to pay up to $10,000 to the retirees filled government lawyers with panic. The government asked for an en banc hearing — that is, that the case be heard by the full court of twelve judges. And they planned how they would bring out the legal equivalent of the nuclear option.

The government estimated that at least 1.5 million retirees were older than sixty-five and that if each received $10,000, the feds would have to fork over $15 billion. To Day and the retirees, this was a moral issue, an issue about a broken promise. Now the government was making it a dollar issue. And $15 billion was an amount that would make any federal judge jump back from his desk.

The court granted the request for an en banc hearing and issued instructions that new briefs should include an analysis of only three issues: 1) Were promises of free lifetime medical care enforceable? 2) In light of retirees receiving free medical care under authorization bills passed by Congress and thus arguably with its approval, to what extent has Congress ratified the promise by funding the military health-care system and permitting the military to make good on its promises to retirees? 3) What relevance, if any, did the National Defense Authorization Bill of that year have? (This legislation contains funding for the military.)

Bud Day would be ready. Or so he thought.

In November 2001 came an event at the Air Force Academy that, while seemingly tangential to Bud Day's story, would have a profound effect on his life.

Brigadier General Robbie Risner, the high-profile POW, was a devoutly religious man. After he retired, Ross Perot had been responsible for his being named director of the Texas antidrug program. Risner and Perot became close friends, so close that Perot asked Risner to speak at his church in Dallas, the Highland Park Presbyterian Church. There Risner told the story of how he had organized the first church service in the Hanoi Hilton, how this resulted in the Church Riot, and how, as he was led away to torture, he heard Bud Day leading the POWs in singing the National Anthem. He recalled how at that moment, "I felt nine feet tall."

Perot had been so moved by the story that he commissioned a sculptor to cast a nine-foot-tall statue of Risner. Perot took verse eight of the sixth chapter of Isaiah, which reads, "Also I heard the voice of the Lord, saying, Whom shall I send, and who will go for us? Then said I, Here am I; send me," and condensed it to "Who will go . . . send me" and had it engraved on the base of the statue. (Perot is one of few men with enough confidence to rewrite the Old Testament.)

Perot wanted the statue placed at the Air Force Academy, where it would serve as a model for generations of cadets. Some claimed that officials at the academy demurred, though Perot denies this. He says the academy always supported the idea. But the truth is that the Air Force prefers dead heroes to live ones. And while it is rare for live heroes to have buildings named after them, it is even rarer for a live hero to be honored with a statue. In addition, Risner was not an academy graduate; in fact he had come up through the cadet program and had only a high school education. Finally, the idea for the statue had not originated at the academy.

But Perot was relentless, and not only did he succeed in getting the Risner statue placed at the academy but he also ordered the creation of a duplicate cast to stand in front of the Weapons School at Nellis AFB, and a bust made from the statue to be displayed at Randolph AFB.

But those who know Perot and his relationship with the U.S. military were not at all surprised. One of the great untold stories in America is how Perot, a man frequently criticized and ridiculed by the national media, has spent millions of dollars on the military. He has financed military museums, libraries, research centers, and statues, and has flown dozens of active-duty military people — particularly in the Special Operations community — to Dallas for specialized and expensive medical treatment. Just to identify what became known as the Gulf War syndrome, he spent close to $100 million — every penny against the strong opposition of the Clinton administration, which did not want the government to pay disability to troops affected by this new disease.

It is safe to say that in the history of America, no private citizen has spent as much money on the military as has H. Ross Perot. (He is an Annapolis graduate who served a tour in the Navy.) And no private citizen is more respected by those who have served. When the POWs hold their reunions, Perot is always there — and when he enters the room, they stand up. Perot can pick up the phone and contact any one of the Joint Chiefs of Staff and they will take the call. (In 2005, in the middle of the Iraq war, all of the chiefs came to a Dallas party that recognized Perot's contributions to the military.) So, in the end, the Air Force Academy could not say no to anything Perot wanted.

On Friday, November 16, 2001, the Risner statue was dedicated. Bud Day was the keynote speaker. He began by recognizing several dozen former POWs whom he called "my fellow criminals." After Day's speech, in which he said the statue was "life-size," the POWs came onstage and reprised that magic moment from three decades earlier when Day led them in singing the National Anthem. They were old men now and their voices were faltering. But this was a military audience, and the story of the Church Riot was taught throughout the military — it was history come alive.

The next day, Saturday, was one of those crisp late-autumn perfections that sometimes comes to the Front Range of the Rocky Mountains — a day that is both a remembrance of summer and a hint of spring. The sun was blinding, the air was clean, and visibility was unlimited. Risner and his fellow Yankee air pirates were guests of honor at a football game on Falcon Field, where, as usual, the academy was losing. At halftime, UNLV was ahead by a score of 13-10, and the cadets — rightly, as it turned out — probably figured this was another defeat. They needed something to celebrate.

Then came the announcement that General Robinson Risner and Medal of Honor recipient Colonel Bud Day were about to lead a group of POWs onto the field. Risner and Day were up front. Like most pilots, they had rarely marched even when on active duty. But Day was calling cadence and had them marching like Marines: shoulders back, heads high, legs swinging in unison. Many in the stands would not notice, but one of the POWs was being helped along by his comrades on either side — he had multiple sclerosis. But he was marching. As they came out of the shadow and onto the field, the sunlight glistened on their white hair, and had they not been so old, you would have sworn there was a touch of swagger in their march.

The cadets came to their feet and the stadium erupted in a cheer that must have been heard all the way to Denver. Day marched the POWs to the center of the field, where they halted, pivoted, and faced the cadets. Risner ordered, "Present arms," and the POWs saluted the cadets. The cadets popped to attention and returned the salute.

In that frozen moment, nothing was said. But much was understood. Cadets barely in their twenties and long-retired officers in their seventies were joined across a half century. The cadets, every single one of them, must have wondered, *If the time ever comes, can I do what you did? Can I bear up? Can I uphold the honor of America?* And the POWs, in effect, were saying, *Yes! You know what the standard is. Carry on.*

ON the morning of March 6, 2002, Day dressed for the en banc hearing before the U.S. Court of Appeals for the Federal Circuit.

Day was not unaware of the unique position he held, and he was prepared to use that influence on behalf of the retirees. He reached into his suitcase and pulled out the black case that contained his Medal of Honor. Then he stood before a mirror as Doris reverently clasped the medal around his neck. He again reached into his suitcase and picked up his silver command pilot's wings, buffed them on his sleeve, and pinned them on the left breast of his suit.

Day almost never is flustered. But that morning he was as nervous as Doris had ever seen him. This was more than the usual dry mouth before oral arguments. Doris was running late so Bud went ahead by taxi. On the way to the courthouse, he had to stop and have a bowl of soup. Then he broke out in such heavy perspiration that he had to take off his jacket.

The courthouse was crowded with retirees, some of whom had driven seven or eight hours to be there. They came from all across the eastern side of America, from the South, and from as far west as Texas. They were not as trim as they once had been and most of them had white hair — that is, if they had hair. Many wore glasses. Some were on walkers and crutches. Several carried oxygen bottles. They would have looked like refugees from a geriatric ward had it not been for their eyes. They might have been old geezers, but they were tough old geezers.

When Day entered the courthouse, stooped over, arm pumping, the Medal of Honor around his neck, it set off a ripple effect. As soon as they saw him, every retiree in the lobby and in the halls and on the stairs stood at attention. They could not stand as straight as they could when they were young men, but they could still get their heels together and hold their heads up. And when Day entered the courtroom, dozens of retirees stood as one. He smiled and nodded and motioned for them to sit. But they waited until he found his table at the front of the room before they sat down. His partner, Tim Meade, was already there.

Day opened his briefcase and pulled out his documents and his legal pad. He placed his pen atop the pad and looked over his shoulder. His mouth was so dry he could not speak. He needed Doris behind him; he needed to know she was here and to feel her great strength.

He knew without looking when she entered the courtroom. But the chamber was so packed there was no place for her down front. Robert Geasland asked for two volunteers to give up their seats so Doris and Marilyn Reinlie, wife of one of the plaintiffs, could sit behind Bud.

Military people rarely volunteer for anything unless it involves sacrifice. Every retiree in the front row stood and offered Doris and Marilyn his seat.

With Doris behind him, Bud Day was ready.

He was seventy-seven years old; William Schism was seventy-six and Robert Reinlie was eighty-one.

The court had a newly appointed judge. One of the judges who had been on the three-judge panel was in a semiretired status but was present. So Day was looking at thirteen judges, one more than planned.

As the arguments ended, Day prepared to leave the courtroom. But Chief Judge H. Robert Mayer looked at Day and said, "Just a minute." The judge looked at the government lawyers, looked across the courtroom filled with retirees, and announced, "I have something to say and it has nothing to do with this case."

Everyone in the courtroom froze. What was about to happen?

The judge stared at Day, paused, and said, "Colonel Day, on behalf of everyone in the room, for the veterans in the audience, for the lawyers at both counsel tables, and for every member of this court, I thank you for your great service to our country."

For a moment the courtroom was silent. Then almost every person in the audience stood and applauded.

DAY was happy as he left the courthouse. Even to the most cautious of legal minds, it was clear that, once again, he had prevailed in court. Usually, Day is a reserved man. Now he was babbling away. Day is a man who needs his sleep. But after his court appearance he did not go to bed for twenty-three hours. Doris had never seen him like this. It was just a matter of waiting for the court to hand down its decision.

OUT in Sioux City, Brendan Burchard, the command chief master sergeant of the 185th Air Refueling Wing, had done a lot of research about Bud Day and was appalled. Small Midwestern towns have few heroes. Anyone of any accomplishment at all from nearby towns in Iowa or Nebraska or South Dakota had been recognized in some fashion. But Siouxland had done nothing for Bud Day. Burchard and Master Sergeant John Sandman decided to change this.

Many people in the 185th had gotten to know Day over the years, so Burchard figured it was appropriate that any recognition of Day begin with the military. Renaming the airport to "Colonel Bud Day Field" seemed a good idea. But this would take the support of airport officials and the city council.

Burchard went to the wing commander, Colonel John Janson, and presented his case. Janson was easily convinced and ordered that a video of Colonel Day's life be put together "that will make it impossible for people to say no" to the renaming idea.

The fifteen-minute video was so compelling that when it was shown to airport authorities, they sat in stunned silence for about twenty seconds.

Bud Day was a national hero. Why had his hometown not honored him?

The city council had the same reaction.

Word of the video spread, and soon the members of the 185th were showing the tape to civic groups around Sioux City.

Plans became more ambitious. In addition to renaming the airport, what about a statue of Day to be placed inside the terminal?

After approval for renaming the airport was granted, members of the 185th began calling Day's old comrades, Mistys and former POWs, for information and for items they could place in an airport exhibit. They were overwhelmed at the emotion they encountered. Bill Douglass, as usual, wept when he spoke about Bud Day and the Mistys. "You just don't understand what this man means to us," he said.

Among the memorabilia Day sent out to be placed in the airport exhibit was a set of boxing gloves imprinted with a gorilla. Members of the 185th could not figure out their significance, and they were reluctant to ask.

The airport renaming was on May 25, 2002, and coincided with a NAM-POW reunion in Dallas. Perot piled as many of the former POWs as he could on his corporate jet and flew them to Sioux City, where they taxied up near the speaker's platform. As the jet approached, word buzzed across the crowd of several hundred people, "The POWs are here." When the door opened and the men began filing out, they were greeted with a spontaneous round of applause.

Orson Swindle was there. Jack Fellowes, who had nursed Day after his torture ended in the fall of 1969, was there. John McCain was not, but he sent a videotape in which he said, "I have never known a tougher, more ornery, disciplined leader than Bud Day. Neither have the North Vietnamese." McCain went on to say that Day had taken beatings for those under his command in Hanoi and ended with, "I have never had a dearer friend and never known a finer man."

Perot was the featured speaker. Afterward the media wanted to talk with him. But as is always the case in these events, he would not speak to the press. This event was to honor Bud Day.

Now Day had joined the ranks of men whose names can be counted on one hand: men who, while still alive, have had an airport named for them.

The only thing missing was the statue.

The 185th wanted a bust of Day to be placed in the airport. But preliminary inquiries indicated a bust would cost at least $5,000. The money could not be taken from tax funds, and it was too much for the 185th to raise. It appeared that, other than an exhibit of pictures and POW memorabilia, there would be nothing to represent the man for whom the airport was now named.

Then one day Colonel Janson picked up his telephone to hear, "Colonel, this is Ross Perot. Here's what we're gonna do." And off he went talking about a nine-foot statue of Bud Day. A conversation with Ross Perot often is not really a conversation; it is a matter of listening while Perot talks. So Janson listened. Dealing with the casting of a statue for a retired officer is not the business of a wing commander. So Colonel Janson delegated to Major Stephanie Samenus, who was in charge of community relations, the job of coordinating all details of the statue.

Ceilings inside the airport were ten feet, so airport officials were having trouble with the idea of a nine-foot statue, especially since it was to stand atop a four-foot marble base. Clearly something had to give. Perhaps Mr. Perot would consider a smaller statue, maybe a bust of Bud Day?

Absolutely not. He said everyone in Room 7 was nine feet tall the day of the Church Riot. The height of airport ceilings was irrelevant.

(The Bud Day statue also had to be nine feet tall because the sculptor used the same mold as he had used for the Risner statue — only a different head.)

ON November 18, 2002, the U.S. Court of Appeals for the Federal Circuit handed down a 9–4 ruling against the retirees that rejected every argument that the three-judge panel had embraced.

The judges said only Congress, and not military recruiters, had the power to authorize free medical care.

For Day it was a stunning and unexpected reversal. What happened? Why did nine judges revolt against a decision by the chief judge? Dissenting from the majority were the same three judges who earlier ruled in Day's favor. Another dissenting judge had once worked for the Air Force as a civilian lawyer.

It hadn't been his argument. Indeed, Day's courtroom performance had particularly impressed the 235,000 members of the Young Lawyers Division of the American Bar Association. They realized that if Day won it would mean a $15 billion settlement and a $1.5 billion fee. The Young Lawyers named Day "Lawyer of the Year" and presented him with the Fellows Award for the best trial performance of the year.

So what had happened? How could the court make such a turnaround? Day read the majority opinion and was appalled. His assumption was that judges at this level were masters of abstract thinking; that they were penetrating legal scholars able to pierce to the heart of any issue no matter how complex. Day wondered if the judges had simply turned everything over to young law clerks and if they had seen what went out over their names. Within the majority opinion the absurdities were endless and showed a fundamental lack of knowledge about the military. Day wrote in the margin alongside one comment, "This was written by some nonmilitary draft dodger w/o a clue what these words mean."

Day's beliefs appear to have been shared at least in part by one of the dissenting judges. Justice S. Jay Plager added a telling comment: "Perhaps the problem is that, with the demise of compulsory military service, too few of our citizens today have the experience of knowing firsthand what the military is about." His remark was a direct slap at eight of the nine judges who wrote the majority opinion — the eight who had no military experience.

Later, Day researched the biographical sketches of the eight judges and found that most of them were of college age during the Vietnam era. "Hell, they could have been hanging out with Hanoi Jane," he said.

Day would ask the U.S. Supreme Court to review the ruling.

He was not optimistic when he found that the court, as then constituted, had only three justices who were veterans.

After Day announced he would take the dispute to the Supreme Court, several retirees gathered. One of them mused that with the passage of TRICARE for Life and its accompanying pharmacy program, the retirees had regained almost everything taken from them by Bill Clinton. Why was Bud Day still fighting?

"Because it ain't over till the fat lady sings," said another.

A third man nodded and paused. Then he said, "As far as Bud Day is concerned, the fat lady *never* sings."

AIRPORT officials in Sioux City eventually decided to put the Bud Day statue near the front door of the airport, in sight of every-one who entered or departed. Colonel Bud Day Field is a small regional airport served by six daily flights, all Northwest Airlines feeder flights to and from Minneapolis.

The statue arrived on December 9, 2002, the day before it was to be dedicated. Coincidentally, Bud and Doris arrived on a flight about the time the flatbed truck pulled up out front, and they watched the statue being placed atop the pedestal.

The next morning, on the sixtieth anniversary of the day he joined the Marine Corps and a day that Bud celebrates every year, the statue was dedicated.

Orson Swindle delivered the keynote speech. He told how he and Bud Day met in 1971 when their jailers moved the "bad apples in the barrel" — the Hells Angels — to the terrible prison known as Skid Row.

The former Marine, then serving on the Federal Trade Commission, alluded to the lawsuit and whether or not it would be heard by the Supreme Court. He closed with a partial verse from "Sir Andrew Barton," one of the ballads in *Percy's Reliques*, pub-lished in 1765. Barton had been wounded in battle.

"Fight on, my men," Sir Andrew sayes,
"A little Ime hurt, but yett not slaine;
He but lye downe and bleede awhile,
And then He rise and fight againe."

After Swindle's speech, Day's daughters pulled away the parachute that covered the statue.

Perot had inscribed on one face of the pedestal, "Prisoner AT war," an inscription that caused some confusion; people thought it must be a typo. Perot also insisted that a specific inscription be engraved on another face of the pedestal. The inscription reads, "Never give in. Never give in — Never, Never, Never." It is attributed to Winston Churchill.

What Churchill actually said on October 29, 1941, to students at the Harrow School was somewhat different. But Perot had already rewritten the Old Testament. Churchill was small potatoes.

WILLIAM O. Schism, one of the plaintiffs in the suit against the government, died on March 30, 2003. And by July, of the original thirteen CAG volunteers who worked in Day's office, seven had died.

Now the only plaintiff was Reinlie. It was not widely known, but Reinlie had colon cancer and diabetes. If he died before the Supreme Court heard the case, the case might end.

But Reinlie was alive in June 2003 when the Supreme Court of the United States declined to hear the case. This meant that the decision of the Washington appellate court stood: it was regrettable that recruiters made promises to the "greatest generation," but those were empty promises and Congress did not fund empty promises.

The irony, as many retirees noted, was that Chief Justice Rehnquist, who served only three years in the military, was being provided with free medical care at Walter Reed.

* * *

BUD Day decided to fight on. It was clear that President George W. Bush had forgotten his campaign promises and his speech about the retirees. Like Clinton before him, he was trying to cut costs at the expense of the retirees. But maybe Congress would use its powers to specifically fund the free medical care.

Bud Day and CAG were not finished.

19

One More Mission

BEFORE Day's story can move to another part of the national stage, three bits of background are necessary.

First, the military invented the Internet, and military people are among the most Internet-savvy people on the planet. Many veterans and retirees stay in regular online touch with the members of their old units. Most active-duty military units have Web sites, and there are Web sites for every type of aircraft flown by military pilots, even the aircraft of Vietnam, Korea, and World War II. Many of these sites transcend interservice rivalries and, through various links, reach active-duty or retired members of every branch of the military.

Almost all of these sites are for members only. Webmasters rebuff attempts by outsiders to contact members of the network. Some Web sites, and messages sent through those sites, have enormous weight and credibility. At the top of that list is the NAM-POW Web site.

This military side of the Internet is parallel to the Internet that most people know; it is there but is neither visible nor accessible without proper credentials. And while it is impossible to quantify the number of people who can be reached through military-connected sites, the number is certainly in the hundreds of thousands.

The second bit of background concerns the military caste system. MOH recipients are at the top of the system. Many civilians believe the Medal of Honor is awarded for killing enemy soldiers. (Think Audie Murphy in World War II.) But in real life, the medal often is awarded for defying death in order to save a comrade: falling on a grenade to protect others or landing a helicopter under heavy fire to perform a rescue. That is why many MOH awards are posthumous. Most of the living recipients would have died but for a twist of fate.

POWs are up there pretty close to MOH recipients. Next in the military caste system are the DAV, the Disabled American Veterans. Many members are amputees or severely handicapped. You don't get into this club unless you have left your blood and pieces of yourself on a battlefield.

If a man is in all three categories — an MOH recipient, a POW, and a member of the DAV — then he has really pushed his luck. He should have been dead many times over.

Bud Day is one of very few of these men still alive. To several million young active-duty officers and enlisted personnel, seeing these men and hearing them speak is not unlike having George Washington step from a painting and issue marching orders. When Bud Day sends an e-mail signed "Bud Day, MOH," it is as close to holy writ as can be found.

Finally, and in light of what was about to take place, the most crucial bit of background information is to know something about military culture, particularly the inviolate concepts of honor and duty, of adhering to *principle*. (The overtly corrupt world where Congress, the military, and the defense industry come together, and the political world of generals, are obvious exceptions.)

If a civilian can't get his arms around the simple fact that honor and patriotism and adherence to a code of conduct are the inviolate core of the military heart, then he will never begin to understand the men and women in uniform.

Now we can pick up Bud Day's story.

* * *

In July 2004, at the Democratic National Convention, Senator John Kerry became his party's nominee for president of the United States. He began his acceptance speech by saluting and saying he was "reporting for duty."

That salute was a big mistake.

Bud Day exploded in anger.

The next morning he called a friend and said, "You know, I thought the reason God saved my life so many times was so I could be in jail in Hanoi. Then, twenty years later, I thought God had saved my life so I could work to restore medical benefits to the retirees. But I was wrong. Now I really know why my life was spared. I have one more job, one more mission before I die."

There was a pause as the friend thought through Day's past and wondered what there was at his age that could galvanize him enough to sally forth into battle again. "What is it?"

"To do everything I can to keep that traitor John Kerry from being elected."

And then Bud Day sat down at his computer and began firing off e-mails through the NAM-POW list and his own list of hundreds of names. To each one he added in the abbreviated system of POWs, "Pls fwrd to ur net." Many recipients, proud that they were on Day's mailing list, forwarded the message to those on their own e-mail lists. And those people did the same with their lists.

It is easy to say Day was motivated by party politics. After all, he had been an ardent Republican for more than thirty years. He had worked for Reagan and for Bush — father and son — and for McCain. On August 10, when President George W. Bush campaigned near Fort Walton Beach, Day met him at the airport rally and led the Pledge of Allegiance.

Later, after his speech, the president went to Day and said, "Bud, I thank you for your support."

"It can be no other way," Day replied.

But on the other side of the coin was a matter of principle.

When Kerry had saluted, the bitter memories had rushed in: Once again it was April 1971, and Kerry was testifying before the Senate Committee on Foreign Relations. All the newspaper and television reporting about the Vietnam War flooded back too, coverage that many Vietnam veterans believe is the longest-running hoax ever perpetrated on the American public. And here was the man they believed responsible. Many in the military community suddenly realized John Kerry could be elected *commander in chief.*

It was time for John Kerry to be held accountable.

It was time for a great wrong to be righted.

Night and day, dozens of military sites flashed impassioned messages across the Internet. No one could read the volume and sense the intensity of the e-mail traffic and not know something big was beginning.

What happened next, in the late summer and early fall of 2004, has never before happened in American politics. And today, the backstory of those tumultuous months remains either generally unknown or widely misunderstood.

In previous presidential elections, if the national media — television networks, major daily newspapers, and news magazines — ignored a story, there was no story. But the anti-Kerry movement surging through the Internet soon would make it embarrassingly clear to the traditional media that this no longer was the case. For the first time in the history of presidential campaigns, the traditional media faced off with the "new media" — the Internet. The agility of the new media, aided and abetted by talk radio and cable television, enabled it to own one of the most important stories of the year, a story that changed history. And because the traditional media believed they were the only media that mattered, they never realized they were roadkill until long after events had passed them by.

In early August, retired major general Patrick Brady, an MOH recipient, published an emotional and angry Op-Ed column in an obscure veterans' newsletter in Missouri. Usually, maybe a hundred people would have seen the column. But in this instance someone scanned it, added his own comments, attached it to an e-mail list, and hit the "send" button.

The column talked of how Vietnam veterans had suffered more than any veterans of the past century. "What Kerry/Fonda and the media elite did to the Vietnam veteran and his family is deplorable," General Brady wrote. He said even the men who died in Vietnam suffered because their families wondered if they were war criminals.

He said real heroes do not use their medals for political gain and that after Kerry had thrown away his medals, he then used the same medals as the basis for his political career. He added that Kerry's medals were "unchallenged by mainstream media." The column rocketed through the military network for days.

In the September 6 edition of the *Army Times* was a full-page ad paid for by Dexter Lehtinen, a former Army Ranger who had been wounded in Vietnam and who then came home to graduate first in his class at Stanford Law School. He later served as a Florida state senator and as U.S. attorney in Miami. His ad told how in 1971 he was wounded in Vietnam and awakened days later on a hospital ship, where he learned of Kerry's congressional testimony. He said the wounds he suffered on the battlefield eventually healed, but the wounds inflicted by John Kerry continued to bring pain to him and to other Vietnam veterans. He said these wounds "go to the heart and soul. These wounds never go away." Contents of the ad circulated widely through the military community on the Internet, again with numerous supportive comments.

In midmonth came a column by Barbara Stock on FrontPageMag.com that was widely circulated. "Revenge Is a Dish Best Served Cold" told how John Kerry's salute and his "reporting for duty" had resurrected the anger of Vietnam veterans; how Kerry "had shredded their honor without a thought and climbed over the bodies of their fallen friends to launch a political career."

The important thing here, the near universal sentiment in the military, is the deep sense of anger that Kerry's salute evoked and how this time the military was going to hold him accountable.

One group, the highly vocal "Swift Boat Veterans for Truth," or "Swifties," as they came to be known, began putting ads on television that talked of Kerry's service in Vietnam, the circumstances under which his medals were awarded, and the details of his discharge. Holy writ for the Swifties was a book published in May, *Unfit for Command* by John E. O'Neill and Jerome R. Corsi. After its publication, the Swifties asked Kerry to release his military records to the media, a standard and long-existing campaign practice. Kerry refused, never releasing the full details of his military record. (After the campaign he released *part* of the record to selected reporters.)

Kerry loyalists and the media declared the Swift Boat campaign underhanded and sleazy for wanting to go back thirty years into a candidate's past. But while the media generally supported Kerry's position that his military records were off-limits, George Bush's National Guard records were a major media event. Bloggers and the military side of the Internet — along with the *Boston Globe* — months earlier had discredited the source for the anti-Bush stories. Nevertheless, CBS continued with a story, claiming Bush had used political connections not only to avoid being shipped to Vietnam but to avoid even showing up for his National Guard postings, and the network suffered great embarrassment when it aired spurious allegations. The self-inflicted wound resulted in the firing of a producer and the resignation of three senior executives, and was a factor in the retirement of CBS anchor Dan Rather. When it became known that the producer had given the source's phone number to the Kerry campaign, it did little to improve the image of CBS — or the national media — in the military community.

The media's refusal to examine Kerry's military background with the same energy with which they examined Bush's did something else: it reinforced the belief of veterans that television networks and major daily newspapers were liberal to the core, were biased, had little or no concerns about military interests, and rather than reporting the news were generating propaganda for John Kerry. And all this made those opposed to Kerry even more determined.

The Swifties, in large part because of *Unfit for Command*, continued to hammer Kerry's military record. One of the authors, John E. O'Neill, was a Naval Academy graduate who took command of Kerry's boat after Kerry's four-month tour in Vietnam. O'Neill, who had attacked Kerry back in 1971 in a debate on *The Dick Cavett Show*, said, among other things, that Kerry lied about the circumstances under which his medals were awarded and did not deserve the medals.

The book was such a scathing denunciation of Kerry that Kerry loyalists threatened to sue bookstores that carried it. The controversy put the book on the *New York Times* bestseller list for five weeks and resulted in some 800,000 copies being sold. The national media savaged the book but were never able to disprove the allegations.

From a military standpoint, what the Swifties were doing was unprecedented in U.S. military history or in the history of presidential campaigns. It is an inviolate principle of the military that officers do not criticize fellow officers in public. But 253 Swifties, Kerry's entire chain of command up to and including Rear Admiral Roy Hoffmann, commander of all Swift Boats in Vietnam, publicly opposed Kerry's candidacy. They did not believe he was fit to be president.

The civilian equivalent of this would be if a governor announced he was running for president, and his chief of staff and everyone who worked for him or with him opposed his candidacy.

The widespread perception that Kerry had broad military support is simply wrong. His "band of brothers" was few in number.

The anti-Kerry buzz on the military side of the Internet began to move to talk radio and then to cable television.

After about a six-week delay, Kerry responded to the Swifties by questioning their patriotism and motives. He reminded people that he was a Vietnam veteran who wore a Silver Star and three Purple Hearts. He diverted the thrust of what the Swifties were saying by claiming they were part of the "Republican attack machine" and were guided by Karl Rove of President Bush's staff and financed by Republican fat cats. The last point is certainly true. But no evidence points to the GOP or to Karl Rove.

Finally, John McCain publicly weighed in. McCain declared that the Swifties' going after Kerry's military records was "dishonest and dishonorable." (He also said — and this was not widely reported — that Kerry's 1971 testimony was fair game.) McCain was one of the few men in America who could have single-handedly stopped the Swift Boat Veterans. His comment carried enormous weight with the media and with much of America. But it engendered great anger in the military community. The Kerry campaign earlier had floated McCain's name as a possible vice presidential candidate. Now it seemed McCain was demonstrating that for him the brotherhood of the Senate was stronger than the brotherhood of the military. And veterans believed he was splitting hairs by opposing opening Kerry's military records and minimizing what to most veterans was the real issue — Kerry's 1971 Senate testimony. Still, McCain's statements, when coupled with the strength of Kerry's response — and how widely it was reported — dispirited the Swifties. They thought they were dead in the water.

And John Kerry thought he was wounded. From August 9 until September 21 — forty-three days in the middle of a presidential campaign — Kerry did not hold a news conference. He knew reporters wanted to talk about the Swift Boat Veterans.

After McCain's comment, Bud Day closed his office door and spent hours reading and rereading Kerry's 1971 testimony. The testimony, to him, was the main issue. Then he made a very difficult decision to publicly oppose his old and dear friend. He called McCain and, in his words, "chewed his ass out." Then he sat down and, on October 4, wrote an e-mail saying that while he and McCain were friends, McCain was wrong and the Swift

Boat Veterans were right. In the letter he compared Kerry to Benedict Arnold. He ended by saying, "John Kerry for president? Ridiculous. Unthinkable. Unbelievable. Outrageous." He signed the letter "Col. Bud Day, MOH, POW, USMC, US Army, USAF" and hit the "send" button.

In the military community, Bud Day's moral high ground is considerably above that staked out by John McCain. His e-mail about Kerry may be one of the most widely circulated e-mails in the history of the Internet. It simply would not stop. And suddenly the tide had turned.

OTHER things were happening in the background.

About the same time the Swifties first were planning their course of action, a retired journalist in Pennsylvania came to a turning point in his life. Carlton Sherwood, as a young man, had been a Marine Corps sniper at Con Thien, the remote outpost Bud Day was trying to reach during his escape. Sherwood came back home and went into journalism, and later had the unusual distinction of winning a Pulitzer Prize in 1980 as a newspaperman and a Peabody Award in 1982 as a television journalist. He knew a story when he saw one. But he had a serious heart problem and did not want to come out of retirement to get involved. He spent months trying to motivate his old friends in the media to do some research about Kerry. But they would not listen when he said they should look at the "John Kerry myth."

Sherwood found that reporters and columnists, especially the older ones who had an institutional memory of Vietnam, were afraid of the story. Many of them had made their bones writing that the Vietnam War was an evil war in which it was wrong to serve. They did not want to write a story that would undermine the foundation of their careers. The Kerry mythology was a train that could not be turned around.

But neither could the former Marine. One of Sherwood's closest friends was Bob McMahon, another Vietnam combat veteran who was a Democrat and the mayor of Media, Pennsylvania. McMahon told Sherwood to stop talking and to do the job himself.

Sherwood's ideas revolved around television; nothing else reached so many people so quickly. Perhaps a documentary. But who would be in it? Someone who had not only a military background but a background that included the credentials to speak the truth about Kerry. Participants had to be highly decorated officers whose records were so exemplary that whatever they said would have ecclesiastical weight. They had to be men whose place in the pantheon of military heroes was such that their words simply could not be questioned.

There was only one such group. A documentary exposing Kerry inevitably would be seen as Republicans versus Democrats. Only the NAM-POWs had the moral authority to say that this was a matter of principle, that it was personal and not political.

But the POWs, as a group, do not get involved in politics. Nor are they the sort of men a former Marine sergeant could call on the telephone and say, "Hey, buddy, want to go on television?"

Through McMahon, Sherwood was able to post a notice on the NAM-POW Web site. He gave a brief synopsis of who he was and what he wanted to do, and he asked the old warriors if they would be willing to march one more time.

He was overwhelmed by their response.

Soon Sherwood had a list of POWs who would talk on camera. Bud Day and Leo Thorsness, both MOH recipients, were at the top of his list. For three weeks in July and August, Sherwood crisscrossed the country from Pennsylvania to California to Florida, driven by a seemingly impossible deadline: if it were to make a difference, the documentary had to be edited and ready to go on the air by early September.

Sherwood had no money and there was no time to organize a fund-raising effort. He maxed out his credit card, bumped up the limit, maxed it out again, bumped it up again, and kept taping. His life was airports and taxis and hauling heavy equipment. He was rumpled and exhausted, and several times he fell asleep dur-ing interviews. It was no schedule for a man who had a pacemaker implanted three months earlier. Sherwood did not have time to review the tapes between flights, and every time McMahon called to ask how things were going, he replied, "I don't know. We may have a dozen hours of nothing."

When Sherwood came to Bud Day's house, Day took one look at him and said, "Pal, I think you need to get some rest."

The interview with Day galvanized Sherwood. Immediately afterward, he called McMahon and said, "Colonel Day had his war paint on."

"War paint? What are you talking about?"

"The medal. He's wearing the medal. And if you saw the steel in his eyes, the controlled resolve in his voice. It is unmistak-able. This is a warrior locked again in mortal combat, no quar-ter expected or given. I almost pity John Kerry." He paused. "We have a documentary."

IN the middle of the taping, Sherwood gave in to numerous requests to put up a Web site. Throughout his professional career Sherwood had gauged response by circulation and by how many faces were in front of a television set. It was impossible to quan-tify the Internet, and he was lukewarm toward the idea. But on August 4, www.stolenhonor.com was up and running.

Almost from the moment the site became active, dozens of military sites began linking to it. In less than a week, the site was recording a thousand hits per day, then two thousand, then three thousand.

The reaction fell into two distinct categories. The biggest group consisted of those born after 1971 and who were thus unaware of Kerry's antiwar activities. In this group there was genuine surprise and anger that a man campaigning as a war hero had gone so far in his denunciation of Vietnam veterans. The second, older group vaguely remembered what Kerry had done but were unaware of the consequences and the significance of his activities as an international spokesman for the antiwar movement and that he was such a major author of the image of the Vietnam soldier as a criminal.

While the Web site took off like a rocket, the documentary was running into serious problems. Hollywood, which usually falls all over itself providing film clips to almost anyone who wants them, would give him nothing. C-SPAN would give him nothing. Even local television stations would not send him old Vietnam footage. He eventually found some generic footage. But interviews would comprise most of the documentary, and "talking heads" were considered deadly dull. Plus, a significant part of the American population had not been born, or were infants, in 1971. So Sherwood had to do a lot of filling in, a lot of background, which is even more dull than talking heads.

Once finished, Sherwood's documentary would have been ridiculed by a freshman in a broadcasting class. The production was as simple as it was primitive — just a bunch of old men sitting there talking of things that happened to them back in 1971, of the effect John Kerry's Senate testimony had on them as POWs, of why they believed he should not be commander in chief. To a man, they were calm and soft-spoken.

It was near the end before Bud Day appeared. With his Medal of Honor around his neck, he looked straight into the camera and said of John Kerry, "This man committed an act of treason. He lied, he besmirched our name, and he did it for self-interest. And now he wants us to forget? I can never forget. Treason is a crime that can never be forgiven."

Sherwood called the documentary *Stolen Honor: Wounds That Never Heal.* Broke, Sherwood transferred the forty-three-minute documentary to DVD format, produced a few thousand copies, and put them for sale on his Web site.

The first showing of the documentary was at the Military Officers Association of America building in Washington on September 9. The large ballroom was packed with former officers and their families, POWs, and a smattering of congressional staffers. Reporters lined the back wall and clogged the doorways.

After the documentary was over and the credits had rolled, there was a period of silence. Sherwood thought his documentary had bombed.

Then the room exploded in applause. Almost everyone in the room stood up and continued the ovation.

A former Vietnam combat officer walked up to Sherwood and said, "After seeing this, one thing is certain. No one who has ever served in uniform, in war or in peacetime, could ever pull the lever for John Kerry. He might not vote for Bush. But he cannot, will not, vote for Kerry."

It seemed that as soon as it debuted, the documentary was knocked out of the news cycle by hurricanes in Florida and then by the presidential debates.

But the documentary that in theory was primitive and dull and flat was, in practice, electrifying. This was a view of history, a view of the Vietnam War, a view of John Kerry, that many people had never seen. And it was deeply disturbing. People who had never been in the military sent Sherwood e-mails saying, "I don't want to believe that this is true. But those men, the POWs, are real. I believe them." Bud Day was receiving upwards of three hundred e-mails daily about the documentary. Wherever he went around Fort Walton Beach, he was stopped by people who wanted to talk about the documentary. "I did not know that about John Kerry," they said.

Almost all the buzz was below the media's radar, although Frank Rich, a columnist for the *New York Times*, did write about the documentary. He dismissed it as "a hatchet job." On September 21, Alessandra Stanley reviewed the documentary in the *Times* and said it was a "histrionic, often specious, and deeply sad film . . . ," but — and this was a crucial bit of insight — it will "help viewers better understand the rage fueling the unhappy band of brothers who oppose Mr. Kerry's candidacy and his claim to heroism."

Except for Stanley's review, however, the documentary was virtually ignored by networks and major dailies. They gushed over *Fahrenheit 9/11*, Michael Moore's emotional polemic against

George Bush, as significant social commentary but considered *Stolen Honor* insignificant or a cheap shot financed by ultrapartisan Republicans.

Before he retired, Sherwood was one of those people described as a "distinguished member of the Washington press corps." In addition to winning a Pulitzer and a Peabody, he wore the reporter's ultimate badge of honor: he had been jailed for refusing to name his sources. Now his old colleagues either ignored him, reported false information about his production company, or were indignant that he was picking on their candidate.

The reporters who did call Sherwood were openly contemptuous of him as a Republican lapdog, and all they wanted to know was who financed the DVD. They would not accept that it was a solo effort on his part. A reporter for the *Los Angeles Times* called three or four times and was so adamant in insisting that the NRA was behind the DVD that a frustrated Sherwood finally said, "I haven't taken a dime from the NRA. I haven't heard from the NRA. I don't know anyone at the NRA. But if the bastards want to write a check, I'll take it."

In the flurry of the presidential race, it was easy to think of the documentary and the Swift Boat campaign as one and the same. There was some cross-fertilization, but they were two separate groups. While the Swifties were organized as a Section 527 organization, Sherwood's production company was incorporated as a for-profit Pennsylvania S corporation. He did this for two reasons: First, while raising money as a Section 527 organization or a 501 (c) (3) nonprofit would have been much easier, to do so would have put the documentary in the political category. Second, Sherwood did not want what he described as a "historical news documentary" to be subject to federal election restrictions. The Swifties and Sherwood, until they combined forces in October, not only were separate groups but had separate agendas: the Swifties went after Kerry's medals and combat records while the documentary went after his 1971 Senate testimony.

In late September, the Swifties were still wallowing. But they were sitting on millions of dollars. Sherwood's documentary had no traction, and he was broke.

Then, in quick succession, came a series of events that turned everything around.

The Sinclair Broadcast Group, a company with sixty-two television stations, announced it was going to run *Stolen Honor* in mid-October. Meanwhile, the Swifties talked to the POWs about joining forces. The truth is that while the Swifties' attack on Kerry's military record and his medals had hurt the Democrat, it also had backfired — the Navy will not retract medals — then stalled out. The media lost interest. Now, in an effort to regain momentum, the Swifties asked the POWs who had appeared in *Stolen Honor* to join them. On October 2, the two groups met in a Washington, DC, studio to tape a series of television ads.

Several in the room outranked Day. But he took charge and set the tone of the gathering. Today, there will be many who will laugh when they hear what Day said: "We have no choice in this battle. This is something each of us must do. But I want it understood by all of you that this is not political. This is a matter of principle. And it must not be tainted with politics. We will simply tell of our own experiences. No one in this room must gain anything from the administration. And to prove that it is not political, we must continue this battle after the election. No matter how the election goes, we must stay together to see that Vietnam veterans get the respect they deserve. At bottom, that is what this is all about, the truth of Vietnam — regaining the honor of those who fought in Vietnam."

There is a story about British admiral Lord Nelson that, even if apocryphal, is relevant here. The story has it that during a cold night at sea, one of Nelson's subordinates offered him a cloak against the cold. He refused, saying his zeal for king and country kept him warm. Nelson, because he was Nelson, could utter such lofty beliefs with absolute sincerity. So could Bud Day. And he could sound so old-fashioned, so nineteenth century, in a way that resonated with his comrades but which utterly baffled the Frank Riches of the media world.

The format of the television ads was simple and doubtless was influenced by Sherwood's documentary. Again, the old men simply told their stories — gut-wrenching stories that often brought them to tears.

One of the most powerful commercials shot that weekend was one in which Bud Day, Medal of Honor around his neck, looked straight into the camera and asked John Kerry, "How can you expect our sons and daughters to follow you when you condemned their fathers and grandfathers?"

The day after the ads were taped, the Sinclair plans to air the documentary leaked. The Kerry campaign immediately made the documentary an FCC issue — that is, if it ran, they would challenge Sinclair's broadcasting license. When eighteen Democratic senators stood on the floor of the U.S. Senate and denounced the documentary, Sinclair backed off and said it would run only part of *Stolen Honor* inside a broader program.

Since the Garden of Eden, people have wanted forbidden fruit. And now, in the second week of October, not only were the new Swift Boat ads appearing but *Stolen Honor* was picking up steam.

Orders for the DVD flooded into Sherwood's Web site. His site, which had been getting around three thousand hits per day, experienced a jump to around a million hits per day. In the next few weeks, Sherwood said, he recorded fifty-one million hits. And Sherwood, the man who thought he knew and understood the media, realized he knew nothing. The Web site had tapped into something he did not understand. The more the old media attacked Sherwood and the documentary, the more the new media wrapped their arms around him.

On October 16, Kerry loyalists filed two lawsuits against Sherwood. The intent was to completely shut down distribution of the documentary. Kerry loyalists made it clear they would sue anyone who aired the program. Movie theaters canceled plans to exhibit it.

When a theater just outside Philadelphia announced it would show the documentary, Kerry loyalists responded with threats of violence and civil unrest. The theater canceled the showing. Two other theaters in a Philadelphia suburb canceled showings for security reasons. The Kerry campaign even threatened to sue those who showed the documentary in private clubs or organizations.

Then Sherwood did something remarkable: he put the documentary on his Web site, where it could be watched for free. He announced he would grant full rights, without fee or restriction, to anyone who wanted to show *Stolen Honor*. Unlimited free usage.

It was the tipping point.

Through phone lines and cable modems and DSL wiring, *Stolen Honor* went underground. Suddenly it was being shown widely in Ohio, Florida, Pennsylvania, and Iowa, all crucial states in the election. The documentary was aired in private homes or hastily organized packed houses in movie theaters. Local Republican clubs all around America were showing it. It was being watched in firehouses and in city halls. In Fort Walton Beach, Bud Day's Lutheran minister and church officials stood on street corners and passed out flyers telling when *Stolen Honor* would be aired. They packed the local civic center.

The traditional media either knew nothing of this or dismissed the showings as insignificant gatherings of Republican zealots. All the while, Kerry loyalists darted all over the country, threatening lawsuits anywhere *Stolen Honor* was aired. But it was like trying to stop a virus; it was showing everywhere, but they rarely heard about it in time to do anything. The more that Democrats complained about how underhanded and unfair and unethical it was to air the documentary, the more people wanted to see it. And now, in addition to the documentary, the Swifties were back — and the POWs were with them.

George Will, the nationally syndicated columnist for the *Washington Post*, saw a copy of the DVD and later said he had thought that "it was deeply powerful; that it would be — as it was — deeply and properly injurious to Kerry; that it would have a difficult time getting the mainstream media to credit it as a legitimate part of the campaign."

He was right on every count.

Conventional wisdom has it that in a presidential campaign there are too many special interest groups and too many issues to isolate any group or any issue and say it was the deciding factor in the campaign. Nevertheless, both *Time* and *Newsweek* said Kerry's inability to deal with the Swifties and the POWs ultimately cost him the election. A top Kerry campaign official later said on national television that the campaign's biggest mistake was underestimating the Swifties.

There was much gloating over the Internet in the days after the election. Had mainstream media or Kerry loyalists read the postings, they would have dismissed them as mawkish conservative ramblings. To do so would be to miss the point that these were the sentiments of untold thousands. For his part, Day fired off a long e-mail saying veterans had done something unprecedented in political history: they had turned around a presidential election. He ended with "We had the right message: Hanoi John and Hanoi Jane." Russ Vaughn, a member of the fabled 101st Airborne Division who had served in Vietnam, published a widely circulated poem that told how the Swifties had won the "last battle of Vietnam." The poem ended with "To our Brothers, forever, on that long black wall / You've been vindicated now, one and all."

But the most poignant posting was from a proud Vietnam vet. "Kerry's defeat," he said, "was the parade we never got."

Epilogue

THE life of those men whose time on earth justifies a biography follows a necessary pattern: birth, early years and education, followed by the reason for the story — the man's personal or professional accomplishments — and then his death, which offers the opportunity to put the span of his years in perspective.

With Bud Day, such a progression is impossible. In 2006, he turned eighty-one and was still as active in his law practice and as involved in military-related events and as outspoken about public and political affairs as he had been at seventy-one. Or sixty-one. Or fifty-one.

So perhaps the best way to end the story of a life that is far from ending is a series of vignettes — small stories that, like stitches in a tapestry, comprise the ongoing saga of Bud Day.

DAY is in Washington for a NAM-POW reunion and is annoyed that McCain has not showed up. He called McCain several times before the reunion and McCain said he would be there. The hotel where the reunion is held is about five minutes from the Capitol and no more than ten minutes from McCain's condominium.

But McCain doesn't appear. Later, when asked why, he says, "I know there is a lot of talk about that. But I just didn't have time."

The reunion falls over Memorial Day, and a Washington radio station calls Day for an interview. The reporter wants to talk about Vietnam, so Day says, "Dan Rather and Morley Safer went over there with the idea they wanted the North Vietnamese to win." He names the most prominent newspapers in America and says they are guilty of "yellow journalism."

Later he goes out to the Vietnam Veterans Memorial known as "The Wall" for a wreath-laying ceremony. The names of eight Mistys are on The Wall. Day searches out the panel with the name Edwin Atterberry, the POW who was killed after the abortive escape attempt in May 1969. Day's lips tremble as he remembers how Atterberry's death was the prelude for his own weeks of torture.

He comes to attention and snaps off a salute.

He searches out the names Connell, Cobeil, and Cameron, the three men taken away and never seen again; he remembers how he almost joined them, and again he comes to attention and salutes.

As he walks up and down in front of The Wall looking for the names, he is frequently stopped and someone will say, "Thanks for your work on behalf of the veterans."

"It's a labor of love," he replies.

One person says, "Thanks for the work you did in keeping Kerry out of office."

He laughs. "Another labor of love."

Later that day he and Doris walk around the corner from the hotel to the Old Ebbitt Grill for a late lunch. He is wearing slacks and a Misty T-shirt. He is stooped, and in the T-shirt his frame is gaunt. To those who do not know him, he is just another old veteran roaming around Washington. The maître d'hôtel looks at the shirt and smiles, and in what is almost a patronizing tone says, "Misty? What kind of a name is that?"

Far back in Day's eyes is a flicker, a glacial hint of warning. He smiles and says, "It's the name of an outfit I once flew with." He is shown to a table.

Behind Day in line are several POWs. One of them has overheard the exchange with the maître d' and tells him who Day is.

The maître d', embarrassed and very solicitous, hurries down the aisle to Day's table and apologizes profusely.

Day could not be more gracious. "That's okay, pal. Don't worry about it."

The maître d' tells the waiter to give Colonel and Mrs. Day a dessert on the house. Then he goes back to his station at the door, where he can be heard telling bar patrons and diners, "We have Colonel Bud Day in the house. He was a POW and he wears the Medal of Honor."

IMMEDIATELY after the 2004 presidential campaign, Day and Carlton Sherwood formed the Vietnam Veterans Legacy Foundation (VVLF) to educate people about the Vietnam War and the men and women who fought there.

The group raised some $200,000 in 2005, much of which went toward fighting lawsuits filed by people close to Kerry. When the VVLF filed a suit against Kerry for defamation, a Kerry spokesman described Day and Sherwood as "serial liars."

Sherwood's pacemaker stopped in early 2005, and he went to the hospital for emergency surgery. Later he had more surgery.

Then he went to work on a documentary about the Tuskegee Airmen, black pilots who gained glory in World War II, and how they helped desegregate the U.S. military — an odd choice for a man the media described as a "Republican attack dog."

Sherwood has a newsman's sense of irony when he talks of the last few years. "This is a free-speech issue. I'm being sued for producing *Stolen Honor*, a documentary in which no one has pointed out a factual error. Yet no one sued Michael Moore for *Fahrenheit 9/11*. No one sued Jane Fonda for what she said about the POWs. It was okay for John Kerry to say American soldiers committed two hundred thousand murders a year and that they raped and cut off ears and acted like the hordes of Genghis Khan."

AFTER the Supreme Court refused to hear the case involving medical benefits for retirees, Day returned to lobbying Congress, urging members to pass a "Keep Our Promise to America's Military Retirees Bill." For several years, he made periodic trips to Washington, where he trudged the halls of Congress on behalf of his comrades.

Part of the effort was the "Brown Bag Campaign," in which veterans from all over America tore away part of a paper bag, wrote a note on it urging support of the bill, and mailed it to a congressman. More than fifty thousand such notes were sent.

In early 2005 Undersecretary of Defense David Chu was quoted in the *Wall Street Journal* saying military pensions and health insurance "have gotten to the point where they are hurtful. They are taking away the nation's ability to defend itself."

It is true that health benefits have become more expensive. But to make retirees the scapegoat, to say that keeping the promise is deleterious to America, is arrant nonsense. If America is losing its ability to defend itself, it is because the Pentagon is buying ever more expensive — and often irrelevant — weapons systems. It is because of flagrant corruption in the weapons-acquisition system.

Nevertheless, as the Pentagon drumbeat of "runaway health costs" continued, Day could sense the retirees were losing the battle. Congress passed bills including hundreds of millions for tsunami relief, for the Sudan, for Iraq, for New Orleans, but nothing for the retirees.

Representatives privately told Day that all of these expenses, the war in Iraq, and now billions for Louisiana, meant there was no money for the retirees. Then the Department of Defense indicated it would raise the TRICARE premium for veterans under sixty-five. Day knew it was only a matter of time before premiums were raised for veterans *over* sixty-five.

In early 2006 Day sent out word he was folding his tent and leaving the field. Even though he had restored 95 percent of what he wanted for the retirees, the battle over Part B in Medicare was lost.

For the rest of his life, Day would feel he had let down his comrades.

But the retirees are pragmatic people. They knew Day had done his best. They knew what they owed him. So they gritted their teeth and soldiered on.

And they thought rather highly of Bud Day.

Bob Reinlie, the surviving plaintiff in Day's suit against the government, has good days and bad days. On his good days, he comes to Day's law office, where an office has been set aside for him. Almost daily the letters still arrive, letters from widows of retirees. There is great fear in the letters. These women do not know how they will pay their medical bills. "Thank you for fighting for us," they write.

Reinlie pounds the desk and moans, "What is my government doing to these people?"

But his is a lonely vigil. His cause is unknown to the public and is ignored by the media and politicians in the Capitol and at 1600 Pennsylvania Avenue.

The Mistys are having a reunion in Colorado Springs and visit the Air Force Academy, where they pay particular attention to a memorial for the Doolittle Raiders of World War II. A large shadow box holds small silver cups engraved with the names of every Raider. Only a few cups are upright; all the others are inverted, signifying the Raider is dead.

Later, at a business meeting, a member points out that the Mistys are growing few in number. Perhaps the Mistys, like several other Vietnam-era military groups, should open up the membership not just to those who were there but to active-duty military officers or even civilians. This will ensure the group lives on.

Dick Rutan jumps up in opposition. He says when he attends a Misty reunion, he wants to look around and be able to say, "I flew with that sonofabitch."

Bud Day smiles and nods in approval. The idea is squelched. It doesn't matter if members are dying and membership declining. It doesn't matter if, like the Doolittle Raiders, the time comes when the Mistys can be counted on one hand. When only one

Misty is left, that man will have his own reunion, and he will hoist a glass to his brothers who flew up north and who were in the shit on every mission. He will drink to those who never came back.

And when the last Misty wakes up on the wrong side of the grass, the book will be closed and that will be that.

But the Mistys will live on. Their story will be told for as long as fighter pilots gather to talk of the long ago, to remember their departed brothers.

It is all part of the continuum.

DAY is in Phoenix attending a reunion of MOH recipients. Some are on crutches or use walkers. Some are too ill to attend.

America is running out of heroes.

On Friday afternoon a retired general picks up Day and brings him out to nearby Luke AFB. There, a colonel drives him down the flight line and tells him of all the squadrons based there, one of which is the "Top Hats," the 310th Fighter Squadron, which is the training squadron for F-16 FAC pilots. Coincidentally, Friday afternoon is when the pilots of the 310th gather for a weekly debriefing by the squadron commander.

Would Colonel Day like to visit, maybe say a few words to the young pilots?

"You bet."

For more years than anyone can remember, every graduating class of FACs has a party, a ceremonial and tradition-wrapped party, the highlight of which is "the drink of the white smoke." The new FACs begin the ceremony with a toast to the Mistys. Then they toast the F-16. There are more toasts. They put dry ice in their glasses and drink to the white smoke that marks the target. The room fills with white smoke, and then they drink to Bud Day and recite one of his sayings: "Gentlemen, clear the smoke and continue the honor of those before you."

As Day walks down the hall, he passes a plaque on the wall that bears that very quote.

The colonel accompanying Day opens the door of the auditorium where the pilots are meeting and summons the squadron commander. He introduces Day. The squadron commander steps back inside and, with a slight tremor in his voice, says, "We have a very special treat this afternoon." He pauses. "Colonel Bud Day."

Day walks in, the Medal of Honor visible against his white shirt. He smiles that boyish smile and waves.

The young pilots, men born around 1980, stare in stunned silence for two or three seconds. Their thoughts are written on their faces:

That frail and stooped old man is Bud Day. That is Misty 1.

The sound of their boots hitting the floor is a thunderclap. They snap to attention. Even after Day waves for them to be seated, they remain at attention for another few seconds.

For the next hour they listen in rapt attention as he tells what it was like to fly FAC missions up north, to muscle that old F-100 down in the weeds and go trolling for trouble at five hundred knots, to scramble for sky when the air was filled with bursts of 57 mm shells.

Down on the Mexican border in McAllen, Texas, in a small house in a neat and crisp little subdivision, Norris Overly lives.

Until Robert Timberg's *The Nightingale's Song* was published in 1995, Overly was generally unknown. But in that book he was identified as the man who saved John McCain's life, and almost overnight he became something of a local celebrity. The newspaper came calling and made him McAllen's expert on military matters. After all, he was a POW.

When John McCain ran for president in 2000, Overly was flown to New York to be interviewed by *60 Minutes*. The only quote used in the program was when he was asked if he had seen McCain since he left Hanoi, and he said no. When asked why not, he said, "You'll have to ask him."

Overly's disingenuous reply left the impression with viewers that McCain had turned his back on the man who saved his life. And CBS, because no one connected with the program knew about the early releases, let it stand.

Veterans who live in McAllen seek out Overly. Occasionally one of those veterans will be traveling or will call a friend in another part of the country and say he has met Norris Overly, the POW who saved the lives of Bud Day and John McCain. Afterward, that veteran will phone Overly and say, "I was talking to a friend and he told me another story about you." Overly will never again hear from that veteran. And they will not again visit him.

"I have nothing to hide," Overly says. "I'm a confident person in that I harmed no one. I have a sense of pride about my life and career."

Ross Perot is in semiretirement, but he comes to the office daily. He still spends large sums of money on military-connected causes. He is the featured speaker at NAM-POW reunions. And when POWs come through Dallas, they often visit with him.

In the spring of 2006, Perot flew to Sioux City, where various events were being held to honor Day: a street was named for him, a college scholarship in Bud's name was announced, and the newspaper said his life story now would be part of the curriculum at local schools. Day was the featured speaker at the Rotary Club. As the program was about to begin, the master of ceremonies announced a special visitor. The rear doors to the room opened and Ross Perot came in to a standing ovation. He made a stirring speech about how important it was that Sioux City was recognizing its native son. Doris and Bud went out to Riverside, where several hundred elementary school children sang a song written for him. It was a stirring and moving visit for Day.

IT is not a widely known fact, but military people are weepers.

They weep when they watch a parade and the flag goes by.

They weep when they hear the National Anthem.

They weep at tales of valor and sacrifice.

And as they get older and their emotions rise closer to the surface, they weep at the memories of the brave men they have known. Bud Day still cries when he tells the story of the first time he saw Larry Guarino.

Day still speaks at Dining Outs. Much has been written about him and much of it is wrong, but it doesn't matter. He is one of those men who, during his lifetime, has moved into the realm of legend.

At every Dining Out, an officer will rise and ask, "Colonel, was it worth it?"

Day stares in disbelief that someone would ask such a question. Then he talks of the greatness of America, how enduring are its values, and finally, in a trembling and emotion-choked but powerful voice, he utters the final words that reach to every corner of the room: "God . . . bless . . . America."

And there are few dry eyes in the room.

DAY lives in a part of the Florida panhandle that is hit with some regularity by powerful hurricanes. Over the years, homes along his street have been severely damaged. Because his house is built so high, he has sometimes been surrounded by water, but the only damage he has experienced has been a slight bit of water seepage. And that happened only once.

Neighbors emerge from the wreckage of their homes and look at Day's house with some bewilderment. After the last big hurricane, when the street was blocked by fallen trees and parts of houses, a neighbor looked at Day's undamaged house and said to him, "God must be protecting you." He put his hands on her shoulders, smiled, and said, "You are right. God realizes I have been through enough. He is not going to let a hurricane harm me."

DAY wheels his white Cadillac into a gas station in Fort Walton Beach. The Cadillac is well known around town, in part because the Medal of Honor license plate with the single digit "9" reveals his identity but more so because Day has a heavy foot and darts into traffic with all the verve of a twenty-five-year-old jet jockey.

The driver of a passing car sees Day, brakes, and stops beside him. The two confer intently for a few minutes.

As the man is driving away, the same thing happens again. "Drop by my office and we'll work out the details," Day says.

He finishes refueling and slides into the driver's seat with a satisfied smile. "Two new clients while I was gassing up. Good clients too. Maybe I should gas up here more often."

BECAUSE he is a U.S. senator, no man is more closely associated with the POWs than is John McCain. And although he has said that talking about his POW years "bores the shit out of me," the POW card is his hole card; he plays it when he must and he plays it well.

He confronted President Bush over the issue of torturing terrorist suspects, and he won. Bud Day and many of the POWs disagreed. They believe that to win the war on terror, America must use every possible means to obtain information. And they know that torture does yield information.

The POWs vigorously lobbied McCain not to oppose President Bush on this issue. When he continued, they were bitter in their private denunciations of him.

A *New York Times* reporter was told that Day opposed McCain on the issue. When the reporter called Day, all he got was a quote saying that McCain knew a lot about torture.

Larry Guarino was not so diplomatic. He still thinks of McCain as a cocky little smart-ass who somehow became a U.S. senator. He wrote a letter to *Florida Today*, his local newspaper in Melbourne, Florida, saying that he had been McCain's superior officer in Hanoi and that he was "disappointed" in McCain, who "has become a media darling and the consummate politician."

With the exception of the one-day drive-by he did in Texas in the mid-1980s, McCain has never attended a NAM-POW reunion. (He did another drive-by in 2006.) And many POWs have grown weary of his stance as POW 1. Guarino's column received wide distribution on the military side of the Internet. He received dozens of e-mails from veterans who believe "McCain has gone overboard" or "McCain has lost his way." Some e-mails point to McCain's low academic standing at the Naval Academy, saying he is defensive about his intellectual reputation and easy prey for those who pander to that weakness.

This has not affected the deep friendship between Day and McCain. They remain two headstrong guys who see things differently but who remain very close. It seems that each time Day is having particularly horrific nightmares about the Bug, or having a bad day physically, the phone will ring, he will pick it up, and the first thing he will hear is McCain saying, "How you doing, buddy?" And if McCain is taking flak or is hurting from his old wounds, somehow Day knows and is on the phone boosting him.

Swindle sometimes is caught in the middle. He explains that Day is a lawyer and a fighter pilot — a mixture of two of the most aggressive personalities on earth — and his battles are inevitably mano a mano. His outlook is that of an advocate. But McCain is trying to get along with senatorial egos and reach a consensus.

McCain himself may have best crystallized the differences between the two men. The July 2005 issue of *Architectural Digest* included a cover story about McCain's home in Phoenix. At the end of the article he claimed his best friends remain the men he was in prison with. Describing Day, he said, "He is one of those people for whom everything is either black or white. It's wonderful to go through life like that. I wish I could."

THE December 13, 2005, newsletter of the VVLF opened with a quote by John Kerry, who recently had appeared on *Face the Nation*, where he said, "There is no reason that young American soldiers need to be going into homes of Iraqis in the dead of night, terrorizing kids and children."

Day wrote that Kerry was "still slandering America's troops" and went on the *Sean Hannity Show* to add that Kerry was "a thoroughly dishonest witness to how our troops operated during Vietnam, and an equally dishonest critic today."

SEVERAL years ago, Day was asked to become dean of the South Dakota Law School. He turned down the invitation; Midwestern winters are too cold for him. "I like living in paradise," he says. But every fall, Day goes back to Siouxland to hunt pheasant. He calls ahead to a hunting lodge near Vermillion, South Dakota, perhaps a forty-five-minute drive from Sioux City, where the manager adds him to a group.

Before he leaves Sioux City, he always has dinner with Frank Work. Paul Jackson has been having health problems, but if he is receiving visitors, he and Day always meet. Jackson has been lobbying Congress for years to promote Day to general.

When Day drives up to Vermillion, he often takes the back ways — the roads he traveled when he was in law school and he and Curly would road hunt. These roads are a maze, some paved, some graveled, some dirt, but Day knows them all. As he drives, Day slows to what is little more than a walking pace and rolls down the windows and takes deep breaths. A smile of pure peace eases across his face.

When he hunts, he can't walk in the tall grass anymore; he just doesn't have the energy. So he walks alone in the open flat ground. And even though he is a guest who was added on to a hunting party, he takes charge. "Let's keep that line straight," he tells the hunters as they trudge across the big fields. They hustle to obey, delighted they are hunting with Bud Day. In the beginning, they keep an eye on him because he wears a hearing aid in each ear and seems almost frail. But when a pheasant erupts from the grass, Day's eyes are good and his hands are quick. He rarely misses.

At the end of the hunt the men gather in the lodge and someone says, "Colonel, may we offer you a drink?" That boyish smile comes forth and he says, "The only time I ever refused a drink was when I didn't understand the question."

The hunters laugh and they cluster around Day, hoping he will tell them of war and prison and of the patriots he has known.

In February 2006, Day turned eighty-one. Almost weekly, one of his younger but long-retired comrades will ask, "Bud, why the hell don't you retire?"

He laughs and shrugs.

Doris says, "What they don't understand is that work is his therapy. He needs to work."

Perhaps the best indicator of how well he is doing as an eighty-one-year-old lawyer is that, at the end of 2005, he received such substantial payments from clients that he groused for days about being unable to spread the money out over several years and was going to take a big tax hit.

At an age when most men are long retired and living off investments or Social Security, he worries about tax breaks.

Day travels often and easily, making several dozen speeches every year. If Doris is with him, and if they sit together at a banquet, they hold hands under the table. They reach out often to touch each other on the hand or arm. After almost sixty years of marriage, he is as considerate and courteous toward her as if he were courting her.

When he makes speeches, Day often is asked, "Colonel, what are you most proud of?" He never misses a beat: "My wife. Because she worked tirelessly on behalf of the POWs."

At a banquet, when Day sits down, he unrolls his napkin and places the fork on the left side of his plate and the knife and spoon on the right, just as his mother taught him. Other habits just won't break. To the bewilderment of many a hotel waiter, Day insists on having his coffee in a Styrofoam cup, preferably with a lid.

Back in Fort Walton Beach, Day zips down the road in his white Cadillac toward his office, listening to music from the 1940s — the big bands — or the songs of Vera Lynn or Frank Sinatra. He likes the music of a less complicated time — a time when the wars were good wars and when America was always right.

Sometimes, around midafternoon, Day might have what he calls a "sinker." He becomes so exhausted and so sleepy he closes his door and lies on the floor, his head on a law book, and naps for a half hour.

It can be difficult for him to get out of a chair. He says he is thinking of installing ejection seats on the lawn furniture.

He has a PSA upward of fifteen and almost certainly has prostate cancer. But he is eighty-one and his doctor figures he will die of old age before he dies of prostate cancer, so he does nothing.

Day has the same "nervous stomach" that his father had. Also, like his father, he has his favorite ethnic stereotypes. He is unable to say "North Vietnamese"; for almost forty years, it has been "gooks," and that is what it will remain.

He is unbending in his scathing criticism of "liberal media," particularly the *New York Times* and what he now calls the "Communist Broadcasting System."

One night Doris and Bud accompanied their pastor and his wife to see *The Passion of the Christ*. During the scene where Jesus is being flogged, the pastor's wife leaned over and whispered to Doris, "Is that the way it was when Bud was beaten?" Doris nodded. She could not speak — Bud was squeezing her hand so tightly she was gritting her teeth.

That night, Day's sleeping pills could not keep the Bug at bay, and the nightmares came. Doris always knows when the Bug is beckoning because Bud begins a low gurgling sound that becomes louder and louder. She curled around him and held him and whispered that all was well.

The next morning he left early for the office, where he shut his door and did not come out until noon.

Once a year Day drives over to Naval Air Station Pensacola, where the POWs go for their annual physical. Because no POWs from earlier wars ever went through what the Vietnam-era POWs endured, the military is studying the long-range effects of traumatic orthopedic injuries. The Navy doctor schedules the men who came home early on days when no other POWs are present.

The doctor knows there are some POWs who, if put in the waiting room with an early release, would — at the very least — cause a scene.

Day's medical problems, most of which originated in Hanoi, worsen with age. After his most recent eye surgery, the doctor told him not to drive for several days. The next morning he was up before Doris and out of the house before she could stop him.

Doris is active in several women's clubs. If she is attending an evening meeting or has an appointment at the beauty shop, Day grabs dinner on the run and always at the cheapest place he can find. No matter how stringy the meat or how unpalatable the food, Day cleans his plate. "I feel guilty about leaving food," he says.

For much of the year he wears his old leather flight jacket, the one with the patch of the 4th Allied POW Wing on the left breast. He is perhaps the most recognized person in Fort Walton Beach. When he goes to the courthouse on a legal issue, his mind is often far away. He walks down the hall, bent over, right arm pumping and eyes straight ahead. People see him coming and step aside.

"Colonel," a few of them murmur.

He smiles and nods. "Hello, pal."

His old friend Orson Swindle shakes his head when he talks of Bud Day. "If he ever dies, they better nail the coffin shut. Because if they don't, he will come out at full throttle with afterburner glowing."

Day says, "I'm not going to die. But if I do, I want to be reincarnated as a twenty-six-year-old captain flying the Advanced Tactical Fighter. I want to come back at two thousand miles an hour."

He pauses and his eyes sparkle. "But before I can be reincarnated, I must die. When that happens, I want to be buried upside down so Dixon and the Bug can kiss my ass."

Day spends weekends puttering in his rose garden. For him, the best thing about trying to grow roses in Florida is that when he is in the yard, he can hear fighters taking off from Eglin.

Sources

Much of the material in this book came from the following sources. They were interviewed by phone, through e-mail, or in person. A large number of those interviewed were once military officers. Because the events of the book took place when they were young lieutenants or captains, and because they retired at higher ranks, I have omitted all military designations to avoid confusion.

Ambrose, Dr. Michael
Amdor, Steve
Bevivino, Ray
Burchard, Brendan
Butts, Thomas L.
Day, Doris
Day, George E. "Bud"
Day, George E. Jr.
Day, Steven
Doub, Jack
Douglass, Bill
Fellowes, Jack
Geasland, Robert
Greene, Mick
Guarino, Larry
Hansen, Robert
Holzrichter, Phyllis Brodie
Humiston, Lee
Jackson, Paul
Janson, John
Kippenhan, Corwin
Lindler, James
Mack, Jim
Mamlock, Stanley
Mattison, Mark
McCain, John S.
McGrath, Mike
Metzner, Al

Milavic, Anthony
Myhre, Larry
Neel, Charlie
O'Neill, John E.
Overly, Norris
Perot, H. Ross
Raymond, Ted
Reinlie, Robert
Riley, Harry
Risinger, Ed
Risner, Robinson
Robinson, P. K.
Rochester, Stuart
Rudman, Mladen
Rutan, Dick
Samenus, Stephanie
Sandman, John
Shanahan, Jack
Sherwood, Carlton
Summers, Charlie
Swindle, Orson
Thompson, David W.
Van Loan, Jack
Walters, William L.
Whitcomb, Darrel
Will, George
Wilson, G. I.
Work, Frank

Bibliography

Anderegg, C. R. *Sierra Hotel: Flying Air Force Fighters in the Decade After Vietnam.* Washington, DC: Air Force History and Museums Program, 2001.

Anderegg, Michael, ed. *Inventing Vietnam: The War in Film and Television.* Philadelphia: Temple University Press, 1991.

"Beyond the Worst Suspicions." *Time* (April 9, 1973): 20, 25–26.

Brace, Ernest C. *A Code to Keep.* Central Point, OR: Hellgate Press, 1988.

Brinkley, Douglas. *Tour of Duty: John Kerry and the Vietnam War.* New York: Harper Perennial, 2004.

Brokaw, Tom. *The Greatest Generation.* New York: Delta, 1998.

Burkett, B. G., and Glenna Whitley. *Stolen Valor: How the Vietnam Generation Was Robbed of Its Heroes and Its History.* Dallas: Verity Press, 1998.

Caputo, Philip. *A Rumor of War.* New York: Henry Holt and Company, 1996.

Chapman, William. "POWs' Nightmarish Ordeal." *Washington Post* (March 30, 1973): A1.

Churchill, Jan. *Hit My Smoke: Forward Air Controllers in Southeast Asia.* Manhattan, KS: Sunflower University Press, 1997.

Collier, Peter. *Medal of Honor: Portraits of Valor Beyond the Call of Duty.* New York: Artisan, 2003.

Davis, Vernon E. *The Long Road Home: U.S. Prisoner of War Policy and Planning in Southeast Asia.* Washington, DC: Historical Office, Office of the Secretary of Defense, 2000.

Day, George E. *Duty Honor Country.* Fort Walton Beach, FL: American Hero Press, 1989.

———. *Return with Honor.* Mesa, AZ: Champlin Museum Press, 1989.

Dittmar, Linda, and Gene Michaud, eds. *From Hanoi to Hollywood: The Vietnam War in American Film.* New Brunswick, NJ: Rutgers University Press, 1990.

Dramesi, John A. *Code of Honor.* New York: Warner Books, 1975.

"An Emotional, Exuberant Welcome Home." *Time* (February 26, 1973): 12–14.

Eschmann, Karl J. *Linebacker: The Untold Story of the Air Raids Over North Vietnam.* New York: Ivy Books, 1989.

Fall, Bernard. "Communist POW Treatment in Indochina." *Military Review* (December 1958).

———. *Hell in a Very Small Place: The Siege of Dien Bien Phu.* Philadelphia: Da Capo Press, 1967.

First In, Last Out. Red River Valley Fighter Pilots Association, Lon Gibby Productions, 1985.

Frisbee, John L. "Surviving in Hanoi's Prisons." *Air Force Magazine* (June 1973): 28–33.

Gibson, James William. *The Perfect War: Technowar in Vietnam.* New York: Atlantic Monthly Press, 2000.

Grant, Zalin. *Survivors: Vietnam POWs Tell Their Stories.* New York: Da Capo Press, 1994.

Gruner, Elliott. *Prisoners of Culture: Representing the Vietnam POW.* New Brunswick, NJ: Rutgers University Press, 1993.

Guarino, Evelyn, with Carol Jose. *Saved by Love.* Cape Canaveral, FL: Blue Note Books, 2000.

Guarino, Larry. *A POW's Story: 2,801 Days in Hanoi.* New York: Ballantine, 1990.

———. "Under the Dirty Blanket of Communism." Unpublished manuscript.

Guenon, William A. Jr. *Secret and Dangerous: Night of the Son Tay POW Raid.* Lowell, MA: King Printing Company, 2002.

Hanson, Victor Davis. *Ripples of Battle: How Wars of the Past Still Determine How We Fight, How We Live, and How We Think.* New York: Doubleday, 2003.

Harmon, Robert B. *John Steinbeck and Newsday, with a Focus on "Letters to Alicia": An Annotated and Documented Reference Guide.* San Jose, CA: privately printed, 1999.

Hershberger, Mary. *Jane Fonda's War: A Political Biography of an Antiwar Icon.* New York: New Press, 2005.

Heynowski, Walter, and Gerhard Scheumann. *Pilots in Pyjamas.* Film. Edited by Gert Prokup, 1967.

Hirsch, James S. *Two Souls Indivisible: The Friendship That Saved Two POWs in Vietnam.* New York: Houghton Mifflin, 2004.

Hobson, Chris. *Vietnam Air Losses: United States Air Force, Navy, and Marine Corps Fixed-Wing Aircraft Losses in Southeast Asia 1961–1973.* Hinckley, England: Midland Publishing, 2001.

Holzer, Henry Mark, and Erika Holzer. *"Aid and Comfort": Jane Fonda in North Vietnam.* Jefferson, NC: McFarland and Company, 2002.

Hubbard, Edward. *Could They Have Done More?* Maxwell Air Force Base, AL: Air University, 1974.

Hubbell, John G. *POW: A Definitive History of the American Prisoner-of-War Experience in Vietnam, 1964–1973.* New York: Reader's Digest Press, 1976.

"Inside North Vietnam's Prisons — How Americans Coped." *U.S. News & World Report* (March 26, 1973): 58–61.

Johnson, Paul. *A History of the American People.* New York: Harper Perennial, 1997.

Kurlansky, Mark. *1968: The Year That Rocked the World.* New York: Ballantine, 2004.

Mamlock, Stanley M. "Use of the Jet Fighter Aircraft as a Forward Air Control Vehicle in a Non-Permissive Environment." Case study. Maxwell Air Force Base, AL: Air War College, 1970.

Maraniss, David. *They Marched into Sunlight: War and Peace, Vietnam and America, October 1967*. New York: Simon and Schuster, 2003.

McCain, John S. "How the POWs Fought Back." *U.S. News & World Report* (May 14, 1973): 46–52, 110–115.

McCain, John S., with Mark Salter. *Faith of My Fathers*. New York: Random House, 1999.

McConnell, Malcolm. *Inside Hanoi's Secret Archives: Solving the MIA Mystery*. Research by Theodore G. Schweitzer III. New York: Simon and Schuster, 1995.

———. *Into the Mouth of the Cat: The Story of Lance Sijan, Hero of Vietnam*. New York: W.W. Norton, 1985.

McFarland, Stephen L. *A Concise History of the U.S. Air Force*. Washington, DC: Air Force History and Museums Program, 1997.

McGrath, John M. *Prisoner of War*. Annapolis, MD: Naval Institute Press, 1975.

McMahon, Robert J. *The Limits of Empire*. New York: Columbia University Press, 1999.

McMaster, H. R. *Dereliction of Duty: Lyndon Johnson, Robert McNamara, the Joint Chiefs of Staff, and the Lies That Led to Vietnam*. New York: Harper Perennial, 1998.

Michel, Marshall L. III. *The 11 Days of Christmas: America's Last Vietnam Battle*. San Francisco: Encounter Books, 2002.

Mikaelian, Allen. *Medal of Honor: Profiles of America's Military Heroes from the Civil War to the Present*. New York: Hyperion, 2002.

Millett, Allan R. *Semper Fidelis: The History of the United States Marine Corps*. New York: Free Press, 1980.

Mock, Freida Lee, and Terry Sanders. *Return with Honor*. Film. Presented by Tom Hanks. PBS Home Video.

"A Needed Tonic for America." *Time* (March 19, 1973): 19–20.

O'Neill, John E., and Jerome R. Corsi. *Unfit for Command: Swift Boat Veterans Speak Out Against John Kerry*. Washington, DC: Regnery Publishing, 2004.

Patterson, Robert. *Dereliction of Duty: The Eyewitness Account of How Bill Clinton Endangered America's Long-Term National Security*. Washington, DC: Regnery Publishing, 2003.

Peebles, Curtis. *Shadow Flights: America's Secret Air War Against the Soviet Union*. Novato, CA: Presidio Press, 2000.

Philpott, Tom. *Glory Denied: The Saga of Jim Thompson, America's Longest-Held Prisoner of War*. New York: W.W. Norton, 2001.

"Plantation Memories." *Time* (June 11, 1973): 23.

Posner, Gerald. *Citizen Perot: His Life and Times*. New York: Random House, 1996.

POW/MIA'S. Report of the Select Committee on POW/MIA Affairs, United States Senate. Washington, DC, 1993.

Proft, R. J., ed. *United States of America's Congressional Medal of Honor Recipients and Their Official Citations*. Columbia Heights, MN: Highland Publishers, 1980.

Rausa, Rosario. "Home from Hanoi." *Naval Aviation News* (December 1973): 9–21.

Risner, Robinson. *The Passing of the Night: My Seven Years as a Prisoner of the North Vietnamese*. New York: Ballantine, 1975.

Robinson, Sue. "I Do. I Really Do." *Ladycon* (March 1984): 48–49.

Rochester, Stuart I., and Frederick Kiley. *Honor Bound: American Prisoners of War in Southeast Asia 1961–1973*. Annapolis, MD: Naval Institute Press, 1999.

Scales, Robert H. Jr. *Yellow Smoke: The Future of Land Warfare for America's Military*. New York: Rowman and Littlefield, 2003.

Schlight, John. *Help from Above: Air Force Close Air Support of the Army 1946–1973*. Washington, DC: Air Force History and Museums Program, 2003.

———. *A War Too Long: The History of the USAF in Southeast Asia*. Washington, DC: Air Force History and Museums Program, 1996.

Schmidt, John F. *A Historical Profile of Sioux City*. Sioux City, IA: Sioux City Stationery Company, 1969.

Sheehan, Neil. *After the War Was Over: Hanoi and Saigon*. New York: Vintage Books, 1991.

———. *A Bright Shining Lie: John Paul Vann and America in Vietnam*. New York: Vintage Books, 1989.

Shepperd, Don, ed. *Misty: First-Person Stories of the F-100 Misty Fast FACs in the Vietnam War*. 1stBooks, 2000.

Sorensen, Scott, and B. Paul Chicoine. *Sioux City: A Pictorial History*. Virginia Beach, VA: Donning Company, 1982.

Stockdale, Jim, and Sybil Stockdale. *In Love and War: The Story of a Family's Ordeal and Sacrifice During the Vietnam Years*. Annapolis, MD: Naval Institute Press, 1990.

Swindle, Orson. "Don't Let Hanoi Off the Hook." *USA Today* (July 1, 1993): 11A.

Tart, Larry, and Robert Keefe. *The Price of Vigilance: Attacks on American Surveillance Flights*. New York: Ballantine, 2002.

Tilford, Earl H. Jr. *Search and Rescue in Southeast Asia*. Washington, DC: Office of Air Force History, 1980.

Timberg, Robert. *The Nightingale's Song*. New York: Touchstone, 1996.

Tuso, Joseph F. *Singing the Vietnam Blues: Songs of the Air Force in Southeast Asia*. College Station, TX: Texas A&M University Press, 1990.

Wyatt, Barbara Powers, ed. *Home with Honor: Thirty Years of Freedom*. Toluca Lake, CA: POW Publications, 1977.

Index